FEAR ON TRIAL

7 ⁹⁵

FEAR ON TRIAL
John Henry Faulk

Foreword by Studs Terkel

 University of Texas Press, Austin

International Standard Book Number 0-292-72443-8;
0-292-72442-x pbk.
Library of Congress Catalog Card Number 82-84409

First University of Texas Press Edition, 1983

Revised and updated with editorial assistance by Don Gardner

To the three persons, Texans all,
who influenced me the most in respecting the liberated mind
and the joys and responsibilities of citizenship:

MY MOTHER AND FATHER AND J. FRANK DOBIE

PROLOGUE

A whole generation of Americans have been born and have come to maturity since the events chronicled in this book took place. For this reason, my editors and I felt that something by way of a prologue or explanatory notes about those troubled times might be in order for this edition of *Fear on Trial*.

As the reader will discover, the book deals with my personal experiences with blacklisting. "Blacklisting" was the term used to describe the practice of systematically denying employment to persons for their alleged political beliefs and associations. It was actually just one of a multitude of cruel manifestations of the McCarthy era in the United States, a period of years in the 1950s characterized by widespread political persecution and repression.

Senator Joe McCarthy of Wisconsin sailed over the national political horizon in 1950, using the charges of treason and subversion to intimidate his political opponents into quaking silence. He was neither the first nor the only political personality of that day to use demagogy, distortion, and falsehood for political advantage. He was simply the most flamboyant. Hence "McCarthyism" entered our political lexicon.

The climate of fear and hysteria that invaded our political institutions and distorted our political processes in that day was carefully encouraged and orchestrated by governmental bodies as well as by private groups. In Congress, the House Un-American Activities Committee (HUAC); its counterpart in the Senate, the Internal Security Committee (McCarthy's Committee); and, in the Executive Branch, J. Edgar Hoover's FBI kept up a steady drumbeat of alarms and exposures. Self-appointed private groups like the American Legion and AWARE, Inc., joined the clamor and din.

That respected maxim of American justice which says

that a person charged with a crime is presumed innocent until proven guilty by due process of the law was stood on its head and became "a person charged with holding dissenting views is presumed guilty until proven innocent."

Senator McCarthy, in 1954, began to have hard times, for the Army-McCarthy televised hearings gave the public a good look at his tactics, and the United States Senate voted to censure him. His influence faded quickly, as the excesses and injustices of the McCarthy era became increasingly apparent to the public; the governmental and private organizations that had been so vocal in support of him lost popularity rapidly. Those two national tragedies, the Vietnam War and Watergate, both at least in part due to the secrecy in government that was institutionalized during McCarthy's time, resulted in some in-depth studies of governmental and private vigilante groups. The HUAC withered and fell off the vine. Severe controls were placed on the FBI's function as a political police force. These accoutrements of political repression became, for a while, almost moribund.

Today, however, there are disturbing signs on the political horizon. As we move into the 1980s, forces are active in the land that carry echoes of the repressive days of McCarthy. Bellicose talk and the emphasis on astronomical defense spending, accompanied by executive orders directing the FBI and the CIA to institute secret *political* surveillance of American citizens who are neither suspected nor charged with criminal activities, are frightening. Political surveillance is the sine qua non of repressive politics. Numerous members of Congress have signed up for the re-establishment of the infamous HUAC with its awesome subpoena powers. Charges of disloyalty and subversive activities are beginning to be bandied about in the present administration's attacks on its opponents.

It is hoped that the publication of this edition of *Fear on Trial* will, to some small degree, serve as an aid to those readers who would avoid the injustices and harm to our free institutions that public or private vigilantism creates.

THE PEOPLE

Val Adams *radio/TV reporter, New York City*

Louise Allbritton *actress; wife of Charles Collingwood*

Marvin Antonowsky *statistician; expert on Pulse ratings; testified at trial*

Leslie Barrett *actor; member of AFTRA; opposed to AWARE*

Frank Barton *executive of Lennen & Newell advertising agency; testified at trial*

Orson Bean *comedian; organizer of Middle-of-the-Road slate (with Faulk and Collingwood)*

Jackson Beck *announcer; turned against Faulk*

Roy Bedichek *naturalist; philosopher; friend of Faulk*

George Berger *assistant to Paul Martinson*

Harry Blackburn *executive of Rheingold Brewery; testified at trial*

Thomas Bolan *attorney; lawyer for AWARE*

Himan Brown *producer, director, and packager of TV shows; testified for Faulk*

Alan Bunce *actor; friend of Collyer; AWARE supporter; opponent of Faulk*

Nelson Case *radio announcer; AFTRA member; withdrew support from Middle-of-the-Road slate*

Roy Cohn *attorney; lawyer for AWARE*

Charles Collingwood *CBS commentator; president of AFTRA; and witness for Faulk*

Clayton (Bud) Collyer *radio/TV personality; supporter of AWARE; opponent of Faulk*

Samuel Dalsimer *executive vice president, Grey Advertising; testified at trial*

Sidney Davis *attorney in Louis Nizer's office*

Chris and Merle Debuskey *friends of Faulk*

Gerald Dickler *business manager and agent for Faulk*

J. Frank Dobie *writer; professor; friend of Faulk*

Elaine Eldridge *actress; member of AFTRA; opposed to AWARE*

Faye Emerson *actress; member of Middle-of-the-Road slate of AFTRA with Faulk*

John Henry Faulk

Harold Gary *actor; member of AFTRA; opposed to AWARE*

Lee Grant *actress; member of AFTRA; opposed to AWARE*

Justice Geller *judge in trial*

Mark Goodson *TV producer; witness for Faulk*

William B. Greene *attorney at WCBS; testified at trial*

Vincent Hartnett *board member of AWARE; defendant in lawsuit*

Vinton Hayworth *president of AFTRA; member of the board of AWARE; opponent of Faulk*

Peter Hilton *president of Kastor-Hilton advertising agency; testified for Faulk*

Del Horstmann *singer; joined Faulk in union fight*

Kim Hunter *actress; witness for Faulk*

Henry Jaffe *attorney for AFTRA; AWARE supporter; opponent of Faulk*

Laurence Johnson *supermarket owner; member of AWARE; defendant in lawsuit*

John Lang *assistant to Bolan and Cohn*

Myrna Loy *friend of Faulk*

Allen Ludden *program manager at WCBS*

Rex Marshall *actor; AWARE supporter; opponent of Faulk*

Paul Martinson *partner of Nizer; attorney for Faulk*

Harry Matusow *FBI informer; friend of Johnson; withdrew support from defendants and helped Faulk*

Paul Milton *officer of AWARE; opponent of Faulk; testified in trial*

Garry Moore *radio/TV personality; joined Faulk on Middle-of-the-Road slate; witness for Faulk*

Tom Murray *advertising executive; witness for Faulk*

Ed Murrow *radio and TV personality; supporter of Faulk*

Conrad Nagel *actor; AWARE supporter; opponent of Faulk*

Louis Nizer *attorney for Faulk*

Cliff Norton *actor; AFTRA member; withdrew support from Middle-of-the-Road slate*

Ted Poston *reporter for the* New York Post; *testified for Faulk*

Tony Randall *actor; witness for Faulk*

Kenneth Roberts *announcer; supporter of Faulk; testified in trial*

Janice Rule *actress; joined Faulk in union fight*

Godfrey Schmidt *member of AFTRA; attorney for defendants*

John Sibley *reporter for the* New York Times; *testified in lawsuit*

Sam Slate *program director at WCBS; friend of Faulk*

Everett Sloan *actor; testified for Faulk*

Dick Stark *announcer; member of Middle-of-the-Road slate; turned against Faulk*

Ed Sullivan *TV producer; opposed Faulk*

David Susskind *TV producer; witness for Faulk*

Luis Van Rooten *actor; AFTRA member; withdrew support from Middle-of-the-Road slate*

Carl Ward *manager of WCBS; testified in Faulk lawsuit*

Lester Wolff *advertising executive; testified at trial*

Jack Wren *advertising executive at Batten, Barton, Durstine & Osborn; testified at trial*

FOREWORD

Some thirteen years ago, when this book was first published, I read it. I raced through it; it was that suspenseful. It was something else, too. Even now, this moment, as I write these words, my sense of rage returns, along with my rising blood pressure and, paradoxically, my feeling of exhilaration. John Henry Faulk faced the bastards and beat them down.

Don't misunderstand. This is not a story of machismo. It is not a "saga" acted out by Clint Eastwood or John Wayne or Charles Bronson. It is not about two-for-a-nickel, ersatz heroism that has too long been our model. It is precisely the opposite. It is a reply to what Faulk, in the opening passage of this book, calls "the violence of vigilantism." It is about something genuine in our makeup that has too rarely been called upon; it is about a man who said no at a time when it was far from fashionable to say no. John Henry took his lumps; but he is around and his detractors are gone.

It would be comforting to think the phonies who equate dissent with treason are no longer about. But experience has taught us they are always about, especially in times of national crisis. That's why this new edition is as contemporary as when the work was first published.

Fear on Trial is more than a chronicle of the blacklist in the world of entertainment. It is more than one man's test in the shameful fifties, an epoch that Lillian Hellman has so succinctly called "scoundrel time." The Cold War was at its most freezing. The coyotes were howling. Joe McCarthy had things going all his own way. Richard Nixon was flowering. J. Edgar Hoover was the sacred cop. The House Un-American Activities Committee was *The* Committee. They were judge, jury, and executioner of reputations and careers. Only fools would challenge them. The silence of the majority was as the silence of the tomb. Respectable liberals were so respectable that, though they disapproved—in Aunt Emma's fashion—of the techniques of the demagogues, they "understood." Such has always been understanding in matters of this sort; playing it safe was the order of the day. Oh, it was a time, children.

Right in the middle of this mess was John Henry Faulk. A maverick Texan, he just didn't know any better. You see, his was the tradition of speaking out. Silence was not for him; certainly not in a time of such venality. And if he saw that the emperor had no clothes, he said so. He couldn't help it. John Henry was—and indeed is—a talker. He is one of our funniest, most eloquent, and most perceptive. He is in the tradition of frontier talkers: Opie Read, Petroleum Nasby, Mark Twain. He could no more be shut up than Canute could hold back the waters. Something had to be done about this troublemaker.

Consider this. He was a quite popular entertainer in the employ of the Columbia Broadcasting System. He was reaching out toward millions. He was revealing brutes and bullies for what they were: clowns. And he was not about to apologize for having spoken out on behalf of causes considered unfashionable by those who were determining the fashion of the day. He was a stubborn one.

Well, they got John Henry. "They," in this instance, refers to a couple of wretches who recognized a good thing when they saw it. The witch hunt enabled one, Hartnett, to make a fairly good buck. He published a rag called *Red Channels* in which were listed actors, singers, announcers, writers and directors in radio and television, whom he considered subversive. This obscene journal became sacred in the executive offices of the networks, of multimillion dollar advertising agencies, and powerhouse sponsors. Though Faulk's name wasn't included, he became one of Hartnett's pigeons.

The other Fury was a Syracuse grocer named Johnson. He threatened to institute boycotts of sponsors of Faulk, among others. As a result of their efforts, John Henry was fired. Soon enough, he was flat broke. He sued his detractors and won an unprecedented award. Irony: the defendants had limited funds. The emperor had no clothes. And that is what this book is really about.

The culprits are not really these two petty scoundrels. They are bad enough, sure. It is the others, though, the powerful ones, the television networks, advertising agencies and sponsors, whose behavior was so execrable. Their cravenness was appalling. They shamelessly genuflected—to what?

Archibald MacLeish, in his poetic drama, *Fall of the City*, tells of the conqueror who enters the gates. The others fall on their knees before him; in their terror, they do not look up. The conqueror opens his visor. Nobody is there. The visor is empty. The others don't see this. They are too busy trembling and cheering. MacLeish, who wrote this in the thirties, was prescient. It applied to the fifties, as well. John Henry Faulk was shouting: The visor is empty. Why did he have to suffer all those slings and arrows to make his point?

Can Scoundrel Time come upon us once again? Of course. All it takes is forgetfulness. *Fear on Trial* is a reminder, a necessary one. It also tells us, in an unassuming way, of Hero Time. Not just John Henry Faulk alone; but those gentle people who stuck up for him. The gallant ones were pitifully few; but there they were, a Gideon's Army. And that, too, is what this book is about. The glory of our times as well as the disgrace.

An ironic footnote: In 1975, over the Columbia Broadcasting System, a two-hour dramatization of "Fear on Trial" was telecast. It was enthusiastically received by the public as well as by critics. The Columbia Broadcasting System had fired John Henry Faulk in the fifties. Though it honored him in the seventies, it made him no job offer whatsoever. Is the blacklist, in all instances, really a thing of the past?

Studs Terkel

FEAR ON TRIAL

I

This is a story of violence. Not violence involving physical brutality, lust, or bloodshed, but a more subtle kind of violence—the violence of vigilantism. In a society that has achieved rule by law, rule by vigilantism is a violence not only against those immediately affected, but society itself. Like all stories of violence, this one took place against a background of intrigue and fear. The story began, for me at least, with a telephone call.

I had a radio show on WCBS, the flagship station of the Columbia Broadcasting System, in New York City. It was a one-hour show each afternoon, five days a week, and it was pretty much a talk program. I spun a few yarns, reminisced about my childhood in Texas, and commented on the news of the day and the foibles of the world.

I was sitting in my apartment study on February 12, 1956. The phone rang. It was Val Adams, a radio and television columnist for the *New York Times*. He apologized for bothering me at home and then asked if I had seen the bulletin that AWARE, Inc., had just issued, attacking me for pro-Communist activities.

AWARE, Inc., was a self-appointed group of people operating as something of a vigilante organization in the supercharged atmosphere of that period—the McCarthy era—when the simple suggestion of dissenting opinions got one branded as a subversive. It put out bulletins from time to time accusing performers in radio and television of Communist or pro-Communist activities. It had played havoc with the careers of dozens of performers; any performer it attacked was blacklisted throughout the industry.

Val said the bulletin listed some alleged pro-Communist affiliations I was supposed to have had. I asked him if I might see the bulletin before I commented. He agreed and promised to leave it at the *New York Times* office for me. I tried to sound casual about the matter with Val, but after I hung up, I gave way to a quaking fear. I knew AWARE was a powerful influence in the affairs of the American Federation of Television and Radio Artists, known familiarly as AFTRA.

AFTRA is a national union and all performers in network radio and television are required to belong to it. Since the early 1950s, the board of directors, who were elected from the membership, had been controlled entirely by one faction, and AWARE supported that faction. The same faction was elected year after year, and in keeping with the national hysteria of that day, anti-Communism was their sole issue. A number of board members were also officers of AWARE, Inc.

In the AFTRA election of 1954, a slate of candidates ran against the entrenched board of directors. The insurgents were soundly trounced, and shortly after the election, AWARE put out a bulletin attacking their patriotism. This bulletin was dutifully circulated to all the employers in radio and television, and it laid the groundwork for the blacklisting of those AFTRA members whom it attacked. It also served as a stern warning to other members of the union; anyone who wanted to run in opposition to the AWARE-supported slate of officers had better think twice.

The AWARE-supported faction, however, did not have control over the feelings of the membership of the union. In March of 1955, at a membership meeting of the New York local, a resolution was offered to condemn AWARE for its unwarranted interference in AFTRA affairs. It was a stormy meeting. One union member after another got up and blasted AWARE and its destructive practices. Not one member of the board of directors spoke against AWARE; on the contrary, most of them defended it.

The membership voted overwhelmingly to condemn AWARE, but the AFTRA board of directors remained in office.

Instead of heeding the obvious desire of the membership to curb AWARE's influence and oppose the blacklisting of union members, the board of directors countered that the vote to condemn AWARE was part and parcel of a Communist plot. It was about this time that I began to take an active interest in AFTRA's affairs.

That summer, 1955, practically every group I ran into was talking about the goings-on in AFTRA and the vote to condemn AWARE. Orson Bean, a talented actor and comedian, lived near me. We had long talks about AFTRA affairs and agreed that we ought to do something. Then and there we decided that we would run for office against the incumbents the following December. We knew that even if we were elected to the board, we wouldn't have much chance of changing things, since there would be thirty-three other members of the board to oppose us. But at least we could make our voices heard; we could dissent.

Charles Collingwood, a news commentator at CBS, was a friend of mine, and I talked to him about the matter. Charles had never been very active in union affairs either, but he felt pretty much the way we did. He agreed to run with us, and his wife, actress Louise Allbritton, said she would join us too. The more we talked about it, the more enthusiastic we became over our chances of stopping AWARE's blacklisting. Charles said if we were going to run, we might as well get a whole slate of officers to join us. Charles and I rounded up Garry Moore, Faye Emerson, Janice Rule, and a number of other well-known performers who belonged to AFTRA and got them to run on our slate. It wasn't easy to find people who would join us since there was a great deal of fear of reprisals from AWARE.

We managed, however, to get thirty-three people in all. We called ourselves the Middle-of-the-Road slate and put out a statement setting forth what we hoped to do for the union. Among other things, we declared that while we were opposed to Communism, we were also opposed to the blacklisting and we intended to do something to put a stop to it. The announcement that there was a Middle-of-the-Road slate running against the AWARE-supported slate created quite a stir among the AFTRA membership in New York.

At election time, in December of 1955, we swept into office. The Middle-of-the-Road slate won twenty-seven of the thirty-five seats on the board. This meant that we were firmly in control of the New York local as far as numbers were concerned. Collingwood was elected president, Bean first vice-president, and I was elected second vice-president of the local. We took office in January of 1956.

We had rough sledding from the start. Most of us were inexperienced in the administration of union affairs and had a great deal to learn. But the biggest problem we had was the strong and continuous opposition we met. We had soundly defeated the AWARE-supported faction of the union, but we hadn't silenced them. In fact we had only stirred them up. Several of their strongest and most effective members were among the eight who had been re-elected to the board. There was Clayton (Bud) Collyer, who for years had been a big wheel in AFTRA and a leading spirit in the old administration. There were Alan Bunce, Rex Marshall, and Conrad Nagel. For years they had all been officeholders in the union and had the advantage of experience. They offered unyielding opposition to everything the Middle-of-the-Road slate undertook to do, both at board meetings and outside. There was also Henry Jaffe, who for years had been the legal counsel for AFTRA, both local and national; he made no secret of his dislike for the Middle-of-the-Road slate. Although he was only an employee of the union, not a member, and consequently was not entitled to vote, he attended every board meeting and never hesitated to speak in opposition to us. To add to our problems, a couple of weeks after we had taken office, the House Un-American Activities Committee, in its annual report, let go with a blast aimed at the Middle-of-the-Road administration. It declared among other things that the issue of blacklisting was being used by the Communist forces to reinfiltrate the union. This report was released to all the papers and was widely publicized.

Now, to top it all off, hardly a month after we had taken office, AWARE, Inc., had come out with the bulletin (the one Val had called me about) attacking the Middle-of-the-Road slate.

I alternated between fear and seething anger after Val's call. I knew I had best call my business manager, Gerald Dickler. When I reached him, I could tell he was greatly disturbed at the news, but he suggested that I pick up the bulletin and bring it up to his office the next day before we discussed it further.

2

As I picked up the AWARE bulletin the next morning, I got the same angry-scared feeling that had followed Val's call the day before. I hailed a cab, gave the driver Dickler's office address, and sat back. My hands trembled a bit as I tore open the sealed envelope and unfolded the bulletin. I noticed that it was even longer than I had anticipated—some five and a half pages, single-spaced on legal-sized paper. It was headed "AWARE, Inc. An Organization to Combat the Communist Conspiracy in Entertainment-Communications." It was dated February 10, 1956, and was presented as a "News Supplement to Membership Bulletin, AWARE Publication 16."

It started off by saying that in a recent AFTRA election, "a caucus styling itself 'middle of the road'" had won twenty-seven out of thirty-five seats, "choosing its candidates by two standards: their opposition to AWARE, Inc. and also their opposition to 'blacklisting and Communism.'" Then it advised that "the term 'blacklisting' is losing its plain meaning and becoming a Communism jargon-term for hard opposition to the exposure of Communism."

There followed a paragraph stating: "The 'middlers' attack on AWARE and relative silence on Communism require some comment." Then it called attention to the fact that the "unqualifiedly anti-Communist slate was defeated for the first time in eight years."

Will the "middlers" enforce AFTRA's constitution which bars from union membership those who maintain membership or knowingly aid the Communist party or other officially designated subversive organizations?

Will they enforce AFTRA's National Rule, which provides disciplinary measures against union members who refuse to answer when asked by a Congressional committee if they are or have been Communist Party (CP) members?

After listing the names of fifteen members of the New York local who had refused to cooperate with the House Committee on Un-American Activities in August and October of 1955, it demanded:

> What will the "middlers" do about enforcing AFTRA's Constitution and National Rule against these 15?

The bulletin said that we had been critical of AWARE but had said nothing about the "many CP fronts that have operated in the entertainment field," and it added, "silence is sometimes more eloquent than words." It related how AWARE had been condemned by AFTRA membership the year before, hinting that the condemnation was a dark Communist plot, but it magnanimously declared that "AWARE did not then, and does not now, suggest that to be opposed to AWARE is necessarily to be pro-Communist. It is a tragic fact that most Communist successes have come about with the help of non-Communists won over by slogans."

After these preliminary remarks it got down to the business of working me over:

> John Henry Faulk was further quoted as saying that "all (middlers) were chosen for their opposition to Communism as well as their opposition to AWARE." In most cases, this may well be true. But how about Faulk himself? What is his public record?

There followed seven allegations:

> [1] According to the *Daily Worker* of April 22, 1946, "Jack Faulk" was to appear at Club 65, 13 Astor Place, N.Y.C.— a favorite site of pro-Communist affairs.
> [2] According to the *Daily Worker* of April 17, 1947, "Johnny Faulk" was to appear as an entertainer at the opening of "Headline Cabaret," sponsored by Stage for Action (officially designated a Communist front). The late Philip Loeb was billed as emcee.

[3] According to the *Daily Worker* of April 5, 1948, "John Faulk" contributed cabaret material to "Show-Time for Wallace," revues staged by the Progressive Citizens of America (officially designated a Communist front) in support of Henry A. Wallace's candidacy for the presidency of the U.S. Although Wallace was the officially endorsed candidate of the CP, by no means all his supporters were Communist or pro-Communists. What is in question here is support of any candidate given through a Communist-front setup.

[4] A program dated April 25, 1946, named "John Faulk" as a scheduled entertainer (with identified Communist Earl Robinson and two non-Communists) under the auspices of the Independent Citizens Committee of the Arts, Sciences and Professions (officially designated a Communist front, and predecessor of the Progressive Citizens of America).

[5] Vol. 3 Nos. 1 & 2, of the Bulletin of People's Songs (officially designated a Communist front) named Faulk as one who had sent greetings to People's Songs on its second anniversary.

[6] "Johnny Faulk" was listed in a circular as an entertainer or speaker (with Paul Robeson and two others) to appear at "Spotlight on Wallace" to be held in Room 200 of the Jefferson School of Social Science on February 16, 1948. The Jefferson School has been found by the Federal Government to be what it is, the official training school of the Communist conspiracy in New York.

[7] "John H. Faulk" was a U.S. sponsor of the American Continental Congress for Peace, staged in Mexico City, September 5–10, 1949, as shown by the official "call." The Congress was later described by the HUAC as "another phase in the Communist world 'peace' campaign, aimed at consolidating anti-American forces throughout the Western Hemisphere."

Having dispensed with me, the bulletin turned to Bean and Collingwood. It pointed out that Orson Bean had done a satire on the House Un-American Activities Committee as recently as August 1955 and reported on a letter written by Charles Collingwood in January in answer to the HUAC's attack on the Middle-of-the-Road administration. The bulletin also summarized the HUAC counsel's public reply to Collingwood.

Tavenner further stated that there is not only no blacklist at all, but some of the named individuals have been finding it easy to secure employment. He added: "It is significant to note that the election of the so-called anti-blacklist candidates in the recent AFTRA election [the 'middlers'—A.] has been greeted enthusiastically by the Communist press."

The bulletin ended by expressing great dismay that President Collingwood would dare take issue with the HUAC.

This, then, was the AWARE bulletin. It was a cleverly constructed piece of work. The way it had positioned my name in sentences with "Communist Party" and "Communist front," its use of phrases like "officially designated a Communist front," and its skillful mixing of half-truth and falsehood suggested the work of a hand skilled at innuendo.

I sat pondering the matter as the cab moved slowly through the mid-morning Manhattan traffic. I had a vague, uncomfortable feeling of guilt. But I had done nothing wrong. Why should I feel guilty? I realized at that moment that I was going through the frustrations and anxieties that had been experienced by countless other performers when they had found their names linked with subversion by AWARE.

Up in Gerry's office, I handed him the bulletin. He took it without a word and began to read.

Gerald Dickler was not only my business manager, he was my friend and professional adviser. He had a definitive knowledge of affairs in the radio and television industry, gained through years of intimate association with those media. I relied heavily upon him and his guidance, and I had profited greatly by this direction. He was also intimately acquainted with the affairs of AFTRA and had been for many years. He knew all of the personalities and the conflicts in the union. He had cautioned me against getting into the AFTRA squabble: "You've got a career to look after, Johnny. Besides, you're up against a tough, experienced crowd. They're professionals. You're not." When we had won the election he had told me: "It's a fluke, Johnny. Your Middle-of-the-Road slate is a sandlot team. You have accidently beaten the New York Yankees for one game. Watch out for 'em. The men who have controlled this union for many years have a vested interest in keeping that control. They're not about to let you and your Middle-of-the-Road slate take that control away from them."

As Gerry finished reading the bulletin he looked at me with a troubled frown.

"This is bad, Johnny. It could mean real trouble."

"Yes, I know. What do you reckon my first move should be?"

"I think you should take this to Sam Slate at WCBS at once. Get it to him before the AWARE crowd does. Sam's on your side. Ask him what you should do at CBS about it."

"Do you think CBS will stand by me, Gerry?"

He nodded. "Yes, I think they'll stand by you—that is, for a while. They don't want to lose you. They don't like AWARE any better than you do. They won't do anything un-less they begin to get some real pressure from the agencies or sponsors. Then it will probably be a different story."

"How long do you think that will be?"

"It's hard to tell," Gerry said thoughtfully, "hard to tell. They really can't risk firing you outright. Can't afford it. It would leave them open to too much public criticism for let-ting AWARE pressure them. And, if they did that, you would have a legal action against them. The blacklisting business doesn't work that way."

"And besides, Gerry," I said hopefully, "I'm pretty well liked there at CBS. I happen to know that most of the execu-tives there don't like AWARE any better than I do. Maybe they'll line up with me in this fight."

Gerry shook his head. "There's not an executive at CBS that is your enemy, Johnny. There's probably not a one there that likes AWARE. But on the other hand, there is not a sin-gle one of them that wouldn't fire you if a decision is made to do so. Don't forget that."

"I thought you just said they wouldn't fire me—that is, outright."

"The way this thing works, Johnny, is subtle and strictly behind the scenes. The networks and the agencies want to

avoid making an issue of it. So they ease along until a legitimate reason comes. A reason that sounds perfectly logical
on the surface. They they let a man go. However, you take
this on up to Sam Slate. See what he has to say."

"Well, if I get fired from CBS, or even if I don't get any
more work, I could certainly prove it was because of this
damn bulletin."

"That's where you're wrong, Johnny. There's not an executive in radio or television in New York today who would
come in and say he had fired you or refused to hire you because of this. They simply wouldn't do it."

"Who do you suppose went to all the trouble to write this
damn bulletin, Gerry? To get up all this nonsense? It must
have been a lot of work."

"Vincent Hartnett, in all likelihood. He's the mainspring
of AWARE. He and Laurence Johnson of Syracuse helped
start AWARE. Hartnett makes his living out of this sort of
thing. He's a pro."

I had never set eyes on Vincent Hartnett. But his name
was legend on Madison Avenue in those years. He was not
only one of the founders and moving spirits of AWARE, but
he had published a book back in 1950 called *Red Channels*.
In this book Hartnett purported to reveal the extent to
which the international Communist conspiracy had pene-
trated the communications industry. Although the book's
authors were careful to point out that the persons who were
listed inside its pages were not necessarily Communists, or
Communist sympathizers, or even subversive, the book had
a devastating effect on the careers of dozens of performers
whose names were listed in it. *Red Channels* became something of a semi-official guide for employers in the radio and
television industry—a guide in the sense that it was widely
used in deciding whom not to hire. It made money for
Hartnett.

Hartnett's friend Laurence Johnson owned a number of supermarkets. He and Hartnett shared the political philosophy
of Senator McCarthy. But Johnson was not merely a philosopher; he was also a man of action. Sponsors who advertised
in radio and television had to sell their products through
Johnson's supermarkets. When Hartnett protested the appearance of an actor or an actress on a program that was

sponsored by a company whose product was sold in Johnson's store, Johnson obligingly went to the sponsor himself and demanded the artist's dismissal.

I pounded my fist into my palm and declared, "Well, one thing's sure! I'm not going to sit and do nothing! I figure maybe we can get the union lined up behind this thing. After all, it is their fight as much as it is mine. It's their fight more than it is mine, really."

Gerry pursed his lips and gazed at me speculatively. "That's right. It's very important that AFTRA support you. But to be perfectly candid with you, Johnny, I don't believe that you can get AFTRA to act in this matter."

"Why? After all, we swept into office on an antiblacklist ticket. The membership censured AWARE only last year. Our Middle-of-the-Road slate has been attacked by this bulletin. We're in the majority on the local board. We're in control, at least here in New York."

"That's the hell of it, son"—Gerry shook his head—"you're not in control of AFTRA. Not even in the New York local. Henry Jaffe, Bud Collyer, and the men who have run AFTRA for years are in control. They don't like you one damn bit. You'll certainly get no help from them. On the contrary, they will take advantage of this AWARE bulletin to completely undo the Middle-of-the-Road slate. This bulletin is calculated to panic your entire slate. That's one of its purposes. It will probably succeed there."

His observation irritated me.

"Now wait a minute, Gerry. Remember last fall when we started our Middle-of-the-Road slate? Practically everyone, you included, said that we could never defeat Bud Collyer and his crowd. But the membership supported us. If the Middle-of-the-Road slate stood together then, if we stood firm then, why not now?"

"You might as well face it, Johnny. You Middle-of-the-Road boys have been under attack since you were first elected. This is simply the crowning blow. Every member of the Middle-of-the-Road slate knows as well as you do that this bulletin goes to executives in agencies and networks. That fact alone would be enough to scare most of them to death, start them thinking of ways to become disassociated from you and the Middle-of-the-Road slate. Not only that, but remember, your slate has already had its defectors. Take Luis Van Rooten and Cliff Norton, two of the most vocal members of the slate when it was running for election. They've both been voting with Collyer and his clique since you have been in office. They have not supported a single one of your Middle-of-the-Road resolutions at board meetings. You had better stop right now and reflect on the fact that you haven't been able to get one clear piece of action on a single one of the promises that you made to the membership when you asked for election."

Gerry went on to predict that in a fight against AWARE's bulletin, there would be many members of the Middle-of-the-Road slate who would publicly denounce the slate and me. They would do it in a frenzy of fear of being tarred with the same brush that had tarred me. Then he took a slightly more optimistic tone.

"I'll tell you what we should do right now, Johnny. Let's go over the list of names of the Middle-of-the-Road slate who you know will stand with you in this fight. Get hold of Collingwood and Bean, Garry Moore, Faye Emerson, Del Horstmann, Ronny Graham, and the others. Tell them how important it is that you all stand together in this and not let the opposition pick you off one at a time. But you're going to have to move fast."

A thought occurred to me. "You know, come to think about it, since I'm the main target of this AWARE bulletin, it's kind of embarrassing for me to go around to my slate members and ask them to get into the fight. I sure wish that some of them would volunteer to pick up the cudgels themselves. It puts me in the position of asking them to help pull my chestnuts out of the fire. I don't like that. What if they won't do it?"

"You have no choice, Johnny," Gerry said. "Somebody has to take the initiative in this thing and do it fast. It's no time to stand on formalities. Of course if they won't stand with you, you'll be in the soup. So will they, for that matter."

"If they won't support me, what then, Gerry?"

"Then, I'd say, you'd better forget the union and start looking out for number one. If you can't rally enough members of the Middle-of-the-Road slate, or other union members, behind this fight, you'd be a damn fool to keep going. In fact you wouldn't have any choice but to start to figure out a way to save John Henry Faulk's hide, and forget AFTRA. You'd have but one way out there. You'd have to make peace with AWARE. Kiss and make up."

"The hell you say!"

"I know how you feel. I guess it's pointless for me to tell you this, because I know you won't do it. But I'm telling you right now that if you don't do it, you can start looking for some other kind of work."

I started to argue the point with him, but thought better of it and changed the subject. Shortly after, I took the bulletin and left his office.

Sam Slate was program director of WCBS and my direct superior. He was the one who had hired me, back in 1951. We had remained close personal friends since that time. I frequently visited in his home and he visited in mine. He had an enlightened, civilized attitude on social and political affairs. We had discussed them many times. I knew that he resented the inroads that McCarthyism had made in the radio and television industry and had little use for the ridiculous anxieties of some of his colleagues about controversial matters. I respected him and I trusted him.

I had discussed my intention of running for office in the union with him before we ever launched the Middle-of-the-Road slate. He had agreed that AFTRA should be cleaned up for the benefit of the whole industry and was quite pleased when our slate won.

I went in and handed him the bulletin. He puffed his cigar as he read it. Then he put it down on his desk, frowning.

"That's a hell of a note, isn't it, Johnny? This bunch is sore at you because you licked them in that union election." I nodded. He smiled. "Most of those things they claimed you did were nearly ten years ago. Couldn't they find any current subversion to charge you with?"

"I guess not." I relaxed. "But I wanted you to see it, Sam. If there's anything there you want me to explain, I'll be glad to do it. After all, I think you've got a right to know what's true and what's false about it."

"I don't think it's worth paying any attention to, Johnny.

It's all hogwash. Hell, you've been here five years. You're no more red than I am. I personally don't think anybody pays the slightest bit of attention to these fools."

He pushed the AWARE bulletin toward me, then said, thoughtfully, "But you know, you'd better take that in to Carl Ward. Let him see it too. Just so he'll know what it's all about in case he gets a call on it or hears about it from somebody else. If he wants to talk to me about it, tell him I'll discuss it with him."

Sam was so unperturbed and so understanding about it that I began to feel that Gerry and I had overdramatized the whole thing. I thanked him and took the bulletin over to Carl Ward's office. Carl was general manager of WCBS. I had a strong feeling that he did not have the least interest in the union's affairs, nor the rights or wrongs of blacklisting— except where such matters affected the interest of WCBS.

As I handed him the bulletin, I explained that I wanted him to be acquainted with its contents before he heard of them from some other source. He thanked me and started reading it. He was obviously not interested in the labored matter with which it dealt, for he had only scanned it. As he folded it and handed it back to me he was smiling.

"I notice they said that Collingwood is a CBS news commentator, Johnny, but they don't even mention you in connection with WCBS. You ought to speak to them about that. Thanks for bringing it in to me."

I was feeling pretty good as I went into my office and sat down at my desk. Slate's reaction was reassuring. And Carl Ward's reaction was certainly nothing to be alarmed about. Neither Slate nor Ward asked me if the charges were true or false. I appreciated that.

I called Gerald Dickler. "Well, I showed it to Sam Slate and Carl Ward. Sam was almost jovial about it. Put his finger right on the trouble spot—our beating the AWARE crowd in the union. He said not to pay it any mind." Gerry grunted approvingly.

After I finished doing my program that afternoon, I started calling up the members of the Middle-of-the-Road slate. I caught myself joking about the bulletin. Each member, in turn, expressed himself strongly on the matter. Each one wanted to do something at once.

I finished my telephone calls and prepared to leave the office. Just as I was closing the door behind me, the telephone rang. It was Nelson Case, a prominent and successful announcer. He had worked hard for the Middle-of-the-Road slate and had been effusive in his praise when the slate won. His voice sounded strained as he asked me if I would write him a letter stating that he was not a member of the Middle-of-the-Road group and that he had never been one. It was such a strange request that I thought for a moment he was joking. But his voice had a note of impatience and anger. I explained that I didn't consider it my role to write him such a letter. If our side had a leader at all, it was Charles Collingwood. I told him I would ask Charles to write him a letter. He asked me if I would have Charles do it at once. I told him, of course—if Collingwood wanted to do it. I couldn't force him to do so. He said that he thought he had better call Collingwood himself, and I agreed with him. After he hung up, I stood for a moment, baffled. Suddenly, I understood it. He had probably seen the AWARE bulletin.

3

During the next few weeks I did not hear a murmur of disapproval from my employers at CBS. On the contrary, everything seemed to be going along fine there. I became so involved with trying to get action started in the union that I almost forgot that my professional affairs had been jeopardized.

I continued to work hard in the union because I knew if we lost, it would be, in part, because of my own inadequacy. I understood very well that there were many mitigating factors over which I had no control. I was loath to face the unhappy fact that many of the Middle-of-the-Road members had lost their appetite for the fight against AWARE.

This fact became apparent to me after Henry Jaffe and I had an encounter at a general membership meeting some weeks later. Jaffe's suggestion was that I could parry AWARE's attack on me by bringing charges against members of the union who were suspected of having Communist ties. It seemed to me that Jaffe's motive was to get the Middle-of-the-Road slate so hopelessly entangled in legal issues that we would have no time for anything else. But, as he continued, I realized that he was quite sincere in his belief that this was how I might escape AWARE's attack. Jaffe was even willing to locate people who had given evidence against their fellow union members. I thanked Jaffe for his suggestion, without mentioning the revulsion that I felt at such an idea.

Immediately after the meeting, I called several members of the Middle-of-the-Road slate together to discuss Jaffe's suggestion. To my amazement and disappointment, several of them felt that it was a wise solution to our problem. When I argued that I could never be a party to buying my personal security at the expense of another performer's reputation and career, one of the members said:

"Hell, Jaffe's just saying that if you are really anti-Communist you can show it by taking some action."

It was clear that the opinion of the Middle-of-the-Road slate was too sharply divided for comfort. I went home depressed and frustrated.

There was a great deal of sentiment in the Middle-of-the-Road slate for taking action under our National Rule. This rule provided that members of the union who had defied the House Un-American Activities Committee could be subjected to discipline at the discretion of the board of directors of the local to which they belonged. Charles Collingwood consulted some of the best legal minds in the country concerning the constitutionality of such a rule. He was advised that there was a serious question as to whether a member of the union could be disciplined for exercising his constitutional rights and that the matter should be examined at great length. Charles was cautioned that if the union did take the action against a member and the action was unconstitutional, the member would have a real action against the union for damages. Collingwood then appointed a committee, with me as chairman, to study the matter and report back to the board on what action, if any, should be taken.

We had been timid in the matter of a legal counsel for the New York local. Jaffe had been counsel for AFTRA for many years and had the enthusiastic support of the faction that opposed us; in fact, he was so closely identified with the opposition that many members of our slate felt that he should be replaced by an attorney more congenial to our point of view. The anti-Jaffe forces represented a considerable majority on the board of directors and they now demanded that Jaffe be fired at once. Both Collingwood and I argued against this, saying that in all justice, and for the sake of Jaffe's professional reputation, he should be allowed to resign. Collingwood and I prevailed. Collingwood had a meeting with Jaffe on the subject and Jaffe agreed to resign as counsel to the New York local and agreed to give as his reasons that he desired to devote his time to his private practice and to production in television.

The announcement of Jaffe's resignation set off a first-class earthquake. The Bud Collyer faction reacted as though we had announced we were dissolving the entire union rather than merely allowing its counsel to resign. Jackson Beck, an announcer who had supported the Middle-of-the-Road slate in its early days, came charging into my office at CBS and demanded to know what we meant by firing Jaffe and replacing him with Harry Sacher, a lawyer who had been disbarred for defending eleven Communists on trial. He refused to tell me who had told him this piece of idiocy. I began to receive phone calls both at home and at my office, from unnamed persons who announced that they knew for a fact that Jaffe had been dismissed on the instructions of the Communist Party. Ed Sullivan joined the chorus through his column in the New York *Daily News.* He announced that sinister forces in the union were seeking to take over, and he urged the membership of AFTRA to attend an upcoming membership meeting, alerting them that there were real dangers in store that they must be prepared to counteract. Garry Moore called me to say that Bud Collyer and Henry Jaffe had come to visit him and asked him to present a resolution calling for a unanimous vote of confidence for Jaffe. Garry said that he did not know Jaffe and knew little of his reputation, but that Collyer and Jaffe had seemed so agitated that he had agreed to do so.

The membership meeting was held on the afternoon of April 11, at the New York City Center. When I arrived, I realized that it was a near record turnout, with a heavy sprinkling of AWARE members and their supporters. Collingwood first recognized Garry Moore, who introduced his resolution asking for a vote of approval for Jaffe. This was followed by one Jaffe partisan after another coming to the microphone with a ringing tribute to Jaffe and his great services to the union. Most of the speeches contained thinly veiled attacks on the Middle-of-the-Road slate. Those of us who had been responsible for Jaffe's resignation could do little but sit and smart. I rationalized that at least we had gotten rid of him. That was the important thing.

As the pro-Jaffe sentiment reached a fevered pitch, the resolution was passed. Charles Collingwood seemed relieved when the vote was finally taken. He came to the rostrum to continue the business for which the meeting had originally been called. I glanced around at the faces of my fellow board members. They seemed to be as relieved as Collingwood that this part of the meeting was completed. I felt fatuous and ineffectual to think that we who were ostensibly in control of the local board had had to sit by stupidly while our opponents turned the meeting into an all-out rally for Jaffe.

I saw Dick Stark, an announcer and one of the original Middle-of-the-Road board members, go forward and ask Collingwood for the floor. He desired to make a very important statement. Collingwood told him that this was out of order, but he allowed him to speak. Stark then delivered himself of a ringing denunciation of the Middle-of-the-Road slate, charging that a faction on the local board had been holding secret caucuses and were trying to pass resolutions contrary to the best interests of the union. He carefully avoided specifying what the resolutions were. He confessed that he had once been deluded into running with the Middle-of-the-Road slate, but that he was now disillusioned and sought the counsel of the union members as to what he should do. I seethed with indignant fury. Stark knew as well as I did that he had not attended more than two board meetings since we had taken office and he had never expressed the slightest disagreement with our actions or policies. This was obviously a putup job. His speech set off a mighty rumble among the members. I leaped to my feet to answer him. Garry Moore restrained me, saying that Bud Collyer actually had planned much worse for us and that Stark was being mild. I told Garry that I didn't care what Bud Collyer did—I *expected* him to oppose us. But I wasn't going to sit by and listen to a man who had voluntarily joined us publicly misrepresent the facts.

Collingwood recognized me and I went to the microphone. I was too furious to make a coherent speech. Even if I had, it would have done no good. The sentiment of the meeting was running strongly against us. As I gazed out over the faces, I saw only cold disdain. Ed Sullivan and a hard core of our opposition were sitting in the front rows, staring up at me with unfeigned contempt. A terrible feeling of impotent rage overcame me as I sat down.

Cliff Norton, another member of the Middle-of-the-Road slate, went to the microphone and, like Stark, denounced the slate and disassociated himself from it. Those Middle-of-the-Road members who remained firm were so bewildered and confused by the proceedings that they said nothing. Collingwood, always strictly neutral when he was presiding over a membership meeting, could only comment that it seemed highly inappropriate that such matters should be discussed at a membership meeting.

I departed, alone and depressed. I sensed that this was the end of any fight against AWARE in the union. It was probably the end of the Middle-of-the-Road slate. We had tangled with the wrong boys. They had shown us what real fighters could do.

When I got back to my office at WCBS, I received a phone call from Art Woodstone, a reporter for *Variety*. He told me that he knew what had happened at the meeting and asked me if I had any comment on it. I asked him how he had found out so quickly. He informed me that he had been told about it the day before.

The following morning Ed Sullivan's column in the *Daily News* was to carry a report of the heroic onetime fighting marine, Dick Stark, and the heart-warming exhibition of his courage.

As I sat there at my desk reflecting on the chaos that had overtaken our Middle-of-the-Road slate in the union, Sam Slate sent word to me that I should meet him at once in Carl Ward's office.

4

When I got into Carl Ward's office, I found him sitting behind the desk, looking as if he had just lost a good friend. Sam Slate was standing near the window, fingering his cigar and frowning. It turned out that we had lost something just about as close to Carl as a friend: an account. Carl told me he had just learned that Laurence Johnson was in New York, going up and down Madison Avenue, seeing my sponsors and demanding that they withdraw from my show. I was still so punch-drunk from the drubbing I had received at the union meeting that afternoon that I could only mumble, "Well, I'll be doggone."

"This is serious, Johnny," Carl said. "Libby's Frozen Foods account just cancelled today. It looks like you'll lose Libby's Canned Vegetables account this week, too. If Johnson forces all these people off your show, you'll lose your commercial value to the station." Carl was courteous and concerned. He wasn't mad at me. And he wasn't indignant at Laurence Johnson. He was upset at losing an account.

"How'd you find out about it, Carl?" I asked.

He shook his head quickly. "I'm afraid I can't tell you. I'm sorry. I hope you won't press me on that."

"Carl," I said, "you've seen that damn bulletin. You know it's a bunch of trash. It's a shame to let a man go around with that thing and destroy my livelihood without getting back at him somehow or other."

"Perhaps," he said, "you could take this bulletin and answer each one of the allegations. Put it in the form of an affidavit. We could give it to our salesmen to give to any sponsor who raises a question about you. If there are things in there that you didn't do or are just plain lies, say so. If there are things that you did because you were a chump or a dupe, say so. Shoot straight. An affidavit might help."

We talked for a few more minutes about the affidavit and I went back to my office. I pulled the AWARE bulletin out of my desk and looked at it. I was sore at Ward and Slate for taking what I thought was a pretty indifferent attitude toward my interest in the matter. But when I got to thinking about it, I realized that they were really trying to help me. I had a lot of good sponsors, which meant a lot of money for the station. If for no other reasons than those of good business, Ward and Slate would try to hold on.

If the world won't be saved, dammit I'm not going to break my neck trying to save it, I thought. I'm going to look after my own interests. I'll answer this bulletin. I'll give them what they want. Maybe get Dickler to call AWARE. He could tell them that I'd made a mistake and wanted to call the whole thing off. At the moment I felt utter defeat.

I took up the AWARE bulletin and started to read it. Ward had said that I should answer each allegation candidly. I intended to do just that. As I read and reread the portion devoted to me, an astonishing fact emerged—*there was nothing to answer!* I was being asked to reply to nebulous, fatuous assertions that had no bearing on either my patriotism or my loyalty to the United States. Suddenly, the whole shoddy methodology of the McCarthy period and those who exploited it, became crystal clear. This discovery was accompanied by a strong surge of elation. Ward wanted an affidavit and I would give him one. I would make sure that it was worded in such a way as to serve notice to CBS that I did not expect them to be so craven as to pay any mind to AWARE's claptrap.

In the affidavit, I stressed my association with WCBS, my overseas Red Cross service, my army record, and my long years before the public eye.

I pointed out that I had made hundreds of appearances before dinners, conventions, and patriotic groups. I cited the awards that I had received from the D.A.R., the National Press Club of Washington, D.C., the American Legion, and dozens of Protestant, Catholic, and Jewish organizations. Then I stated my reasons for taking office in AFTRA—solely to help eradicate blacklisting. I pointed out that the first time in my life, and certainly to CBS's knowledge, that I had ever been attacked was after I became an officer in my union. I was confident that WCBS did not want to be party to the scurrilous doings of a discredited organization like AWARE.

I ended up by pointedly stating that I did not consider the allegations by AWARE of any relevance or importance, and said that a great number of executives at CBS, who had known me for years, could advise anyone who wanted to know about my integrity and patriotism.

I was proud of that affidavit as I finished it, and still am.

The next day, April 13, 1956, I signed the affidavit, had it notarized, and took it in to Carl Ward.

It happened that on that very day I had a luncheon appointment with Sidney Davis, a young lawyer from Louis Nizer's office. I had met him through a mutual friend, columnist Harriet Van Horne, of the New York *World-Telegram and Sun*, who had suggested that Sidney Davis would be an excellent counsel for the union. I had arranged to meet him and discuss the matter. Now, after the shellacking I had received at the meeting, there seemed little point in having that discussion. But I had heard so much about Louis Nizer, and about his spectacular victory over Westbrook Pegler, that I decided to keep the date after all.

At our luncheon I told Davis just what had happened. I explained that I was no longer in a position to influence the union to retain him as its counsel. Now, I told him, I had to fight to prevent my enemies, in the union and outside it, from cutting off my livelihood. I would not go down without a real struggle; if I could get hold of something to hit them with, I intended to let fly. I asked him if he thought Nizer would be interested in taking the case should it come to a lawsuit. He said he would discuss it with Mr. Nizer.

That evening, after my show, I had a drink with Gerald Dickler, who told me that Charles Collingwood had called him earlier, greatly alarmed at the news that Johnson and AWARE were hitting my sponsors, and had suggested we come over to his house to discuss what could be done to save my job. We found Charles at home, looking as though it was he, not I, who was about to be blacklisted. We quickly agreed that, as far as the union was concerned, our course had been run, and that we were in total defeat there. We then turned to the matter of my relations with CBS.

Charles said that he intended to do everything within his power to save my job and that he was open to suggestion. I brought up the matter of suing AWARE. Dickler very quickly pointed out that there was no basis on which to sue. Neither Ward nor anyone else who had information would be willing to get on a stand and deliver it. Besides, their testimony would probably be only hearsay—Johnson hadn't been to see them.

Then Gerry turned to me, a little impatiently and said, "Forget about suing. I want you to concentrate on holding your job."

A couple of days later, Sam Slate came into my office. He said that Tom Murray, an account executive with the Grey advertising agency, had come over to CBS quite infuriated at having received a call from Laurence Johnson, followed by a vicious letter attacking me.

Johnson had warned Murray that unless Murray removed the Hoffman Beverage account from my program, he, Johnson, would boycott Hoffman's in his supermarkets and would sic the American Legion on them. This made Murray furious. Sure enough, within a couple of days, along came a letter from an American Legion post in Syracuse. Sam had a copy of the letter and gave it to me. I knew that at last I had the goods on them. Now, for the first time, a performer had been allowed to see the charges. Murray came over. I wanted to embrace him. He knew Johnson and AWARE. He said that he would not be party to any more of their character assassinations. He said, quite undramatically, that even if it cost him his job and his reputation, he intended to help stop them. I was so moved by this honest, decent man, that I thanked him over and over, to his great embarrassment.

I called Sidney Davis and told him about the letter I now had. He said that he had spoken to Nizer about the matter and that it was time for me to see Nizer myself. Mr. Nizer would see me the next day.

The offices of Phillips, Nizer, Benjamin and Krim are located high over the Times Square area of Manhattan, occupying an entire floor of the Paramount Building.

As the secretary ushered me in, Louis Nizer rose from behind his wide, polished desk and came forward to meet me. He is a man of medium height and powerful build, and I was struck at once by his warmth and geniality.

He invited me to sit in one of the heavy leather chairs in front of his desk, seated himself in a high leather swivel chair behind the spacious desk, and suggested I relate my grievances against AWARE. As I went through the recitation of the events that had led up to my present situation, I was only barely aware that Nizer was quietly but firmly moving me past trivia to important points in the case. He never hurried me. He just moved me along, listening gravely and nodding.

When I had finished, he asked me if I understood the implications of filing a lawsuit against a group like AWARE. I told him that I thought I did. I knew that my opponents would give me a mighty hard time, if that's what he meant. He nodded; but he said he meant more than that. He said that I should know that it might take several years to bring the case to trial. During that time, great pressure would be brought to bear on me—not only economic pressure, but subtle emotional pressures. He then detailed a rather black picture of legal procedures. It all added up to a grim warning.

I told him that I was prepared to go through whatever might be necessary in order to bring this group of people to trial in a public courtroom. I felt the issues involved were vital ones.

He fell silent, reflected for a moment, and then smiled warmly. He said, "I have deliberately tried to discourage you. I don't want you to be misled that this would be an easy case. It won't be. This action will be a long one. But you will win in the end. I will represent you."

His voice did not change as he made his final statement, but it had a certain quality that lifted my spirit and reassured me.

He said that he wanted me to meet Paul Martinson, a partner of his, who would prepare the necessary papers for filing the suit.

Paul Martinson is a man of kindly face and thinning auburn hair. As he went through various papers, asking me questions, I began to experience the same comfortable, secure feeling that I always had with scholarly, pleasant professors at the university. By the time he had finished his questioning and had written down the information that would be the basis of our formal complaint, I knew that I was talking to a very fine legal mind. I soon conceived a great affection for him. His grasp of the entire case was immediate and complete.

I went home, lighthearted and excited. Up and down Madison Avenue, word would go out that John Henry Faulk had Louis Nizer fighting his case.

I started calling up friends to tell them that I was going to sue AWARE and that Louis Nizer was taking the case. A friend of mine, Palmer Webber, came up to see me, and as we discussed the case, he asked me how much of a retainer Nizer was charging. I brushed his question aside with a glib statement that Nizer wasn't charging any retainer. Palmer, knowing that I could be carried away with my own enthusiasm, explained to me that Nizer's office would probably require an immense retainer to take such a prolonged litigation. After all, Nizer was a million-dollar lawyer. I had better get ready to cough up $50,000–$100,000 as a retainer fee.

I was dumfounded. Nizer had said nothing about this. Palmer pointed out that he probably took it for granted that I knew it. Just getting Nizer to take the case was enough. But in a lawsuit such as this one promised to be, Nizer's firm would be out thousands of dollars just in expenditures.

I called Charles Collingwood and asked him if he'd ever heard of this retainer business. Charles agreed that in all likelihood, Nizer would require a rather large retainer.

Deciding that I had better talk to Nizer about the matter at once, I called him and asked for an appointment. The next morning I went down and asked him about a retainer. I told him what my friends had said about a retainer. I told him candidly that it would be impossible for me to raise that kind of money. I didn't even know whether I would be working.

To my relief, Nizer told me that my friends had misinformed me. Ordinarily his firm did require a large retainer. In the instance of my suit, it would be $10,000, which was minimal for a major case. He explained that this retainer was not for legal fees, but for actual out-of-pocket expenses. I didn't tell him that my savings did not nearly amount to the money required.

During the next several days, I frantically called friends, trying to raise money. They were all willing and anxious to help, and several did. But I was far short of the whole

amount when the day arrived for payment. Not everyone, by
any means, felt that I was wise to sue.

Ward of CBS felt that it was a very dubious move. He felt
it would call the public's attention to my troubles with
AWARE. Sam Slate felt a little differently. He thought it
would probably shake up Madison Avenue and raise a real
question about me. However, he said that with Nizer guiding my case, it would very likely knock AWARE out of the
pitcher's box. Gerry Dickler was doubtful. He pointed out
that his chief concern was for my career; he did not want to
see me become a martyr. He also pointed out that after the
suit was filed, I could be sure that the defendants would increase their pressure on the radio and television industry to
starve me out. They would have real incentive now.

I argued that this was an opportunity of a lifetime. I could
expose their fraud in open court. If no one else realized what
a travesty they made of patriotism, I had to go through with
it. Gerry pointed out that I would find few friends in the industry who would support me during the trial.

Several days later Martinson called me to say that he was
filing the suit. He said the evidence indicated a conspiracy
between AWARE, Vincent Hartnett, and Laurence Johnson
to carry out the blacklisting.

The day after the suit was filed, all of the New York papers
carried the story. One of them, the *New York Post*, filled its
entire front page with big, black headlines on the subject.

I was still $7,500 short of the amount needed for the re-
tainer. I was embarrassed to go to Nizer and tell him that I
couldn't raise it. He might get the idea that he had taken
on a pauper. As I was sitting at my desk at CBS, racking
my mind for someone to call and borrow money from, Edward R. Murrow called me from his office upstairs.

He said that he was terribly glad that I had filed the suit,
and that Carl Sandburg had sent word: "Whatever's the matter with America, Johnny ain't." He said that he was mighty
happy about the suit and that his door was always open
to me.

I had known Ed Murrow for a number of years. My teacher
at the University of Texas, and friend, J. Frank Dobie, had
become acquainted with him during the war years in Europe
and had me look up Ed when I first came to New York. I told

Ed that I wanted to see him at once and went up and laid the matter before him.

I told him that I lacked $7,500 of the retainer fee. He expressed surprise that CBS was not paying the expenses of the trial since I was the one who was doing the fighting. I told him that, if anything, the executives to whom I had spoken were strongly opposed to my filing a suit. He said, "Tell Lou Nizer, Johnny, that he will have the money tomorrow."

I protested. "Look, Ed, I can't borrow $7,500 from you. Hell, I might lose my job. And even if I win the suit, there may be no money to repay such a sum as that."

Ed looked at me evenly and said, "Let's get this straight, Johnny. I am not making a personal loan to you of this money. I am investing this money in America. Louis Nizer must try this case. These people must be brought into court. This blacklisting racket must be exposed. This is a very important suit. I don't know whether even you realize how important it is."

And so it was that on June 26, 1956, the lawsuit *Faulk v. AWARE, Laurence Johnson, and Vincent Hartnett* was filed in the New York State Supreme Court.

5

I had no illusions when I began. I knew good and well that I was putting my reputation on the block. I understood very well that the defendants had many allies throughout the country and that they would go over my background with a fine-tooth comb.

There was one area in which I was completely naïve. I thought that the radio and television industry would believe that I was taking a bold step and that they would admire me for it. I had the notion that once the news of my lawsuit got around, the radio and television executives—long oppressed by AWARE's vigilantism—would lose their timidity. I was more convinced of this than ever when, within a week after the suit was filed, I received hundreds of letters at CBS from listeners, all of whom approved and sympathized with my action. Many of them expressed outrage that such a lawsuit was necessary and that I was put to the trouble of having to defend myself.

The men who directed the affairs of Madison Avenue, however, reacted as though I had announced I had highly contagious mumps. It wasn't long before I realized that instead of improving my employability, the lawsuit had had an adverse effect upon it; I had become more controversial than ever.

Few, if any, of the radio-TV fraternity believed for a moment that I would win the suit—at least among the impartial executives. The Susskinds, Murrows, and others of their persuasion, never doubted for a moment that I would win.

My greatest personal disappointment came with the union's lack of reaction. There was not a voice raised in my behalf in the union, save for a couple of close friends and loyal Middle-of-the-Road members. I was still a member of the local board; indeed, I was still a vice-president. However, I had had my ears whipped down so soundly that I was not much of a power in union affairs anymore.

The defendants began to stir themselves. They did not take kindly to being sued. Godfrey Schmidt became attorney for the defendants. He went on a radio program and declared that he was confident that AWARE was right and that obviously I was a man who could not be trusted. He said that he welcomed the opportunity to try the case in the courts of the land.

When he filed his answer, he asserted that I had no cause for action: there was nothing libelous in the AWARE bulletin. They had not called me a Communist. They had only repeated what was the public record of my past doings. If they had made a mistake, it was an honest one.

Nizer challenged these answers as unresponsive. Justice Saul Streit upheld Nizer and dismissed the defendants' answers. In fact, Justice Streit handed down a decision that was one of the cornerstones of our case. It held that the defendants had, indeed, sought to raise a question of my patriotism by innuendo and that the bulletin was a libel per se. The only full defense was for the defendants to plead the truth of their innuendo: that I was a Communist, at least pro-Communist. They had to prove it by my acts and words. They could no longer hide behind what I was alleged to have done.

The defendants immediately gave notice of appeal to the Appellate Division of the New York State Supreme Court. They couldn't let Justice Streit's decision stand. It struck directly at the heart of McCarthy-type blacklisting—that of character assassination by innuendo.

Although literally hundreds of people had been involved in blacklisting in one form or another, locating witnesses was a tedious task. Under Martinson's direction, the accumulation of evidence was begun. Dozens of performers, writers, and directors who had been damaged were contacted, but the majority of them showed reluctance to becoming involved in any way with my lawsuit.

John Crosby, radio and television columnist for the New York *Herald Tribune*, had for many months been writing scathing columns about the doings of AWARE and about blacklisting. AWARE, sometime prior to the filing of my suit, had sued John Crosby and the *Herald Tribune*. The *Herald Tribune*'s attorneys had investigated AWARE and

Vincent Hartnett before they came to court, and they had accumulated a sizable library of factual material concerning
Hartnett and AWARE. When we filed our suit, the *Herald
Tribune*'s lawyers came forward and offered us detailed
material, and it proved to be of great assistance to us in preparing the suit.

Another very interesting source of information on blacklisting became available to us at about that time. In the
summer of 1956, the Fund for the Republic published an
excellently documented study of blacklisting in the radio,
television, and motion picture industry. In response, the
House Un-American Activities Committee hauled John
Cogley, editor of the report, down to Washington, and instead of investigating the charges he had made, they investigated Cogley. Not a single person in the radio and television
industry came to Cogley's defense. He was understandably
bitter about this. We made good use of his book in assem-
bling the evidence for our case. And in no instance did we
find him inaccurate.

Although my show at WCBS retained most of its sponsors,
when one would cancel, we would never know whether it
was because of some backstairs pressure or for a wholly unrelated reason. Before long, it became obvious to us that the
television field was rapidly closing to me. Dickler and I discussed it many times, and he said that in spite of all his
efforts to stir up interest, the doors remained closed. He suggested that I reconcile myself to the notion that until the
lawsuit was over, nothing in the way of additional work
would be forthcoming.

In December 1956, WCBS renewed my contract with
them for another five years, and I breathed easy. Although by
its terms I could be dismissed at the end of any thirteen-
week cycle for certain reasons, I believed that WCBS was actually giving me a vote of confidence. I was making good
money out of that one show, and I had no reason to com-
plain. As the spring of 1957 flowered across Central Park, I
was completely resigned to forgetting about more ambitious
plans for my career until the suit was brought to trial.

Collingwood and I had been re-elected to the local board,
but we were hopelessly outnumbered. We could do little but
sit in board meetings and watch the other side have its way.

The new board took office in January 1957. Their first several meetings in office consisted of rescinding nearly all of the resolutions that had been passed by our board the year before.

Then to make sure that no wild-eyed radicals like the Middle-of-the-Road people ever got a chance to win an election again, the local board introduced a resolution making it necessary for all candidates for office in the union to submit any statements they intended to mail to the membership to the local board for censorship before mailing. I stopped going to the local board meetings shortly after this.

Meanwhile, the defendants had failed to file their appeal from the ruling of Justice Streit within the proper time. Nizer threatened to ask for judgment by default. Schmidt agreed to a stipulation providing for pretrial examination—which is not mandatory in libel cases in New York State—and granting us the right to examine the defendants prior to their examining me. (New York Supreme Court procedure calls for the plaintiff to submit to pretrial examination before the defendants, unless otherwise stipulated.) This was just one of the many brilliant and valuable legal moves that Nizer accomplished before the case came to trial.

In April 1957, the Appellate Division unanimously sustained Justice Streit's decision declaring the AWARE bulletin libelous per se.

This knocked the props from under the defendants. The only complete defense in a libel suit is truth. This decision meant that they were going to have to come into court and prove that what they had alleged about me was the truth.

That same month a reassuring change occurred in the management of WCBS. Ward was promoted to a position in the television network, and the position of general manager of WCBS was left vacant. To our delight, Sam Slate was appointed to the job of general manager in May.

Sam's elevation to the job, I felt, meant that I had a real ally against any sneak attacks on me from AWARE or the other defendants. Now, since I had managed to retain most of my sponsors, and with Slate as the general manager of WCBS, I decided to take my first real vacation since I joined WCBS. I looked around for a place to go to and discovered that Ocho Rios, Jamaica, filled the bill exactly.

I got back to New York on Sunday night, August 5. After a good night's sleep, I awakened early and sat down at my desk to write a journal of my holiday. About nine o'clock in the morning the phone rang. It was Gerald Dickler. His voice carried a note of alarm. He asked me to come directly to his office.

When I reached his office, he stated at once that I had been fired while I was away. He handed me a registered letter which he had received in my absence, announcing the cancellation of my contract with WCBS. The news hit me like a bolt of lightning. I could only sit and blink. In the past year I had become overconfident. Of course, I had been expecting the news subconsciously since the AWARE bulletin had come out, but I had successfully pushed it out of my conscious mind.

I had told myself many times that if worse came to worst and I did get fired, I would be man enough to stand it. Now that that time had arrived, I was not prepared for it at all. It took my breath away. Gerry said he was sure that there was only one explanation. They had taken advantage of the fact that I was several thousand miles away on vacation. He pointed out that this was really the first opportunity that WCBS had had, since the filing of my suit, to make such a move and cover it up with plausible reasons. He said, "Of course, none of their reasons really make any sense. You're doing as well as almost anybody at the station, and better than most of them. You've got a good record at WCBS as an earner."

I just sat there looking at the registered letter. "The plain facts are," Gerry said, "they don't want you there any more, Johnny. Somebody got to them. How or when, I don't know. But you became the source of embarrassment to WCBS. They picked up what excuses came to hand, took advantage of your absence to make the move. That's all there is to it."

"Well," I said finally, "now that it's done, it's done. Where do we go from here?"

Gerry looked glum, and shook his head. "Nowhere, I'm afraid."

"My God, I'd never have taken that vacation if I had known this was coming. Have we got any money left?"

Gerry nodded. "Yes, I've been working on that. I figure

that if we're real cautious with what you have in the bank, you can get through for three or four months. Possibly until Christmas. But you are going to have to cut down on every expense—right to the bone."

He suggested that I go on up to see Slate at once since he had promised Sam that he would send me directly to him. He said that we would get together later that afternoon and discuss plans—if any.

I went to Slate's office. I was embarrassed. I got the impression that he was too. Sam began by saying that he had made the decision entirely on his own, and that no one else was responsible. He then gave me several reasons for having reached the decision. He said that Arthur Godfrey and the network had pre-empted part of my time, that I had been in the same place too long, and that perhaps a change would do me good. He said, too, that my ratings had slipped some.

I felt terribly sorry for him. I tried to reassure him that there were no hard feelings. And when I left his office I was certain, and I still am, of one thing: Sam Slate sincerely regretted having to fire me from WCBS.

Allen Ludden was program manager at WCBS at that time. I went in to see him. Allen told me that Slate felt very badly about my being fired. He also told me that as program director he took full responsibility for the decision. They were planning to change the program format of the station.

This somewhat baffled me. A few moments before, Sam Slate had said that *he* took full responsibility. I left Allen's office rather confused. I went into my office and called Louis Nizer and told him what had happened. He wasn't confused at all; he was angry; he knew the ax had fallen at last.

6

At home that night, alone, I sat down and stared out over lower Manhattan. The impact of my situation hit me full force. I could not think of a single move to make. It seemed like the end of the road.

What was really happening to me? Nothing that I had not anticipated. What did I really believe about my society? About America? What had Daddy really believed about our society when he'd catch a bus and ride for an entire hot summer's day to try a case for a Black who could not even afford to pay Daddy's bus fare? I was allowing self-interest to become paramount, it was that simple. Good Elmer Davis had said: "America was not founded by cowards, and it will not be saved by cowards."

The society I believed in rested firmly on the bedrock of freedom. The genius that had founded our society and written into its laws: "Congress shall make no law respecting an establishment of religion, or prohibiting the free exercise thereof; or abridging the freedom of speech, or of the press, or the right of the people peaceably to assemble, and to petition the government for a redress of grievances"—that genius had placed a heavy obligation on me. I accepted it. I believed with every fiber of my being that America's greatness stemmed directly from those great dreams and ideals. The enemies of these ideals—the House Un-American Activities Committee, AWARE, Inc., the Ku Klux Klan—no matter what powers or shapes they assumed, they could not change that conviction.

I went back to my office and pondered the matter. It was all right for Dickler and Nizer to be convinced that WCBS had fired me under pressure. But I realized that neither one of them had had the long and close association that I had; I felt that it placed me under a certain obligation to accept WCBS's explanation until it was proved conclusively not to be so.

I was to do Lanny Ross's program for the next two weeks.
His program was scheduled to come on from four o'clock to
five, the hour before mine. One of the secretaries brought in
his commercial schedule for the day. As I casually glanced
over the list of commercials, I made an interesting discovery.
I got out the commercial schedule for my own program and
compared them. I was astonished to find that Lanny Ross
had only about half as much commercial time on his program as I had on mine.

A radio station—whatever public service posture it may
strike—is in business to make money for its owners. That is
fundamental. My program was making a profit, and a handsome one, for WCBS.

I swiveled around in my chair and gazed out the window.
The decision to cancel my contract had had nothing what-
ever to do with my ratings or with program changes at CBS.
From that moment on I never believed otherwise.

7

My forty-fourth birthday arrived August 21, 1957. That evening I realized for the first time what a terrifying thing it must have been for the tens of thousands of other men in their mid-forties who had suddenly lost their jobs or had their professions swept away from them. I had never understood what a painful thing it was. There they were—just as I was—with no takers for their particular training and experience. How could they bear it?

It might take three or four years to bring my case to trial. These would, ordinarily, be my prime, most productive years. And they were precisely the years in which I would be doing nothing.

For a time, in the early fall, things began to look brighter. I had an offer to become the new radio personality on WCCO in Minneapolis. At the same time I got a call from Joe Hyman, a theatrical producer on Broadway. He said that they were producing a play called *Fair Game* and that its author had suggested me for a part. The author had in fact written the part with me in mind.

My hopes soared. I asked the producers of *Fair Game* if they would hold open the part while I went to Minneapolis to see about the radio offer. They said they would try, and I took off for Minnesota.

While in Minneapolis I was treated as a celebrity, wined and dined, and introduced to practically everyone in the city including the governor. I flew home encouraged.

But back in New York I found that the play had been cast and was already in Philadelphia. Then the program director at WCCO called and said they didn't want me.

In October 1957 the long wait began—the long wait to confront AWARE face to face before a bar of justice. Before, there had always been an income to lean on. Now unem-

ployment had come to sit in our house like a turkey buz-
zard—roosting there, watching, waiting.

Louis Nizer and Gerald Dickler had anticipated what
waiting out the lawsuit could do to me, if I were unemployed. After I returned from Minneapolis, Lou had a long
talk with me. He recommended that I not for one moment
consider myself unemployable. He said that I should not regard any door as closed until I had tried it.

I made a list of everyone I could think of who could be instrumental in getting me work in radio and television. All of
the network and independent stations' executives, advertising executives, independent packagers of shows—everyone.
I made a vow I would follow each lead to its end—no matter
how tenuous it seemed to be.

I was meticulous in my search and contacted everyone on
my list. Some were encouraging; some even came forward
with what seemed like definite offers. But always, after a few
days of consideration, the answer would be the same—they
didn't have anything at the moment.

As Thanksgiving-time drew near, I had begun to run out of
contacts, persons to call on in search of work. I found it more
and more difficult to make calls. I tried to read. I couldn't
concentrate. I began to wonder about my talent. How did I
know I was being refused employment because of the blacklist? No one had called me in and said, "Look here, you're
blacklisted. We can't use you." How did I know it wasn't my
own inadequacies as a performer that were keeping me out
of work? The doubts set in.

8

Shortly after New Year's 1958, Dickler suggested I had better not wait until I had no money whatever left in the bank before I made plans to borrow some. I had been very squeamish about this.

I promised him that I would sit down at once and figure out just what to do about borrowing money. Going to a bank for the loan was out of the question; unemployed and without security as I was, that would be about as pointless as going to AWARE and asking for money enough to tide me over until the suit came to trial. I made a mental inventory of possessions that might be hocked.

I knew that whatever loan I got would have to be made on exceptionally flexible terms, such as one could arrange only with a friend, one who could lend me the money without having to have it back at any specific date. I wrestled incessantly with the problem; I couldn't sleep at night trying to figure it out. I persuaded myself that my stake in the lawsuit constituted some kind of security; I could ask some of my wealthy friends to lend me money against the sum that I would recover in court. Then I realized there might not be any recovery. Nizer had told me that after years of litigation and a verdict in our favor, the jury might only award me one dollar for damages. The costs of the case were mounting astronomically. The chances of having much money for the repayment of loans after the suit was over were slim indeed.

Obviously, I concluded, the only thing that I could do was to go to a prospective lender and candidly tell him the facts.

I made a list of well-to-do friends whom I could consider as prospects. Then I started working out an approach to them. I rationalized that in a way I was fighting the battle of all right-minded people in this country.

I realized that I would run myself ragged trying to raise the amount I needed if I asked for $50 or $100 at a time. So I might as well start at $500.

The first friend I selected was Herbert Steinmann. He and his wife, Anne, were generous, intelligent people, with a deep sense of social responsibility, and a great affection for me. We had been warm friends and had served together on the board of a mental health clinic. When it came to the matter of actually calling him up and asking for an appointment, however, I hesitated. What if I were being completely unrealistic about this business? What if Herb, who was a good social friend, were to feel that I had presumed on our friendship by asking him for what amounted to a gift? We would both be terribly embarrassed.

When I finally screwed up enough courage to visit Herb, he was eager to know all about the progress of the lawsuit. I told him the latest court news. Then I began relating a little of my experiences in job hunting. He suddenly interrupted me. "Oh, by the way, Johnny. Forgive me for interrupting you, but the thought just struck me, and I might forget to mention it later. Would you consider letting me give you a check for a thousand dollars? You know, just to help you along right now? After all, this is my fight too. I think you ought to let me participate—even if it is just in the limited way of giving money."

I don't recall what else I said during that visit, but I presume it was inspired.

Sometime later, in April 1958, I received a letter from Wendell Campbell, who offered me a job on station KFRC in San Francisco. It was not only a big job, but one that would earn me a lot of money. Campbell had known me and my work at WCBS and said he was sure that I was just the personality he was looking for. He asked me if I would be available.

I was in a state of acute ecstasy. I wrote a letter to Campbell telling him I was not only available for the job, but was eager to give it a go. Then I sat on pins and needles awaiting his reply.

9

Campbell was a friend of Slate's, so later I called Slate and told him about the San Francisco offer. He suggested that I come down to his office. There he told me that Campbell had already called him from San Francisco and had told him that he was very anxious to bring me to KFRC.

However, Sam said, Wendell was concerned over the lawsuit in which I was involved. In fact, he and Sam had discussed the matter and agreed that there would be real drawbacks to my signing a contract in San Francisco as long as I was involved in a lawsuit in New York. Sam then suggested that I should give serious consideration to dropping the suit. He pointed out that we had won our points over Hartnett and Johnson in court. He said he was sure that now the defendants would be perfectly willing to make a public apology. That is, if I would drop the suit. I asked him how he knew this, and he said it was his impression that they were very anxious to have the suit dropped.

He seemed to have information that he did not care to disclose, but kept suggesting that if I forced AWARE to fight, they would come out on top. Nevertheless, I appreciated Sam's concern and told him so. I told him that I would give his suggestion serious thought.

After leaving Sam's office, I called Nizer and told him what Sam had said. Nizer wanted to call Campbell in San Francisco and assure him that the litigation would in no way interfere with my moving to San Francisco. The case would not come to trial for another year or so at the very least, and we probably could arrange matters so that I would attend the trial during a vacation period. When I asked Nizer what he made of Sam's insistence that my wisest course now would be to settle for a public apology, Nizer chuckled. He said that Sam was probably accurate, which meant that now was a propitious time to call the first of the defendants for his ex-

amination before trial. In the meantime, I should continue
to push the San Francisco deal with all my power.

Papers were served on Hartnett directing him to come to
Nizer's office for examination before trial. Martinson explained to me exactly what an examination before trial, or
EBT, was. New York Supreme Court procedure provides that
each party to a civil suit may examine the other party before
trial. The chief purpose of this is to ascertain exactly what
will be at issue when the case comes to court. This narrows
the area of disagreement and prevents either side from taking the other one by surprise with unexpected evidence or
issues. The EBT is conducted in the presence of a court reporter, the witnesses are sworn, and all evidence given is
part of the official court record.

About a week before the Hartnett examination, I received
a subpoena to appear before the House Un-American Activities Committee. I was directed to appear on June 17, 1958.
Nizer told me not to worry about it however, and to sleep
soundly and forget the matter. But I couldn't go to sleep that
night.

I was deeply concerned over this latest turn in events. I
had no love for this particular committee and I knew that
Vincent Hartnett had been in communication with them
quite frequently. It angered me to think that an agency of my
government might join the defendants in the persecution
of me. It occurred to me, as a matter of fact, that it was
probably a clumsy attempt on the part of the defendants to
frighten me into settling the suit.

My reasons for distrusting the HUAC ran back a number
of years. I knew, for instance, that in the days before World
War II the Dies Committee, as the HUAC was known at that
time, had enjoyed the praise and support of some of America's most unsavory pro-Hitler groups. Names like Gerald L. K. Smith, Joseph P. Kamp, Merwin K. Hart, Gerald
Winrod, and other like personalities had been among the
committee's earliest and staunchest supporters. The Dies
Committee had made headlines in Texas papers back in
1944, by claiming that the University of Texas was a hotbed
of Communists. When the president of the university, Dr.
Homer Price Rainey, had demanded that Dies either put up
or shut up, Dies apologized. He even declared that the Uni-

versity of Texas was a model American institution. But the harm had already been done, and serious harm, to the university.

Later, Representative John E. Rankin of Mississippi and Representative John S. Wood of Georgia had taken over the Committee. They were notorious for their violent anti-Semitic and anti-Negro speeches. In the late forties, when J. Parnell Thomas was the chairman of the Committee he had been sent to prison as a common thief, but not until after his Committee had wrought havoc in Hollywood with its reckless hearings. I remembered how in his magazine *The Cross and the Flag*, Gerald L. K. Smith had boasted that his Christian Nationalist Party deserved the credit for pushing the HUAC into Hollywood investigations. The Committee had even so far overstepped itself that it subpoenaed President Harry S. Truman—or attempted to. They didn't get very far. It didn't stretch my imagination much to believe that an organization like AWARE, Inc., would urge the Committee to attack me, and that the Committee would likely oblige them. I knew that the HUAC was a great favorite with most of the vigilante groups, such as AWARE, across the country. They doted on its so-called findings, but worst of all, HUAC furnished a platform and Congressional immunity to an assortment of crackpot witnesses.

My concern over the subpoena was overshadowed by the arrival of June 5, 1958, the date set for Vincent Hartnett's first day of EBT. My excitement was at high pitch. Nizer had explained the procedure to me. Hartnett would be examined, then Johnson, and then, perhaps, several of the directors of AWARE. Then the defendants' attorneys would examine me, and the trial date would be set.

Shortly after ten o'clock, three men entered the room. I recognized one of them as Godfrey Schmidt and presumed another was Hartnett. They noticed me sitting on the sofa at the far end of the room, and they nodded curtly. Then one of them commented, "That's John Henry Faulk." Schmidt came forward and shook my hand, explaining that he had thought I was an attorney. He then introduced me to Vincent Hartnett.

I was relieved to see Nizer come into the room. Hartnett was sworn by the court reporter and his EBT began.

Nizer's manner was courteous and correct. Vincent Hartnett, obviously at ease, puffed away on his big cigar, giving
his answers easily and clearly. If a question was asked that
Schmidt thought improper or irrelevant, he would object.
The lawyers would then talk off the record, and if a colloquy
between Schmidt and Nizer failed to resolve Schmidt's objection, that line of question was dropped until the record
could be taken before a justice of the New York Supreme
Court for his ruling on it.

The questioning went along the lines of Hartnett's background and the origins of AWARE. At one point Nizer asked
a question about some person, and Schmidt objected on the
grounds that the person and the question did not relate
to John Henry Faulk's case. Nizer explained that we had
charged a conspiracy, thus, he was entitled to cover a great
many other matters relating to AWARE, its operations and
origins, and other persons who had been affected by its
practices. Schmidt seemed surprised at this explanation, as
though he had not realized before what the "conspiracy" in
our original charge meant. He and Hartnett exchanged a
brief whispered conversation. From the expression on his
face, and his general manner, I gathered that this was the
first time he really recognized the width and breadth that
our lawsuit might assume.

A little later Nizer asked a question that involved an accusation against Hartnett. It was the first stinging question
that had been put. It upset both Schmidt and Hartnett.
There was a brief argument, off the record, between the lawyers. Hartnett was clearly annoyed. "Mr. Nizer," he snapped,
"I would remind you that I'm not on the witness stand, and
you're not a district attorney."

Nizer eyed him intently for a moment. Then he remarked
quietly to the court reporter, "The following is on the record." Looking directly at Hartnett, his voice cold, but without rage, Nizer said: "Do I understand, sir, you presume to
instruct me in the conduct of this examination? Are you,
sir? How dare you impudently speak of district attorneys
and witnesses! You sir, you who have sat as judge, jury, prosecuting attorney, and executioner on the lives and careers
of hundreds of loyal, innocent victims! You, sir, who have
drawn the noose of starvation around the neck of that inno-

cent man sitting there, seeking to starve his children and destroy his reputation. You dare, sir, instruct me in the conduct of this case?"

The eloquent outrage in Nizer's voice sent Schmidt and Hartnett reeling backward. Hartnett cleared his throat as though to reply, and Schmidt quickly put his hand on his arm and shushed him. Hartnett tried to place a cigar in his mouth and put it in his left ear instead. Schmidt protested that Nizer's remarks were unnecessarily harsh. Nizer replied to Schmidt that he needed no instruction from him, either. It was clear that both Schmidt and Hartnett were shaken not only by the sharp lash of Nizer's words, but as to what the future held for them in this suit.

From that point on, Hartnett answered the questions obediently, and Schmidt showed a definite reluctance and nervousness at objecting. Nizer really opened up on the case then and began to probe for names—names of people whom Hartnett had blacklisted, names of his colleagues in the blacklisting business. I was hearing things that amazed me. Hartnett named personality after personality, and described his method of informing on people, gathering information on them, etc., in great detail. Nizer dug deeper and deeper into the conspiracy. By the time the first session of the EBT was over, Hartnett realized that he was in for a much rougher experience than he had anticipated.

Each day Nizer continued his relentless examination of Hartnett. The names of people who had been Hartnett's aides, the ones who had given him secret information, all came out and were placed on the record. The amount of money Hartnett collected for his services startled me. I had no idea he had such a lucrative business going. He was forced to turn over his income tax returns and explain the sources of his income. Most of it had been derived from furnishing information on entertainers to the various agencies, networks, and sponsors.

On the following Monday I received a telegram from Congressman Walter, continuing my HUAC subpoena from June 17 to July 17. When I showed it to Nizer, he was not satisfied. He immediately fired off a letter to the counsel of HUAC pointing out that July 17 was no more desirable than June 17. He said further that obviously I could not be called before the HUAC before my EBT had taken place. He asked that the subpoena be dropped, or continued, at least, until October 31.

It is an interesting coincidence that on the very next day, June 17, when I was scheduled to appear before HUAC, Hartnett, having learned that I was not going to have to appear, completely capitulated to us in his EBT. I was not present, but Nizer reported to me that Hartnett had not had his heart in the testimony. Then, along toward the middle of the afternoon, both Hartnett and Schmidt seemed to have given up. Nizer phoned me at once and reported that they had made very damaging admissions. They admitted on the record that they had been fed a barrel of false information about me, and had offered to make any public statement we desired them to.

Nizer was almost as excited over the surrender of Hartnett and Schmidt as I was. He had not expected them to go to such lengths in their admissions so soon, he said. Nizer told me that it would now be just a matter of time until we had completely undone them all. He said that he had scheduled a meeting with Schmidt the next day to discuss the matter. I would have turned handsprings had I been able to. I was ecstatic. Now I knew that I would soon be going to San Francisco. This cleared the way entirely. Nizer told me that he would have Schmidt's and Hartnett's testimony printed up so that I might send it to San Francisco at once.

Now, not only were the defendants going rapidly down the drain, but I was being freed to go back to work. Our troubles were over. Of course, I had no way of knowing that they were just beginning. We really hadn't seen anything yet.

10

Though Hartnett and Schmidt had hopelessly compromised their case, there were other defendants to be examined and a great deal more information to be acquired. I was thinking about the day when we would be completely through with Hartnett and start on Johnson and the other defendants. The HUAC had continued my subpoena, so that was off my mind. The San Francisco deal seemed absolutely set. My only problem was whether or not I would take it, now that I was apparently going to be a free man and could probably find work in New York City. In the morning mail of June 28 an airmail letter came from Wendell Campbell in San Francisco. It was filled with pleasant remarks about how well he thought I would do on the radio show. It also outlined in some detail the kind of thing Campbell had in mind for the show I would be doing. It ended with a suggestion that I go down to WOR and cut a thirty-minute audition tape so that he might play it for the other executives at the San Francisco station. He said that he had arranged with a Mr. Leder, of WOR, for me to do the audition at no cost.

I noticed another letter in the same mail addressed to me in an envelope identical with the one I had just opened. In it, however, was a letter addressed to Robert Leder, Mutual Broadcasting Company. It was an original. The thought struck me that perhaps the secretary had made a mistake and had meant to send me a copy of Mr. Leder's letter and had sent me the original instead. I started reading it; it concerned a request that Mr. Leder allow me the facilities of the studios at WOR. The bill was to be sent to Campbell. As I read on, I realized that the secretary's mistake had been a bit more serious than simply sending me the original instead of a carbon. I had an idea that neither the original nor a carbon had been intended for me. Mr. Campbell discussed my victory over AWARE and added that if it was true that I was free of controversy, "Then we will definitely be interested in having John Henry Faulk out here."

As I read the letter over, I realized that here was the first concrete evidence that had come into my hands since I had been fired that AWARE was a factor in my employability. I called Nizer and explained the situation to him. He told me to put the letter in another envelope and send it on to Leder with a note that it had been sent to me by mistake. But before doing so, perhaps, I should have it photostated. I followed his suggestion.

Later in the day I was telling Slate about this strange situation and the fact that Campbell wanted me to do an audition tape. Sam said I was welcome to do it right there, in the WCBS studios. I accepted his gracious offer, made the tape, and sent it out to Campbell.

A day or so later, Martinson called me to say that Schmidt had withdrawn from the case and they were substituting another attorney. He said with a chuckle that I could never guess who this new attorney would be. As irony—or fate—would have it, the new counsel for the defense was Roy Cohn, the dauntless young man who had figured so prominently in the McCarthy investigation days. Cohn, the scourge of subversives. I felt that surely Martinson was pulling my leg.

The next day I called Nizer and asked him when the next EBT with Hartnett was scheduled. I explained to him that I couldn't wait to see Cohn in action.

There was a note of chagrin in Lou's voice. "I'm afraid you're going to have to wait, John. Cohn has announced that he's going abroad for a couple of months. He said he would let us know when it will be convenient for him to continue his clients' EBT. Perhaps in September or October." For a moment I was too shocked to make comment. I had thought that the EBT would go right through to completion. In fact, I had rather banked on that.

"But, Lou," I said, "how can Cohn make a decision like that on his own? He can't just up and declare he will continue this case when it's convenient for him. What about us? Don't we have a right to demand that he stay here and continue right now?"

Lou carefully explained to me that we could do nothing

whatever about Cohn's decision. He counseled me to reconcile myself to the unpleasant fact that the suit was at
a standstill until September, maybe even October. Even
though Hartnett had admitted his error, his malice was yet
to be established.

I called Dickler and told him I wanted to come down. Actually, I wanted to find out what he thought about me trying
to raise the money for a trip to San Francisco. I realized that I
was going to have to have that job now.

When I got down to Gerry's office, the first thing he said
was, "As I understand it, the HUAC continued your subpoena until November 18. They did not quash it. Is that
right?"

I nodded and said yes.

"Have you told Campbell that you are still under subpoena and scheduled to be called on November 18 for the
HUAC?"

"Why, no," I said, "I didn't think it was important. I just
sent him the audition tape."

"Johnny, don't you see what you're up against? They continued your subpoena. They did not cancel it. In other words
you're still under subpoena by the HUAC. Don't you know
why? They might have failed in their effort to call you last
month, but they haven't given up. They're not going to let
AWARE down. Do you think that Campbell, or any executive in radio or television in this country, is going to give a
man a job who is under subpoena by the HUAC?"

Why hadn't I thought of that? In all likelihood, Campbell
had already learned of my being subpoenaed by the HUAC.
The New York papers had carried the story. But even if he
were under the impression that it was over and done with, I
was obligated to tell him that not only was the trial going to
be stretched out further, but that I was still under subpoena.
There was no point in thinking about any kind of work until
that was over with. I cursed the HUAC and the defendants
under my breath.

One night as I sat writing at my desk, I had an inspired
thought. I would tell Texana, my sister in Texas, about my
subpoena.

Texana, my sister, is a year younger than I. In all outward
appearances she is a typical Texas housewife, a devoted

mother, a dedicated member of the Methodist Church, and much occupied with civic and educational affairs in the community—the same community, South Austin, where I was born and grew up and where she has lived all her life. But there is really nothing typical about Teck, as she is universally called. She combines a primitive Protestant ethic with a set of fiercely held egalitarian attitudes. More than this, she acts upon her convictions, with alacrity and dedication. She, like my family, derived her strongly held liberal opinions from our father, who spent his life as a civil-rights lawyer. As Teck puts it: "I love my government, and I love my children. But Lord have mercy, that don't mean that either of them are perfect. Just because I love 'em. It means that I've got an obligation to see that they do right. I'm not going to sit by and watch my children or my government go to the devil simply because it's too much trouble to do anything about it." Inaction and indifference to civic responsibility are deadly sins in Teck's book. She holds, as Tocqueville and James Madison did, that justice is the principal end of government.

I wrote to Texana and outlined exactly what had happened. I really didn't know what she could do or how she could do it. But of one thing I was certain, Texana would do something, and do it at once.

The most punishing aspect of being blacklisted was not the economic hardships that it worked on its victims, but the painful inability to use one's creative resources. It shuts one off from contact with the public at the most important level of existence, the creative level. I would spend frustrating and fruitless hours trying to work on new material. New ideas simply would not take form. I could not create in a vacuum. I knew that others had overcome the difficulty of being isolated from the public, but I couldn't.

In my acute discomfiture I began to understand why some artists had capitulated to the other side—traded their integrity to Satan, as it were—in order to get back into their profession. I knew that the state of mind I was in was exactly what the defendants had planned—going into that fatuous depression, and finally saying, "To hell with it all. I'll settle this deal and get back to work." Well, I thought, if that's their game, they'll damn well be disappointed this time.

I found out that I could make a fast and vast fortune selling mutual fund shares. I spent hours trying to become conversant with all the financial details of stocks and bonds. But somehow or other, it wouldn't stick in my mind. When I tried my approach on my friends, I found I could not convince them or myself that they were investing their money wisely. I did not like gambling with my own money and even less did I like persuading people to gamble with theirs. I found it difficult to make sales and I soon realized being a bond salesman was not my line of work.

Things had picked up considerably about this time in the lawsuit. In the latter part of September, Cohn came back from foreign shores. Martinson, who had taken over the EBT, demanded that Cohn present himself and Hartnett to continue the examination.

On the day appointed for the resumption of the EBT, I

went down to Martinson's office to observe the proceedings.
I had never had the pleasure of meeting Cohn before and was
looking forward to seeing him in operation. He came in, the
very essence of freshness and briskness, along with his partner Tom Bolan. His manner was self-assured and, I might
say, a bit arrogant. As the EBT began, it was obvious that
Cohn was going to put up with no nonsense. His objections
were couched in terms like "Don't answer that!" and "You
can't ask that!" As I watched his performance, I began to
think there was something wrong with me. Cohn had a reputation as a formidable, shrewd, and able lawyer. For the life
of me—and I listened very intently—I could not discover
the slightest basis for such a reputation. As far as I know,
that was the last EBT at which Cohn honored us with his
presence. Thereafter Bolan took charge.

There were several more sessions, in which the attorneys
directed Hartnett to refuse to answer many of Martinson's
questions and to refuse to produce several documents that
had been asked for; and then they indicated that they could
not be bothered with more EBT for the present. It became
necessary for the matters to be resolved by the court. Briefs
were filed before Justice Fine. In November, Justice Fine
handed down his decision, and it was a fine one for us. The
defendants were directed not only to produce all the documents and letters and evidence that Paul had demanded, but
also to continue the EBT on a regular schedule.

In late October, I got a telegram from HUAC canceling my
subpoena. I can only assume that a letter-writing campaign,
led by my sister Texana, had been successful.

Although I enjoyed a feeling of well-being on the legal
front, my financial affairs were in hopeless chaos. I had
slipped further and further into debt.

I had several suits of clothes that were durable and nice,
but they were several years old and, combined with shirts of
equal age, they had a slightly seedy appearance. Much worse
than that, I began to feel seedy.

The most deadening and at the same time painful aspect
of that period was the fact that once I had failed at selling
mutual funds, I didn't seem to be able to think of another
thing that I could possibly do. I got to thinking of myself as a
bum, as a ne'er-do-well. One Saturday evening Myrna Loy, a

long-time friend, dropped by to see me. At the same time, Chris and Merle Debuskey came by. I had not seen any of them for quite a while. They were full of excitement over the latest development in the case, Justice Fine's decision, which had been reported in the papers. The pleasantness of the gathering soon turned to gloom as they began to realize the rather desperate state I was in. Chris and Myrna asked me if I minded if they undertook to do something about it. I laughed and said, "Hell, no." I wanted to do something myself, and anything that anybody could do would be most welcome at this point.

The first week in December, Chris called me and told me that she had rounded up several of the union members who had stood firmly with me, and they, together with others, were planning a huge party for me—a very exclusive one, as a matter of fact, to which even I was not invited. It turned out that they had arranged a sort of benefit for me. Mrs. Roosevelt came, as did luminaries of the show world. Each was asked to contribute some money. They did so, and generously. Dickler took charge of administering the funds. I was so overcome that I scarcely knew what to do. It was as though the hand of providence had reached down and pulled me back from the brink of disaster.

I began thinking about moving down to Texas. After all, I could live more cheaply in Texas and there was bound to be some way of earning a living in Austin.

I went to Austin and got in touch with Cactus Pryor, who was program director of the one television station in Austin, KTBC-TV. He also did a daily radio show. Cactus and I had been friends for a number of years.

I hatched up a notion that I thought I could sell to one of the radio stations. I told the station manager of one of the smallest stations, KNOW, about my ideas for making money for the station and myself. I would use my contacts with sponsors and agencies in New York if the station would give me a two-hour daily show. The manager was enthusiastic and I returned to New York to begin calling on prospective advertisers.

I returned home from a busy day on Madison Avenue and found an airmail special delivery letter from KNOW. It was short and to the point. It stated that the station had programming plans that made it impossible for me to be included as one of its personalities. I guess I had really been expecting the letter all along, but I did not change my plans for moving to Austin. The Texas fever was on me.

12

As I drove south, each mile found the woods and fields turning greener, as though spring were moving north to meet us. And it seemed, too, that each mile I drove toward Texas, my spirits lifted. In my mind, I turned over the prospects before me. Austin was an interesting town. Besides, it was home. I had lived there all my life until I came to New York in 1946.

Austin is as near the dead center of the state as the founding fathers could put it. Although it's only on the western fringes of what in this country is called "the South," it is by background and social custom a Southern town. It has a large Negro population, which, until recently, was rigidly segregated by law and tradition. The University of Texas and the state capital are located there, the former lending a mild intellectual atmosphere to the town, the latter a political air. However, the predominant influence in Austin life during my childhood and youth was a sort of Bible-belt Protestantism.

Flowing down through the wooded limestone hills to the west, the Colorado River runs along the southern border of the business section of Austin. The portion of the town lying south of the river is called South Austin. That is where I grew up. The fashionable and well-to-do citizens of the town all lived north of the river. During my childhood days, South Austin was a rather self-contained community, more rural than urban. Most of our neighbors maintained their own milk cows, chickens, and a garden. Churchgoing was by far the most popular activity.

In those days, the population of South Austin was about equally divided between Southern Methodists and Southern Baptists. There were a few stray Southern Presbyterians about, and among the very poor there was an exotic sect called the Holy Rollers. There was one family in South Austin known to be Catholic, the Gillises. Mr. Gillis was such a charitable and worthy citizen that he was respected and well liked by one and all. His name was seldom mentioned in conversation, however, without his being identified as a Catholic.

My family were all Methodists. Not only religious Methodists, but social Methodists. I was in my adolescence, in fact, before I came to realize that people met in social gatherings not connected in one way or another with the church. My parents were what the community called "pillars" of the Fred Allen Memorial Methodist Church in South Austin.

My childhood was that of any other churchgoing middle-class child in South Austin, with the exception that I was considered something of a sinner rather early in life. This was because I used profanity and knew the facts of life. My nearest and most constant companions from infancy to the first seven or eight years of my life were the children of a Negro family who lived on our place, the Batts. Together we frolicked about the cow lot and barn, through the woods and the fields, finding bird's nests, investigating hay stacks and cedar thickets, and climbing the live oak trees to see the world around us more clearly.

Daddy had been reared a sharecropper. However, he arranged to get an education, was graduated from the University of Texas Law School, and became a lawyer in Austin in 1900. He was a popular young lawyer and had a thriving clientele. However, he had discovered Emerson, Thoreau, and Thomas Jefferson. From them he went to Spinoza. He had long been an avid student of the Bible. His childhood experiences with poverty and deprivation weighed heavily on his mind. He began to move slowly but surely in his philosophy away from orthodoxy toward the wide world of the free-thinker. Mama, who married Daddy in 1902, was a pious Methodist. She was only mildly disturbed when Daddy undertook to explain to her that he loved and believed in the teachings of Jesus Christ but did not believe in the divinity of Jesus. Mama said she accepted his opinion because she accepted Daddy completely. Daddy became concerned with matters of civil rights and social justice. He formed a friendship and correspondence with Eugene V. Debs, who strongly influenced him toward socialism. He began to envisage the unlimited joy and happiness that could come to mankind through achieving a liberated mind.

Yet Daddy identified so completely and affectionately with his Texas surroundings that he was not regarded as alien in the community. I suppose few of them understood what he really believed. He was held in respect and admiration for his ready wit and good humor. In spite of his unorthodox beliefs, he was very active in the Masonic order and a faithful member of the Methodist church. In fact, for as long as I can remember, he was the teacher of the Adult Bible Class at our church. He mixed a strong brew of Spinoza and Emerson with the scriptures and served it out to his nodding listeners every Sunday morning.

By the time I was a senior in high school I had come to appreciate and listen closely to the things that Daddy said and the observations he made. He had a sure and firm grasp on the history of the United States. "We've come a long way, Johnny, and we've got a long way to go. But America has the juice and the power to get there." The "there," to Daddy's way of thinking, was a state of freedom and justice, complete democracy. He was not so vain as to regard himself as a self-made man. On the contrary, he knew that many forces in our society made it possible for him to come from the life of a sharecropper to that of a comfortable and enlightened citizen, and he felt because he had been successful in his climb, that he had a lifelong obligation to assist others who were less fortunate than himself. One of his favorite themes was: "Jesus said, 'As you do unto the least of these, ye do unto Me,' and in a democracy like America, Johnny, as we do unto our least privileged citizen, whether he's Catholic, Jew, or Protestant, Native or foreign born, Negro or white, you do unto America."

Daddy was convinced that bigotry was a two-edged sword that punished the wielder as much as it did the victim. It was during this period that I first heard from him that racial integration would be an accomplished fact, probably within my lifetime. He believed this firmly. He told me that Negroes would go to the University of Texas just as white students did. He also told me that I, as a privileged white Texan and southerner, had a great responsibility to help in hastening that day when the terrible injustice of racial segregation would end.

It was always more or less taken for granted that I would

become a lawyer. I took a prelaw course at the university. However, my chief interest had been literature. I was an avid reader and the world of books was my greatest joy. In my junior year I took J. Frank Dobie's "Life and Literature of the Southwest." Since that time many of my interests and activities have been influenced by Dobie.

Dobie was not only a scholar, he was a humanitarian and a thinker. He gave generously of his time and thought to me. Two other men at the university shared his love for free, searching intellect: Roy Bedichek and Walter P. Webb. The three of them have been my mentors since my university days.

J. Frank Dobie, Roy Bedichek, and Walter P. Webb lived in Austin. As I drove along, a warm affectionate feeling crept over me. I would join their circle again, go out to the Webb or Dobie ranch, sit out late at night talking. Dobie and Bedichek had, perhaps, the greatest influence on my life, aside from my parents. Their conversation, their interests, their observations on the world around us had always fired my spirit, my imagination. Their respect and affection had meant a lot to me, particularly the last three years. I smiled as I recalled how Vincent Hartnett, in his EBT, had testified that he regarded me as suspect, in part, because he had read in *Newsweek* that J. Frank Dobie was a close friend of mine and that I had been greatly influenced by him. In Hartnett's book, J. Frank Dobie was suspect.

My heart was pounding with excitement as we drove up dusty West Live Oak Street, and turned into our old home place. My sister Mary, with her husband, Chester Koock, and their seven children, were lined up, waiting for us. Texana and her husband, John T. Conn, and their three children, my niece Anne McAfee and her husband Bill and their five children, and my brother, Hamilton, and his wife, Bernice, were all on hand to greet us. My other sister, Martha, was teaching school in Houston. Their children had made "Welcome Home" signs of cardboard and brown wrapping paper, lettered in red, green, blue, and yellow crayon: "Welcome New York Cousins" and "Back Home at Last." A great hugging and kissing and general jubilation took place. This was followed by a washing up and a sumptuous meal. Everybody, including the children, babbled at the same time. The scene resembled a Sunday-school picnic more than a family gathering.

I had a long visit with J. Frank Dobie and Roy Bedichek the next day. I recounted all of my experiences with the trial up to that point. I wanted to resume our regular sessions again, but my first order of business would be, of course, to find something to do in Austin. My resources were about depleted. But the problem was not so simple. I had to have a logical reason for my homecoming.

The most politic explanation would be that I had come to my senses and moved back to this true paradise on earth, Austin, Texas. I decided that the wisest course for me was to let it be thought that, having made some money in New York, I had now retired, as any sensible individual would, to Austin to spend the rest of my days.

From the very first week of my coming to Texas, Martinson had been writing letters regularly. It was a practice which proved, for the next three years, to be one of the greatest factors in maintaining my morale. Nearly every week Paul would write to me of what was happening in the lawsuit. His letters were always filled with good humor and affectionate concern for our well-being and little asides on various personalities who were involved in the suit.

He had written that Hartnett was understandably wearing a bit thin with the EBT. Paul had managed to accumulate some 2,500 pages of testimony from him, as well as valuable documentary evidence. Cohn and Bolan had protested that the long EBT was impairing Hartnett's health. They were also refusing to let him answer questions that Paul thought were highly pertinent. This would always cause considerable delay, as Paul would have to draw up briefs and apply to the court for rulings that would compel Hartnett to continue with the EBT, to produce records that had been requested, and to answer questions that had been asked. Nizer, too, made it a practice to send along letters filled with encouragement and good will.

I hoped that the time would come when I would get another shot at my profession. I wanted to keep my hand in by working on new material and developing new ideas. When I would sit down to work over some material, I would discover to my dismay that nothing would happen. My creative juices refused to flow. In my public appearances before civic and business groups, I was forced to fall back on old tried-and-true material from the years past. I simply could not make anything come out right that was new. This was frustrating and painful. The more I thought it over, the more I realized that time was slipping away from me, counting against me. I knew that if I had to wait long enough for my case to come to trial, I would be virtually unknown as an entertainer. When you're in the latter part of your forties, this is a depressing thought. The realization that I would have to begin my career all over again brought on cold sweat.

At times I almost longed for the days when I was blacklisted in New York. At least there, when I suffered a rebuff and hostility, I could salve my ego with the knowledge that the matter did not relate to me personally, it was the blacklist. But in Austin, I did not have even that thin satisfaction. It was not rebuff and hostility I had to contend with. It was loss of status and, more discomforting than that, indifference.

13

In the early part of 1960, Martinson wrote to me that he had completed Hartnett's EBT. There had been "nothing spectacular in his testimony, although it did contain a few bits of the mosaic that we have constructed." In the spring he conducted the EBT of Paul Milton, an officer of AWARE and a collaborator on the libelous publication about me. After they completed Milton's EBT, they began on Laurence Johnson; he, of course, was a key witness, since he supposedly was a multimillionaire and, should we win a judgment, would be solvent enough to pay it off. However, he was an elderly man, and Paul wrote to me that he was having great difficulty in getting Johnson to answer questions. As he wrote, "Johnson's almost universal answer to everything is 'I don't recollect,' and only when confronted with documents will he remember."

Paul's letters also contained a detailed account of his efforts to obtain information from the agencies and networks on the matter of blacklisting. He was refused repeatedly and got very little cooperation from any of them. Although Paul tirelessly and patiently followed out each lead to its end, accumulating a little evidence here and there, with his unbelievable persistence, he was almost bitter in his condemnation of those in the agencies and networks who refused to cooperate.

He reminded me, in one of his letters in the fall of 1960, that when the EBT of Johnson was completed, it would then be my turn to be examined by the defendants. After my EBT was completed, a trial date would be set. I was waiting.

As 1961 rolled around, I had a lengthy, reassuring letter from Nizer, examining the various factors that were causing delays and prolonging our litigation. First the defendants were waging a deliberate campaign of obstruction, and this necessitated time-consuming recourse to the court; second, the business of gathering evidence from the uncooperative and overcautious radio and television industry was a long and tedious one. But, he added in his letter: "rest assured that there will be a judgment day in court. We are determined to bring your cause to fruition, and time, instead of dulling the sword, will only make it sharper when the trial date comes. After all, we went through the same procedure of about five years' delay in the Pegler case. There must have been the same feeling on the part of the defendants that their cause was growing stale. They woke up to learn that our outrage at their conduct had merely accumulated ferocity through the years. So, with deep apology for the delayed trial date, but with renewed assurance of our continued vigor, I send this word to bolster your patience—which fortunately has been robust without these explanations."

In July, Paul Martinson sent me the long-awaited word that I should come to New York for my EBT. I arrived early on a gray, rainy morning, August 24, 1961.

Martinson was waiting for me when I walked into Nizer's office. He introduced me to George Berger, his assistant in the case. George had been working with Paul on the suit for more than a year, and I was pleased to discover that he was as familiar with every detail of the lawsuit and the personalities involved as I was.

Nizer and I walked over to the Algonquin Hotel for lunch.

"Remember at all times during this examination," he said, "you have right and justice on your side. Keep that in your mind. Answer all questions honestly and straightforwardly. But do not volunteer information, and do not be evasive. Be direct and succinct. Above all"—and here he looked at me sharply—"do not try to be clever and witty in your answers. Never try to match wits with Cohn or Bolan, or whoever is conducting the EBT. When a witness does that, the results are usually disastrous."

Cohn's office was on a high floor in one of the tall buildings down near Wall Street. Hung on one wall was a huge photograph of Cohn leaning over the shoulder of the late Senator McCarthy, whispering in his ear. It symbolized the McCarthy era to me, Cohn whispering to McCarthy.

Bolan, a partner of Cohn's, conducted the examination. At his side, at all times, was Hartnett, who had brought a huge package of material from his files, and now and again passed along a piece of material to Bolan for my questioning.

The first day of the examination was taken up with questions of a rather cursory sort about my background. The court reporter, unused to my Texas accent, often asked me to repeat each answer several times, while he wrestled to get it straight. Bolan's manner was both pleasant and courteous, and the examination went along very well.

During my stay in New York, I kept running into acquaintances from earlier days. It seemed that the vast majority of people in radio and television had either entirely forgotten that I had ever been involved in a lawsuit, or remembered it only in terms of my having sued somebody, or somebody having sued me, once in the distant past. I had to face the fact that most of the people in the radio and television industry neither knew nor cared about what had happened to me and would have very little interest in the lawsuit or its outcome. I realized, with a chilly feeling, that they would care a lot less about my efforts to get back into the industry after the suit. I was a kind of forgotten man.

I got back to Austin in the middle of September, with the news that the end of the long wait was in sight. Paul had told me that they would very soon have information on when the case would go on the court calendar.

Shortly after this, Louis Nizer's book, *My Life in Court*, was published. It immediately went to the top of the best-seller list. Friends who knew that Louis Nizer was soon to represent me in my lawsuit in New York treated me with new respect.

On March 16, 1962, the long-awaited call came. Martinson phoned to say that the case was scheduled to begin on April 3. He and Nizer wanted me to be in New York not later than March 28, in order to be fully prepared when we went into court. He told me that I should plan to spend at least six weeks in court. I arranged to stay with Chris and Merle in New York for "the duration."

I loaded my clothes and all the documents and letters that I had on the case into my car. On March 21, as the sun came up, I drove out of Austin toward New York on the last lap of a six-year journey.

14

Martinson and Berger were waiting for me in Nizer's office when I arrived. After a warm and cordial greeting, I detected a strange note in Lou's voice.

"We have no time to waste," he said. "We have an entire case to prepare." I was surprised. I had had the notion that the case was fully prepared and that we could start trying it that very day if necessary. After all, it had been six years in preparation.

I found out mighty soon how wrong my impression had been. Lou began by outlining the hundreds of things that had to be done. "Incidentally," Nizer said, "I would suggest that you make no other engagements at any time. From now on, until the verdict is in, your entire concentration must be on this case. I want you to take good care of yourself, get plenty of sleep, eat well and be in perfect trim. You've got the ordeal of your life before you."

That evening Paul, George, Lou, and I took a taxi to Lou's home. George had three overstuffed briefcases full of notes, briefs, and exhibits. That evening's program was to be a pattern for each evening we spent for the next three months.

Martinson brought up the matter of CBS and what its role in the lawsuit would be. Both Lou and Paul had serious misgivings about CBS and its declared neutrality in the case. They felt that CBS, by its refusal to aid me in the past, had indicated that they would not in any way give me any aid in the actual trial.

Lou explained patiently that I had better be prepared for some pretty grotesque absurdities in the coming days. He said CBS would do whatever it thought served its interest best.

"Yes," I said, "but both Slate and Ward know exactly what happened, they know that Johnson attacked me, they know about the AWARE bulletin, they know all the problems that I had, and if we call them on the stand under oath, they would never lie. They would tell the truth."

"You'd be surprised how much they could forget on the witness stand. They just wouldn't remember," Berger commented.

Lou nodded. "If CBS joins the defendants in this matter and comes down to court and testifies for AWARE, it could hurt us very badly."

A discussion arose over the witnesses we would be able to get for the trial. Lou said that we would have to bring in two or three character witnesses. In addition, there were other witnesses we would have to get who would be crucial to the case, persons who had had experiences with blacklisting.

Martinson said that it was going to be very difficult. Over the past six years he had been able to persuade only one or two to come forth. Paul said that he had talked to a number of network and agency executives who had admitted that they knew a great deal about the matter but were not going to get on the witness stand; they were concerned with their own reputations and their own safety. Lou said I should spend the next week doing nothing but making appointments and sitting down with prospective witnesses and seeing if I could persuade them to testify.

The first name he gave me was that of David Susskind. I knew that this would be easy, for Susskind had taken a strong position on my behalf and had expressed a thorough dislike for the defendants. He had valuable information to give, too, for he had lots of experience with blacklisting.

Next I called Tony Randall. Tony had helped me organize the Middle-of-the-Road slate back in 1955. When I reached him on the phone, he declared he would be delighted to get on the stand and tell what he knew and what he thought about AWARE and its associates. He was preparing to leave the country. He had to go to Turkey to do a movie and would be there for several months.

Lou said that he thought that he could arrange for Tony to be taken out of turn as a witness.

The willingness and enthusiasm of Susskind and Randall misled me: I got the idea that getting witnesses to come would be the easiest thing in the world. But I soon discovered that this wasn't the case. At the end of a week, I still had only two witnesses.

Things changed when I reached Garry Moore the following week. He wanted to know only when I would need him and where; he would be delighted to testify.

Walter Cronkite called me when he learned that I was in town. We had been good friends and had done several shows together. He was acquainted with my fight in the union. He told me that CBS had assigned him to go down to Cape Canaveral, and he might be gone during my trial, but if he was in New York, he would be delighted to appear as a witness.

One of the allegations that the defendants had lodged against me was that I had entertained for an organization called the Southern Conference for Human Welfare back in the late 1940s. When I had been questioned about this on my pretrial examination, I said that I not only had entertained for the organization but also had been a proud member of it, especially since Mrs. Roosevelt had been very active in the organization—had been, in fact, one of its founders back in 1938. Mrs. Roosevelt had corresponded with me several times on the matter of my lawsuit, and she had encouraged me to carry on; now Mr. Nizer felt that it would be excellent if she would give testimony on the Southern Conference. Unfortunately, Mrs. Roosevelt was in bad health and felt that unless her testimony was crucial, she would prefer to avoid going on the witness stand. But she made it clear that if she were needed, she would certainly be on hand. We did not ask her to come.

Lou and Paul felt that we should get as a witness some executive, from an advertising agency or from one of the networks, who had had direct experience with the defendants. I suggested Mark Goodson. Mark Goodson and Bill Todman owned the Goodson-Todman office, which produced many of the best quiz shows on the air and was by far the most successful company of its kind in the country.

Goodson assured me that if Nizer and I thought it would be of value, he would gladly come and tell all he knew about the ugly business. I felt triumphant as I left. Nizer and Martinson were delighted when I told them the news.

That evening, Paul and Lou told me that if I could get two

more witnesses, they would give me a rest. The two witnesses that they wanted me to talk to were Kenneth Roberts, a popular and important announcer, and Kim Hunter, an actress. Hartnett had given both of them a hard time, and they had very important testimony that they could give.

I knew Ken well and gave him a call. He said that he would be delighted to come and testify. He was working for one sponsor at the time. It was a highly paid job, but in spite of any embarrassment that might result, he felt it was very important that he put himself on record in this case. It turned out that his sponsor was cooperative and gave his blessings when Ken announced that he intended to testify.

Paul told me that he thought Kim Hunter would be one of our most important witnesses if we could get her. She had won an Academy Award and had been very popular and in great demand until she crossed swords with Vincent Hartnett and his associates. Their attack on her had had a dismal effect on her career. She had re-established herself and was enjoying great success. While she knew and disliked the defendants, she felt she owed it to her career to stand clear of any further involvements.

Kim's attorney pointed out that while she might come and testify for me and I might win the case, her career could still suffer later.

From the expression on Kim's face, I was sure she was going to apologize, wish me well, and say that she thought it best to stay out of the case. Instead, she placed her arms around my neck and kissed me, and said quite solemnly, "I have decided I'm going to testify. I want to be part of this trial. I'm going to do it for your sake, Johnny, because I admire you. But most of all I'm going to do it for my own sake and in behalf of my children and my profession and my country."

15

The several weeks preceding the opening of the trial are interesting to reflect on, but they were hell to live through.

The days and nights of that period ran together in one long, grueling session of feverish preparation. During the day at the office, Paul and George gathered the voluminous records, documents, exhibits, examination-before-trial testimony, information on prospective witnesses, and the multitude of other matters related to the case. Each night was spent going over it all, sorting it out, examining every detail of the strategy, and fitting the evidence into each planned maneuver of the coming battle.

I quickly learned that a peculiar psychological attitude prevailed in the thinking of Lou, Paul, and George. There were no neutrals for them.

A CBS executive was in a position to do our case a great service, but refused to do so, for no other reason than that he preferred to be neutral in the case. Nizer courteously and patiently reasoned with him for nearly a half an hour on the telephone; then, as the man remained adamant in his neutrality, Nizer's voice took on the deadly tone of outrage. With cold precision, he said, "I do not understand your position. We have spent six years and many thousands of dollars to cleanse your industry of these racketeers. Faulk has placed his career on the line. And you smugly sit there cowering behind a nonpartisan position! You are neither a good citizen nor a good executive!" And he clapped the phone down.

As April 16 drew near, it seemed to me that we had more preparation still to be done than we had when we started, two weeks before. However, on Sunday evening, a few hours before we were to be in court for the first time, Lou announced that we were in good shape and ready for the first skirmish—the selection of a jury.

The next morning I joined Lou, Paul, and George at their office, and we all went down to Foley Square by taxi. The New York State Supreme Court Building stands beside the United States Court House, and is somewhat dwarfed by the great federal edifice.

We took our seats along one side of the long counsel table. George explained to me that the defense attorneys would sit at the same table, directly across from us. And soon they came—Bolan and an assistant, Lang—and took their places there. I hadn't realized that we would be so close to them; for some reason, I had thought we would have separate tables.

Before long, a uniformed attendant shepherded in a group of some fifty well-dressed people, who took seats in the spectators' benches.

Then, the court clerk, standing beside the judge's bench, cried: "The Justice of the Court! All rise!" We all stood, as Justice Abraham Geller, a graying, handsome man about six feet tall, with a stern but pleasant expression, entered in his legal robes. He thanked the veniremen for coming, and then made a statement to the effect that this would be an unusual case, involving some issues that would require rather a long trial. He told the veniremen that those who felt that for substantial reasons they could not serve for as much as a month or perhaps six weeks should come forward and give their excuses. I was shocked to see that over half of the veniremen arose and lined up to go by the judge's bench. I felt somewhat like a performer with half of the audience getting up to leave. As each one in the line came up to the bench, he and the judge held a whispered conference. The judge either accepted the applicant's reasons for not serving and directed him to inform the attendant, or did not accept them and directed him to take his seat again. Two or three of them, as they briefly whispered to the judge, turned and looked in my direction. The judge nodded and excused them. They were persons who knew me too well to qualify as unbiased jurors.

At a signal from the judge, Lou arose and began the process of "challenging" individual prospective jurors. A challenge is an exception taken by either of the attorneys to any of the jurors. It may be a challenge for cause—as, for example, when the venireman is somehow related to one of the parties to the present suit and thus is likely to be prejudiced one way or the other. Or it may be a peremptory challenge, for which the lawyer is not required to state any reason at all. There is no limit to the number of challenges that may be made for cause; but the number of peremptory challenges is limited, usually by agreement between the two sides. In our case, Nizer and Bolan stipulated that each side would have a maximum of eight such challenges.

The selection of the jury turned out to be a fascinating sort of guessing game. Nizer and Bolan both had to decide from a group composed of complete strangers how each would feel about the issues of the case. At one point, a juryman was asked if he had any knowledge of any members of the Nizer firm, and the entire list was read. Then he was asked if he had any knowledge of members of Bolan's and Cohn's firm, and that list was read. The juryman said that while he didn't personally know Roy Cohn, he felt it only fair to admit that he could not give an unprejudiced judgment in a case in which Cohn was even indirectly a participant. He was, of course, dismissed.

One of Nizer's questions to each prospective juryman was whether he had any mental reservations that would make it impossible for him to grant damages amounting to a million dollars or more. One prospective juror said he didn't think that even the President could be libeled a million dollars' worth. Lou thanked him kindly and had him dismissed. Toward the middle of the afternoon, Lou suggested to the judge that it would take another day to complete the selection of the jury. It was agreed to adjourn until the next day. Then, when the jurors and veniremen had left the courtroom, Lou asked for a conference in the judge's chambers. He and Martinson and Berger, joined by Bolan and Lang, went in together.

Our suit as we had filed it in 1956 asked for half a million dollars compensatory damages. Now Nizer submitted briefs and arguments to support the position that, since I had been unemployed for six years as a direct result of the defendants' acts, the original claim was insufficient and that our complaint should be amended to ask for $1 million. Bolan vigorously opposed the motion, but Judge Geller sustained it.

The next day, the selection of the jury continued. After

twelve jurors had been selected, two alternate jurors were selected; they would sit in chairs near the jury each day and listen to the entire trial; then, if one of the regular jurors became ill or for some reason could not continue, one of the alternates would take his place.

The selection of the jury was completed a half hour or so before noon recess. Judge Geller made a rather lengthy speech to the jury. He pointed out that they were to be judges in this case, just as he was, but they would judge the facts, while he would judge the law; it was their business to arrive at a just decision. He cautioned them sternly about discussing the case with one another or with anyone during the trial. He suggested that the newspapers would be carrying accounts of the case, and that they were to avoid reading any of them.

Sitting four feet from me at that moment, was Vincent Hartnett. As I studied his expression, the set line of his mouth, the unyielding expression on his face, I realized that whatever the outcome of this case, his complete and total conviction that he was right and that we were wrong would remain unchanged. I realized at the same time that in all likelihood, Hartnett had never felt the slightest twinge of conscience for the great number of careers he had wrecked. Whatever evidence we might present of blighted careers, anguish and suffering, his self-righteousness would protect him from a feeling of guilt for his acts.

When the judge finished his speech to the jury, he dismissed us all and adjourned court until the following Monday, April 23.

16

About five o'clock that afternoon, we got a call to come into Lou's office at once; an emergency had occurred. We went in to find Lou sitting behind his desk and George Berger standing beside him, both looking grim. George had just returned from CBS and reported that when he had gone to the legal department of CBS with the subpoena to get any records they might have of me, he had been told by the CBS lawyers in charge that Roy Cohn's office had come with a subpoena a couple of weeks before and had taken the records. One of the CBS lawyers then explained to George that they had turned over the original records and had no copies. George had replied that this was unbelievable. It was shocking enough that CBS was obviously cooperating with Cohn's office by making the records available to them, but it was unthinkable that they would give Cohn the originals and not even retain a copy of the records. In fact, George commented, a CBS lawyer had told him that they did not even have a record of which documents had been turned over to Cohn.

I asked Lou what this meant. He was clearly angry. "It means, John, that someone at CBS is incredibly stupid, or that they are openly cooperating with Roy Cohn. I'm afraid it's the latter."

I found this hard to believe. "But if Cohn's office got out a subpoena for the documents, CBS didn't have any choice, did they?"

Lou replied impatiently, "Oh, yes, they did. A very great choice. A *subpoena duces tecom* means that the corporation is directed to present the papers in court at the time of the trial. The procedure ordinarily is simple. On an appointed day, an officer of the corporation or some other authorized person from the corporation goes down to the court with the papers subpoenaed. They are turned over and entered as exhibits. The person in charge of them waits until the operation is completed and then takes the papers back to his company's files."

Paul nodded. "No corporation turns over original records without even keeping a copy of them, especially to a party in a lawsuit—unless the corporation favors that party against the other."

"When I talked to the attorneys at CBS," George said, "they pretended they didn't even know who Vincent Hartnett and AWARE were. They were very evasive." George said the CBS lawyers told him they would try to get the records back immediately, and they promised to call him as soon as they did.

The following day, George Berger received a call from the CBS lawyers. Cohn's office had returned the documents. We could have photostatic copies of them if we desired. We desired! George went bounding over to CBS to get them. Actually, the records turned up very little that was significant one way or the other.

Nizer made it a strict rule throughout the entire trial, that we be seated at the counsel table at least ten minutes before the appointed time for the court session to start. He felt that to arrive late, even by a minute, was an imposition on the court. On that first day I got there thirty minutes early. Fifteen minutes later, George Berger and two clerks from the Nizer office arrived with four crammed briefcases. Paul and Lou followed, greeted me affectionately, and took their places at the table. After a while, the defense entered, Mr. Bolan carrying a small briefcase, his assistant, Mr. Lang, and his client, Mr. Hartnett carrying two heavy suitcases full of papers. They took their places and nodded a curt greeting in our general direction.

Word that Louis Nizer was delivering his opening speech that day brought out a raft of spectators. There were fans of Louis Nizer and a goodly number of friends of mine. It was a standing-room-only crowd. Soon the bailiff called out his "Hear ye! Hear ye!" and we all stood as Justice Geller, in his judicial robe, came in and took his seat. He again pointed out to the jury that each of them would be a judge in this case, just as if he or she were in judicial robes, and that it would be the task of each to judge the facts as they were presented. It was his task to judge the law. He and they were to be something like partners in judging and making sure justice was done.

Suddenly, I was overwhelmed by the realization that *the trial had started!* The trial of *Faulk v. AWARE, Laurence Johnson, and Vincent Hartnett* had actually started! However costly and unpleasant those months and years of preparation had been, I knew now, with quiet certainty, that it had been a small price to pay for this moment.

My God, this is America! Here I sit, a onetime cow-milking South Austin boy who came to New York, felt that an injustice had been done him, and demanded satisfaction. The American people have done the rest—provided all this: a courtroom, a jury, a judge, court attendants, the free press to report the proceedings, and the opportunity to present my complaint and have its merits argued fully. The thought awed me. Everybody in that courtroom—everybody—was there because I, a citizen, felt I had been unjustly treated! I knew that whatever the outcome of the trial, the meaning and impact of this great truth would never escape me again.

As these thoughts raced through my mind, Justice Geller completed his remarks to the jury and nodded to Lou. A hush settled over the courtroom as Lou rose from the table and moved in front of the jury. His easy, poised manner in no way betrayed the exhausting hours of preparation he had given to the case. He appeared quiet and sure as he began to speak. Every eye in the courtroom was fixed on him.

NIZER: May it please your Honor, Miss Tindale, Madame Forelady, and ladies and gentlemen of the jury: As his Honor has already indicated to you, . . . the law, in its wisdom, permits the lawyer on each side to tell you the entire case from his viewpoint , so that when you hear a bit of testimony you know that it relates to the rest of the proof, why it has some relevance to the entire case.

I avail myself, with his Honor's permission, and so will my learned adversary, of that privilege now, the purpose being for me to attempt to explain to you what this suit is about, what we claim in this litigation, what our position is with respect to certain positions taken by the defendants, and they will do the same with respect to us, and then, having a larger perspective of the entire controversy, you will be able to follow particular pieces of testimony a little more clearly. . . .

First, the parties. Who are they? The man who brings this suit is John Henry Faulk. He has sat there from the beginning of the selection of the jury, the third gentleman on that side (indicating).

Lou then went over my entire history, how I had been born in Austin, had been educated in the schools of Texas, and had received my degrees from the University of Texas. He dwelt at some length on the graduate work that I had done in Negro folklore, on my background as a teacher, and on the fellowship that I had received. He outlined my career during the War, how I had tried to get into the army and had been prevented because of blindness in one eye, had gone into the Merchant Marine, and had later become an assistant field director for the American Red Cross in Cairo, Egypt. He told how later I had joined the Army and had been assigned to rehabilitation work at an Army hospital. Then he outlined for the court and the jury my career as a radio and television performer. He went over this in some detail and very effectively.

As he was telling this, I studied the faces of the jurors. Each was listening intently, his eyes following Lou as he moved about. Nizer summed up my career in radio and television.

NIZER: . . . So here was a man who was rising as one of the great stars in radio and later television . . . when a certain situation arose in a dispute in which he was charged with being either Communist or pro-Communist, and just cut off his career sharply as if with a knife.

Lou then turned his attention to the defendants.

NIZER: Who are the defendants in this case? One of them is Vincent Hartnett. He is this gentleman here, seated here, third in this row (indicating).

We will show you about Mr. Hartnett's career. He was a man who earned some $60 to $75 a week in radio in some script department. Then he was out of work for a considerable time, but then fell upon the idea which brought him a great deal of prosperity. That was the idea of collecting data, becoming a so-called consultant on radio artists and television artists, and informing the radio companies and the television companies, the sponsors, the people who advertised, or the agencies who placed these programs, informing them of the records of those artists, the so-called records, their affiliation with questionable causes. He was the principal author of *Red Channels*, a book which made these listings of people on the air. He thereafter continued this work, charging sponsors $5 a throw, to put it bluntly, to investigate somebody.

He would decide whether a certain performer was a good American, what his alleged record was, and we will show you how this worked.

If a name came back after a couple of weeks, if the same actor had a second show on radio or television, why, then Hartnett charged less . . . he charged $2, for original performances $5 to check, and in some cases $20, and if it was a little more important for some reason, $50, and we will show you that these payments were made to him, and that a man who had earned $60 to $75 a week was earning $26,000 a year collecting these payments as an alleged consultant.

BOLAN: I object, your Honor.

THE COURT: Overruled as long as he abstains from making comments, but of course the jury has fully in mind, and I will not repeat it again, that this does not constitute evidence whatever. This is merely what counsel intends to prove. Bearing that admonition in mind, just indicate what you intend to prove, but make no comments or arguments with respect to what you intend to prove.

BOLAN: Thank you.

NIZER: Thank you, sir. I realize that the argument will be made in summation. I am trying to limit myself to what we intend to prove from that witness stand, with documents and evidence.

Then, he outlined for some time the methods used by Mr. Hartnett, Mr. Johnson, and AWARE in achieving the blacklisting of artists, and describing how they had worked on me.

NIZER: Let me call your attention to one other thing we will prove. AWARE, Inc., is not an organization that has any authority from the government of the United States. It is a private organization. . . . So AWARE, Inc., has no standing except as a private individual, with Mr. Hartnett cashing in.

Second, we will show you that Mr. Johnson has not been designated. He is self-appointed and self-anointed. He has no authority of any governmental authority to pass upon the lives of American citizens, economically, patriotically, or any other way.

Lou then launched into a lengthy and detailed account of how the quarrel arose between me and the defendants. He went into the union fight, describing it at length.

He then took up the allegations in the AWARE bulletin about me and went over them in great detail. From time to time Justice Geller would interrupt him.

THE COURT: Mr. Nizer, when you go over those items, indicate what you intend to prove without commenting on it and save your comments for summation.

Lou outlined the manner in which AWARE, Hartnett, and Johnson, with the cooperation of an American Legion post in Syracuse, had used the AWARE bulletin to get me completely blacklisted; he described the industry's reaction to their efforts and told how ultimately I came to be fired by CBS. He then dwelt at some length on my efforts to find employment after I was fired. He described it so effectively and heartbreakingly that I found myself about to cry. The jury was watching very closely, listening to every word he said.

At one point he summed up the issues as he saw them from our position.

NIZER: What we have brought, for the first time so far as I know, is an issue before this court, whether an American court of justice is going to approve the kind of blacklisting that went on in this case for all artists, and which John Henry Faulk makes a test of in his own case, and we're going to bring other evidence to you as to how this operated on famous artists.

What we are bringing to this court is a question as to whether private organizations, or as I would call them, vigilantes, can exist in this nation, when we have a court of law by which we can obtain relief.

He then spent some time on the damages that he intended to prove. Lou pointed out that the defendants would certainly try to minimize the damages they had done me. Then he concluded his opening statement to the jury.

NIZER: And now I shall conclude with one final observation. Mr. Faulk will take the stand, and others will follow for the plaintiff. I know that you will observe him closely because, as his Honor has instructed you, that is the genius of our system, that they watch witnesses for credibility.

I plead with you particularly to observe Mr. Hartnett when the time comes for him to take the stand, and Mr. Laurence A. Johnson, when the time comes for him to take the stand. I plead with you to watch them closely and listen to their answers and observe their mannerisms, and see who it was, as we charge, intimidated the entire television industry.

I want you to follow their answers closely. I plead with you in this particular case to take particular note of Mr. Hartnett and Mr. Johnson under oath and under cross-examination, and when you do, I have no doubt that, in what we consider a great cause, Justice will be done not only for this plaintiff but for the great American cause as well.

When Lou finished speaking, Justice Geller declared a recess for lunch. As the spectators rose to leave the room, a number of them pressed forward to shake Lou's hand. Smiling and courteous, he moved them aside and called on Paul, George, and me to go with him directly to Gasner's

Restaurant; he was anxious to discuss the jury's reactions. On our way out of the courthouse, people continued to step forward to greet him. He smiled warmly, but resolutely marched along, obviously preoccupied with our conference at Gasner's.

Gasner's is located in the vicinity of Foley Square, and at lunchtime it is filled with lawyers and judges; it almost seemed that the clientele consisted exclusively of members of the legal profession.

As soon as we were seated and had placed our orders, Lou asked each of us for our impressions of the jury's reaction to his speech. George and Paul discussed the jurors, one by one, and the facial expressions of each when Lou had been addressing them. I was fascinated with this minute attention to detail. Paul would say, "Juror number X seemed to be deeply interested when you mentioned such and such." George would check his notes, and observe, "When you said such and such, I noticed juror number Y seemed indifferent. His eyes wandered and he looked at the ceiling once or twice." I realized now why Lou had been indifferent to the spectators and his admirers in court. He was interested in the reactions of but twelve people for the duration of this trial.

After lunch, when the court reconvened, I noticed that only about half of the spectators present had been on hand that morning. There were some new ones; but some of the benches were empty. It puzzled me and I asked George about it. He smiled and nodded toward Lou. The morning crowd had come to hear Nizer's opening speech. Mr. Bolan's opening speech, to come next, apparently did not have the same appeal.

The judge indicated to Bolan that he could begin. Bolan rose and went before the jury. He was a well-built young man and rather handsome, dressed in the Ivy League fashion. As he began to speak, the jury again gave their full attention.

BOLAN: May it please the court, Miss Tindale, ladies and gentlemen of the jury:

As you probably know, my name is Thomas Bolan and I

am the attorney for each of three defendants in this case. I am assisted by Mr. John Lang, an associate in my office. The three defendants are, as you know, AWARE, Inc. In case there is some confusion in your mind as to the "Inc.," that is simply an abbreviation for "incorporated." AWARE is a New York corporation.

The other two defendants are individuals. Mr. Vincent Hartnett, who lives in Scarsdale, New York and Mr. Laurence Johnson, who lives in Syracuse, New York.

Now, before discussing the complaint, I would like to just speak a few words on the background of the individual defendants. Before I do that, too, I would like to say that my duty is rather a solemn one, because this is not an ordinary case. It is not just a simple case where one party is seeking to get money from another party.

The plaintiff, John Henry Faulk, in support of his complaint, has charged that the defendants have conspired against him. He has libeled them as extortionists, as racketeers, and as intimidators, as terrorists.

So, therefore, in this case there is more than money involved as far as my clients are concerned. Their reputations are at stake, and, in the case of AWARE, its powerful existence is at stake.

Now, the charges that I have read to you, or have mentioned to you are surely all very serious. It is a very serious charge to call someone an extortionist or racketeer, but I assure you those charges, like the other charges in this complaint, are absolutely without foundation. By the end of this trial I am convinced that you will agree that the plaintiff has failed to sustain those charges.

Now, as to the background of the individuals, first of all, AWARE is a New York Corporation. It is a membership corporation, formed under the laws of the state of New York. It was formed in 1953.

It describes itself as an organization to combat the Communist conspiracy in the entertainment and communications field. Among its dedicated purposes are to disseminate information and material concerning the Communist Party, the Communist fronts, and similar areas.

Also among its purposes is to expose situations where known Communists or even strong anti-Communists have unwittingly or unknowingly given their support to either the Communist Party or Communist front groups. That is one of its purposes.

It is a nonprofit corporation: that is, it is not in the business of making money. None of its officers receive any salary or any other sort of remuneration. It relies solely on the dues it collects from its members, and contributions from friends.

It has never received any money for any of its anti-Communist activities. Its members are decent, honorable, and respectable people. They are not extortionists. They are not racketeers. Mr. Alexander Dick is the chairman of the board of AWARE. He sits there now at the end of the counsel table.

Seated next to Mr. Dick, on his left, is Mr. Vincent Hartnett, who is one of the individual defendants. In a few words as to Mr. Hartnett, Mr. Hartnett is a vice-president of AWARE and is one of its founders. AWARE was founded as a corporation in 1953. It had been active as an unincorporated group for about a year prior to that.

Mr. Hartnett is forty-six years of age. He has six children. He attended the University of Notre Dame, where he received two degrees, a B.A. degree and M.A. degree, both with highest honors, both *maxima cum laude*. He graduated with highest honors in both instances.

Bolan then went into Hartnett's background in the radio and television field and his stint as an assistant producer in radio. He outlined at some length Mr. Hartnett's service in the United States Navy as an intelligence officer. Then he continued.

BOLAN: . . . Mr. Hartnett is an expert and a specialist in the field of Communism, the Communist Party front groups. He spent many years of study, read many articles, has written many articles, and has accumulated enormous files on the workings of the Communist Party, and the Communist front groups in particular.

In the course of time many organizations and groups requested Mr. Hartnett to do special work into the backgrounds of prospective actors or entertainers in radio and television, and other related fields.

These people, the producers or sponsors, did not want to take the risk of hiring somebody who either had been identified as a member of the Communist Party or who had a significant record of affiliation with organizations closely tied in with the Communist Party, and they wanted a check made, and Mr. Hartnett was an expert in the field, and he was called upon to do that work.

In the course of time, Mr. Hartnett devoted all of his time, all of his efforts, which were considerable, in this field. He was paid for his services in this area.

He was called on several occasions as an expert witness on Communism, once by the House Un-American Activities Committee, and on another occasion by the Senate Internal Security Committee. He was recognized as an expert in this field. He was a researcher into Communism and the Communist Party, and I may say J. Edgar Hoover sent Mr. Hartnett a letter.

NIZER: I object.

THE COURT: I will have to sustain the objection to that. Let us await the offer of testimony on that, and whether it is receivable.

BOLAN: As this trial will show, Mr. Hartnett is not a terrorist. He was a sincere dedicated man, who was painstaking in his research, and, as you will see, he is scrupulously honest, perhaps more so, I was going to say, than anyone I have encountered, but I objected to a similar statement by Mr. Nizer as to his experience, so I will not say it.

THE COURT: Mr. Bolan, please keep your voice up. I want to hear every word that is said. You dropped your voice.

NIZER: He just announced, your Honor, that he was not going to make a statement, which he then made.

Bolan then described at some length Laurence Johnson—who he was and how he was connected with the case. Bolan pointed out what he considered his main task.

BOLAN: My main job here now is to discuss with you what this case is all about. I submit to you, what the case is all about is right here in the complaint, and the case is about this one simple issue: Did the defendants damage the reputation and professional career of John Henry Faulk? That is the only issue in this case. Did these defendants damage Mr. Faulk's reputation and professional career?

Mr. Faulk said they entered into a conspiracy to do this. He said that the three of them, the three defendants, got together in February 1956, and at that time they entered into an illegal agreement in which they in a sense said, "Let's destroy the reputation and career of Mr. John Henry Faulk."

I submit to you that the evidence will show no such agreement was made, no such effort was ever made by any of the defendants.

Bolan stated quite candidly that AWARE and the other defendants had always been opposed to having identified Communist members, persons who had used the Fifth Amendment or any other amendment, or who had significant Communist-front records, employed in the television and radio industry. He claimed that AWARE had support of the House Un-American Activities Committee in this regard. Nizer objected vigorously to this. Bolan proceeded to claim that AWARE and the other defendants had relied on the very highest quality sources for their information. He listed among these sources the House Un-American Activities Committee and the Senate Subcommittee on Internal Security. He said that he intended to prove that after AWARE's attack upon me in February 1956 my popularity as a radio entertainer went up and up, that in December 1956 CBS hired me for a new five-year contract and gave me a big raise, after which my rating went "down, down, down, down." Then he made his closing statement.

BOLAN: And we will show that beyond any doubt, too, Mr. Faulk's earnings were not affected by anything that Aware did and nobody of the defendants, either Aware, Johnson, or Hartnett, or anybody else, ever went to any of Faulk's sponsors to request that his services be terminated. Nobody in any of the defendants ever collected one cent for the activities with respect to Mr. Faulk, and we will prove that beyond any doubt. . . . Mr. Nizer said to pay attention to Mr. Hartnett and Mr. Johnson on the stand. Of course, you should pay attention. Pay attention to Mr. Faulk, too. Mr. Faulk by profession is an actor. Keep that in mind, too.

Above all, I do urge you to give your most careful attention to all of the evidence, and I am sure that when all the evidence is in, you will find that the defendants did nothing which in any way damaged the reputation or professional career of the plaintiff. Thank you for your attention.

The court adjourned and we went back uptown. We went over each point of Bolan's opening speech. Lou said that it was clear that the defendants were going to try to minimize the damages. That was to be their angle. There was, of course, a chance that they might seek to prove I was a Communist. But nothing Bolan had said indicated that they believed such a thing. Their main emphasis would be their contention that I had not been damaged. "They might spring some surprise witnesses on us," Lou said, "and we want to be ready in case they try to prove the truth of their allegations. In a lawsuit such as this, one must be prepared at all times for the unexpected as well as the expected."

17

When I reached the courtroom the next morning, no one was around. As I sat there, waiting and thinking, I looked at the empty witness stand and tried to picture myself sitting there. Should I fold my arms and look solemn? Or sit relaxed and look benign? Should I lean forward eagerly? Or lean back calmly? Lou had advised over and over again that I should simply be myself. I wondered how the hell a man could know whether he was being himself, sitting there between the judge and the jury, his every word and gesture being observed by the jury and recorded by a stenographer. Then an interesting new thought occurred to me: It was only under such circumstances that I could really be myself; only under pressure, every fiber in my body being put to the test, could I really find out what there was to me. Then, and only then, did I clearly see this would not be an ordeal; it would be an opportunity to prove to myself what I honestly believed about myself. A glorious opportunity!

After a while, several court attendants drifted in, and a few spectators arrived. Then the Nizer entourage came in. Lou, Paul, George, and two clerks from Nizer's office with the inevitable heavily laden briefcases. They greeted me and took their seats. George started laying out on the table material from the briefcases. I eyed the three men who were absorbed in my welfare, spending their days and nights working to achieve a just hearing for me. These three sharply intelligent men were wholeheartedly devoted to my cause; and knowing this, I was deeply moved. The words "Thy rod and thy staff, they comfort me" came back into my mind, and I felt a lump in my throat. This trio of tireless souls were more than my rod and my staff. They were my sword and shield.

I was a little surprised that there were not more spectators present. Yesterday the benches had been crowded with Nizer's admirers who had come to hear his opening speech. I noticed with a pang of resentment that not a single member of AFTRA was present to hear me, save Chris, who was there as a friend, not as a union member.

After an endless spell of waiting, the bailiff came forward and announced the judge. We got to our feet and Justice Geller entered. "At long last," I breathed. I looked at the clock on the wall; it was exactly ten forty-five.

Lou nodded at me and said softly, "Will you take the witness stand, Mr. Faulk?" The bailiff swore me in, and I stepped into the witness box and took my seat. Lou smiled at me, meaning to reassure me. "Will you please state your name and address?" At that point, my life as a witness began.

I have a conviction about witnesses: One who has never sat in a witness chair cannot possibly conceive of what the experience is like. You sit there, with twelve pairs of jurors' eyes fixed upon you, with a judge who is listening to every word, and a courtroom full of spectators and reporters watching your every gesture. If you blink your eyes, scratch your nose, frown, smile, nod your head, or react with any expression whatever, it is observed. The slightest shift in position is noticed. One might think a performer, used to audiences, would be at home, but this is nothing like being on the stage before an audience. An entertainer has some control over himself and the audience. His training, experience, and skill in his craft give him some control over the feelings he engenders in his observers. He knows what to expect of himself in his performance. However, a witness whose function is to supply information that will affect the outcome of a lawsuit is something of a tool or a pawn. He speaks only when he is asked a question, and he'd better not try to do more. He is completely under the control of the lawyer questioning him. To make matters worse, there is a court reporter about three feet below him taking down every syllable uttered. One might achieve some degree of comfort in a witness stand, but I doubt if anyone ever gets sufficiently used to it to enjoy it.

Lou's questions led me through an account of my early life—family, schools, churches, and all sorts of related trivia. He kept me lively in my answers by his tone of voice. He cleverly had me dwell at length on the thesis I had written for my M.A. degree, the first of its kind ever accepted at the University of Texas. It consisted of ten sermons that I had transcribed as they were preached by ten Negro ministers. When I related this, Lou questioned me at length how I came to write it. I told him of my consuming interest in the folklore of the Southwest, how I had been attracted by the epic quality of the Negro sermons, an art form rapidly disappearing at the time I started transcribing them. I described the imagery and the grandeur of the Negro folk sermon. I told him how I had received a Julius Rosenwald Fellowship to record these sermons for the Library of Congress.

By the time Justice Geller adjourned the court for lunch, I was feeling confident, if not comfortable. As we went down the corridor, several reporters eased along beside me, but Lou hurried me along. He was absolutely firm about my not talking about my case to reporters. Murray Kempton, of the *New York Post*, came up and we pumped hands enthusiastically. He is an old friend, and I felt that I had to chat with him. We talked as we walked along. When we parted, I explained to Lou that we had talked only of matters unrelated to the case. Lou commented knowingly, "You'll see whether it's related to the case or not in tomorrow's column."

As Paul, Lou, George, and I sat down to lunch at Gasner's, Lou patted my shoulder. "You did fine as a start, John. But remember, no false modesty this afternoon when we get into the awards you've received. If you received them, you've a right to be proud of them. Now, you speak right up about them on the stand."

And that afternoon I did exactly that for almost the entire session. I warmed up to the subject with vigor as I went along. By the time court adjourned at four o'clock, I figured the judge and jury were quite relieved to have me shut up.

The next day, Lou succeeded in getting the court's consent to introduce an astonishing amount of material that CBS had published on me, that is, promotional material, which was very effusive indeed.

At lunch recess, we got a copy of the *New York Post*. It carried Murray Kempton's first article on the trial. It was entitled "The Return," and Murray seemed to give the whole posture of the case in that one succinct article, which read in part:

Judge Abraham Geller's courtroom was crowded yesterday, as it is likely to be for the next six weeks, because Louis Nizer will be practicing surgery there.

Nizer, of course, was the chief attraction; but, once there, it was surprising how glad many of the spectators were to see John Henry Faulk again. He sat yesterday, still with the wit disguised as country foolishness, as though the business that had stopped his career was faintly comic. He will be sparing and therefore more terrible in his moments of rage. He returns unchanged and intact, the most immensely formidable kind of witness, the one who can laugh at himself. He will take his vengeance without rancor. There is a sense that when this one is over, Aware will never be able to hurt anyone else again.

I discovered that I was getting rather used to being on the witness stand. It was like riding a stiff-legged horse: It's never comfortable, but once you get on it, you don't notice how rough it is.

It was with real pleasure that I heard Lou request the court's permission to suspend my direct examination and to put David Susskind on the stand the following day, Friday. Susskind's testimony would be the jury's first taste of the bitter facts of blacklisting. Indeed, it would be the first time ever that such testimony had been given in a court. And it would be given by a person whose name was news in itself.

A ripple of excitement ran through the spectator section and the jury box when Susskind was sworn in and took the witness chair. It was obvious that every one of the jurors recognized him. Susskind, volatile and creative, had, for a number of years, been unusually outspoken in his opinions. This had won him as many detractors as admirers. My personal experience with him had been a happy one. Since I had first known him, in the mid-fifties, he had always been considerate and generous with me. Never once had he wavered or equivocated in his position of strong support for our case.

Susskind began his direct testimony by telling of his background, how he attended schools in Brookline, Massachusetts, later went to the University of Wisconsin, and was graduated from Harvard University in 1942 with a Bachelor of Science degree *cum laude*. Susskind told of his work during the war with the National Labor Board in Washington and then of having joined the Navy in September 1942. After the war he joined the New York office of Warner Brothers motion picture company, in the advertising and publicity department. He told of how he got into television in 1948. He and one of the men in Century Artists Ltd., formed Talent Associates Ltd. The purpose of the organization was twofold: managing creative personnel, not performers, but writers, directors, and producers; and the creation of new programs, selling them and putting them on the air. Talent Associates Ltd., as Susskind described it, was one of the oldest television program packaging companies in New York. In 1952, according to his testimony, his company abandoned the management of talent and devoted itself exclusively to creating new television programs, selling them and producing them. In the fall of 1948, they had started producing a program called "Philco Television Playhouse," a program that ran once a week, fifty-two weeks a year, for six years.

The court permitted Susskind to testify at length about the number of stars that had been on his program, their names, as well as the directors and writers on the programs. After Lou had established clearly through David's direct testimony that he had had vast experience as a producer of innumerable dramatic shows on television for various sponsors, he took up a copy of the examination before trial of Mr. Hartnett. Bolan objected strenuously, but the court overruled him, pointing out that both attorneys were permitted to read from the EBT of any witness. Lou proceeded to read direct testimony of Mr. Hartnett given several years previously at his EBT. His purpose became very apparent as he read the questions and Hartnett's answers that dealt with Hartnett's arrangement with the Young & Rubicam advertising agency. As everyone in the courtroom listened, Lou read Hartnett's account of how he charged Young & Rubicam for clearing talent for one of Y & R's clients, the Lorillard Company. Hartnett had testified that he had received $9,000 in equal installments for clearing talent on a program sponsored by Lorillard. His agreement was that for a particular period, the first report he would give on talent was $5, for a longer report it might be $20 or more, and for a repeat on a name it was ordinarily $2. The name of the program for which Hartnett cleared the names was "Appointment With Adventure." Lou laid aside the EBT and turned to the witness.

NIZER: Mr. Susskind, I will interrupt at this point in the reading to ask you what was the program "Appointment with Adventure."

SUSSKIND (after the Judge had overruled several objections from Mr. Bolan): "Appointment with Adventure" was a half-hour dramatic program conceived by my company and sold to Young & Rubicam on behalf of the Lorillard Company and it was on, I believe, in March 1955, Sunday nights 10 P.M. and stayed for fifty weeks every Sunday night.

NIZER: And the Young & Rubicam Company, which is the agency you mentioned, is the same agency as the one I have referred to as dealing with this program?

SUSSKIND: Yes, sir, the same.

Lou then took up Hartnett's EBT again and read his testimony on his dealings with Young & Rubicam in clearing names for the Lorillard program. Hartnett had told how one of the people at the agency would call him almost daily on the telephone, read off a list of names of actors and actresses, directors, producers, supervisors, technicians, and all persons connected with the show. He had testified that he had been given the names of assistant stage directors and other peripheral workers to clear, even lighting technicians. After Lou had read at considerable length from Hartnett's EBT concerning the clearing of talent and others connected with "Appointment with Adventure," he turned again to Susskind on the witness stand.

NIZER: Mr. Susskind, I have read certain passages about a program called "Appointment with Adventure," and you have already told us that you were packager, the producer of that program for the Lorillard Company. Is that right?

SUSSKIND: Yes, sir. We created that program. We sold it to Young & Rubicam for Lorillard, and I personally produced the program.

NIZER: When you say you sold it to Young & Rubicam, that was an advertising agency that represented the sponsor of the cigarettes, Lorillard, is that the sequence of it?

SUSSKIND: Yes, sir.

NIZER: Now, did you when you selected various actors and actresses and even the names of technicians or the director or the assistant director, did you submit those names to anyone?

SUSSKIND: Yes, sir, I had to submit the names of everybody on every show in every category to an executive of Young & Rubicam, and nobody could be engaged by me finally or a deal made and consummated, before a clearance or acceptance came back from Young & Rubicam.

NIZER: Did that acceptance deal with the quality of the actor or the technician or the director?

BOLAN: I object, your honor.

THE COURT: Sustained. Reframe your question.

NIZER: When you submitted these names what was the purpose of submission?

BOLAN: I object, your Honor.

THE COURT: Overruled.

SUSSKIND: When I sold the program to the advertising agency, Young & Rubicam, for Lorillard cigarettes, the condition of the sale was that all names of all personnel in all categories on every program were to be submitted for political clearance by Young & Rubicam, and nobody was to be hired until they approved and said, "All right, hire such a person."

NIZER: These names were submitted on the telephone?

SUSSKIND: All the names were submitted by me or members of my organization to an executive of Young & Rubicam or his secretary, over the telephone.

NIZER: How long did it take before the approval or disapproval came back?

BOLAN: I object, your Honor.

THE COURT: Overruled.

SUSSKIND: It generally took forty-eight hours. I was told that I should always anticipate a forty-eight-hour delay on the approval or rejection of any name.

NIZER: Can you estimate how many names on this one program over the year that it ran that you submitted in this way for political approval?

BOLAN: I object, your Honor.

THE COURT: Overruled.

SUSSKIND: I must have submitted over the period of time about 5,000 names, I would guess.

THE COURT: For this one program?

SUSSKIND: For this one program.

THE COURT: Did you state the period of time this program . . .

SUSSKIND: This program was on the air for fifty consecutive weeks.

THE COURT: From when to when?

SUSSKIND: From April 3, 1955 to March 11, 1956.

NIZER: Can you give us the estimate of how many of the names that you submitted came back rejected.

SUSSKIND: I would guess approximately 33⅓%, perhaps a little higher, came back politically rejected.

NIZER: What was the practice with respect to inquiring about a particular name? Describe it in your own way.

SUSSKIND: The practice was that I would telephone the executive at Young & Rubicam. I would have had previously made tentative commitments to actors, writers, producers, directors, everybody on the program, telling them, "We think we want you on this program. We will advise you on this soon definitely one way or another." I would then call the advertising agency executive. I would submit the names. He would, as I say, reject or approve them in terms of their political acceptability.

THE COURT: Can you indicate who you spoke to, Mr. Susskind?

SUSSKIND: If you want me to. . . .

THE COURT: Yes.

SUSSKIND: The executive in charge of this particular program for Lorillard Company was David Levy. He was assisted by other men, but he was the primary executive.

NIZER: Tell us what was said?

SUSSKIND: I said to Mr. Levy that it is extraordinarily difficult to find the right actors for the right parts, the right writers for the right scripts, and the right directors for the right stories, that his rejections were making the program almost unworkable and impossible artistically, and that I could not accept the responsibility for the steady deterioration of the program when this practice was in vogue. I said, "If you reject somebody, let me get that somebody and ask him. In many cases I know these people and they are fine people, and I know that they are acceptable. You only say no or yes to me about them, but you never give me any substantiation." He said, "I can't give you any. I deplore this practice as much as you do. We're caught in a trap. I have no alternative."

I said, "The production of the program is being seriously impaired. Human beings are suffering loss of employment without any substantiation, without any charges, without even their knowing that they can't be hired, and I am being embarrassed constantly with the agents and the lawyers of the actors and the writers and the directors by saying 'I am sorry we cannot hire you on the fact of political rejection.'

"I know a great number of the people you have rejected. I know them socially and professionally and there is no question about their political reliability or their good citizenship or their loyalty to this country, and on all these grounds I beg you to let me confront these people with whatever you have on them and let them answer and you will find that they will be all right and you will have a much better show." And he (Mr. Levy) said, "I am helpless. We are helpless. This is the practice. We have no choice, and we have to pay $5 for every clearance and $2 for every recheck. Do you think we like it? It's costing us a bloody fortune." And I believe he said, "Cut down the number of actors you submit, cut down the number of directors and the number of writers, because you are breaking us. It's $5 a throw, and $2 a throw, and you give us eight actors for each role and then you give us three writers for each script, and then you give us four directors for each show. Somebody is getting rich. We're growing broke. Stop it. Narrow it down."

I said, "I can't narrow it down, because I have learned

that your percentage of rejections is so high I have to have alternative choices to be prepared when you reject them politically." And he said, "I am helpless. Stop this talk. Get on with it. Do the best you can." I said, "If this continues I will withdraw personally as the producer of the show."

NIZER: What was Mr. Levy's position in Young & Rubicam?

SUSSKIND: He was vice-president, and he was specifically assigned to certain accounts, Borden, Lorillard, and so forth.

NIZER: Did he ever send you any list himself?

SUSSKIND: Yes, sir.

NIZER: Were they sent in writing? Were they written communications, is what I mean?

SUSSKIND: Yes, sir. When I sold the Borden Company, Young & Rubicam, a program, television program for the Borden Milk Company, the program was called "Justice," a half-hour weekly series on NBC Thursday nights, based on cases from the Legal Aid Society. A condition of the sale was that a list of the actors would be given me which numbered roughly 150, and that all roles on all programs in this series were to be billed from these politically cleared actors' names, and only such actors could be employed.

NIZER: What took place on this occasion when this happened?

SUSSKIND: I said to Mr. Levy, I mean the executive in charge of account . . .

I said, "It's impossible to cast a program from a list of 150-odd names. There are three thousand actors in the AFTRA union in New York. There are ten thousand actors in the Screen Actors Guild. I can't anticipate every script that will be written, but surely this 150 names will never permit me to do a program of any quality or any workability. It's impossible." He (Levy) said, "The Borden Company in its previous program had so much trouble with politically unreliable actors and pro-Communist sympathizers that they had made up this list." He said, "This white list is the only useful actors list for this program. Take it or leave it. If you don't want to use this list, you don't have the sale. If you will use this list, you can have the sale."

I took the program, commenting at the time, "This list will have to be enlarged and you will be forced to enlarge it. You will come to understand that, and incidentally this list is the most humdrum list of deadbeat, untalented actors I have ever seen."

Nizer then introduced into evidence a letter from Levy, on Young & Rubicam's stationery, to David Susskind, which Susskind testified had accompanied the list of 150 names of usable and approved actors and actresses. Lou also produced receipts that we had obtained from Hartnett at his EBT, and he read Hartnett's EBT testimony to the effect that he had received from the Borden Company $6,905 in 1954, and $10,000 in 1955. Lou continued to probe.

NIZER: When these names came back not approved, rejected for political reasons, what was your practice in dealing with the actors and actresses or director who was not approved? What happened then?

SUSSKIND: Because of the necessity of political clearance, we always booked actors on what we called a hold. That's a technical phrase in the business.

NIZER: Hold?

SUSSKIND: Yes. You say, "We would like Kim Stanley for this part, but we are not quite sure. Will you, her agent, please make her available for a forty-eight-hour period and not let her take another engagement while we make up our minds? We will get back to you." In the meantime, we establish together that her price will be such and such and that she will be available during the period of time for rehearsals and the program. That was a hold, or a tentative, or an option on her services. I only use her as an illustration.

THE COURT: Whom would you say this to?

SUSSKIND: I would say this to the talent agent who represented that client, or the person or management, or in some cases these people are represented by attorney. Then I would put the names in for clearance. When they came back rejected, as part of my instruction at the beginning of the program when I made the sale of "Appointment with

Adventure" and subsequently "Justice" and many other programs, it was stipulated that I was never to tell any rejectee why he was rejected.

Susskind explained at some length how the agency executives had instructed him never to allow any actor or actress to know that they were being rejected for political reasons. Nizer elicited from him that this was the general practice in all television and radio during that period. Susskind then told how, after getting an actor cleared, if he chose to use him on a program some weeks later, it was necessary to get his name cleared all over again.

The spectators and the members of the press, as well as the jury, seemed appalled at the whole clearance business. A kind of tension seemed to be growing in the courtroom. Lou continued.

NIZER: Did you also submit the names even of children on this program? Could you put a child on without getting clearance?

SUSSKIND: Even children.

NIZER: Will you give us an illustration or instance on this program if that occurred for a child?

SUSSKIND: Every one had to be cleared politically, including children.

BOLAN: May I ask this witness be responsive? He was asked for an illustration.

SUSSKIND: I will give you an illustration. In the course of "Appointment with Adventure," sponsored by Lorillard at Young & Rubicam Agency, we required the services of a, I believe, at least a seven- or eight-year-old girl actress, child actress. It was a backbreaking assignment to find a child who could act well enough to be in a professional program coast to coast. We went to all the established sources, the talent agencies. They did not represent children.

BOLAN: Your Honor, he was asked to give an illustration, and not a case history on a search for an actor or actress. Give us the illustration, not the whole story.

THE COURT: Overruled. I will allow it.

SUSSKIND: It was an extraordinarily difficult search involving going to the public-schools system, the United Nations schools. We finally found a child, an American child eight years old, female. I put her name in along with some other names. That child's name came back unacceptable, politically unreliable.

That did it. The whole courtroom, spectators and jurors alike, gave way to an audible gasp. Justice Geller looked the courtroom over sternly and said, "I will not tolerate any outburst of that kind, or I will order the courtroom cleared. This is not a show. This is a courtroom."

There was a continued stirring among the spectators as Susskind continued to testify about how he had urged that he be given a reason that he could not use this eight-year-old child; she surely couldn't be political. The agency finally told him that it was because the child's father was suspect. Bolan, of course, was furious that this testimony was being allowed to go on record. His protest to the court was so persistent that Lou finally said, "All right, I will connect it to page 847 of Mr. Hartnett's examination before trial."

He then read from Hartnett's own statement that he did check children and charged a fee for them. When Hartnett had been asked why he checked on children, he explained that there were two reasons: Some children's parents had left-wing tendencies, and that would make them objectionable or the child suspect, and the other reason was that some children start in on Communist activities on their own. As Hartnett had said, "They are rather enterprising."

Nizer then had Susskind describe in great detail the types of personalities who earn large salaries in television, men like Arthur Godfrey, Garry Moore, Steve Allen, and others.

NIZER: Can you state with reasonable certainty into what category Mr. John Henry Faulk would have fitted into the television broadcasting profession?
BOLAN: I object.
THE COURT: Overruled.
SUSSKIND: In my very considered opinion John Henry Faulk, had he been allowed to continue as a performer on television, would have become a star of the first magnitude, and

would have enjoyed an income and reputation in the company of the stars we previously mentioned.

THE COURT: You say that with a reasonable degree of certainty?

SUSSKIND: Yes, sir.

NIZER: Your witness.

The court then declared a short recess before Mr. Bolan was to begin his cross-examination of Susskind. Mr. Bolan announced that he wanted to make a motion, but not in the presence of the jury. The judge excused the jury and asked whether Bolan would like to go into chambers. Mr. Bolan then stated that he would like to move for a mistrial on the ground that Susskind's testimony was inadmissible.

BOLAN: It is completely inflammatory. He has spent most of his time talking about blacklisting, relating conversations that he had with some third party, with no relationship to any of the defendants.

The jury has been given the impression that the issue here is whether the defendants have been guilty of blacklisting certain other performers and in particular in the television and radio industry, and I submit that the testimony of this witness has not been directed against the defendants, and has been completely prejudicial, and I believe of the nature that does warrant a mistrial.

Justice Geller did not concur with Mr. Bolan's interpretation of Susskind's testimony, and overruled his motion for a mistrial.

After lunch, Susskind went on the stand for his cross-examination. Bolan approached him the way Mama used to approach a chicken snake in a hen nest. Within a matter of moments they were crossing swords, with Lou popping up full of objections, and Justice Geller trying to hold the fort.

THE COURT: Just a minute. Let us get a bit organized here. Mr. Susskind, you answer the questions just to the extent that the questions call for. Do not respond beyond that, but you, Mr. Bolan, give the witness an opportunity to complete his answer.

BOLAN: Did you ever have any discussion with these people as to what was meant by a political rejection or political clearance or political approval?

THE COURT: These people mean who?

BOLAN: The people in the advertising agencies that you say you had these conversations with, particularly, for instance, Mr. Levy.

SUSSKIND: I endeavored over and over again to find out what the charges were so that I could investigate the charges or apprise the actor and give him the opportunity to face the accusation and discover whether it was true and, if it was true, whether it was sufficient to bar him from employment. This opportunity was never granted me by the advertising agency or firms or anybody else who made the final determination.

BOLAN: Do you have any idea that these charges related to Communist Party membership or Communist Party front group membership?

SUSSKIND: I know of specific instances where I do know things about the charges, in the case of a particular actor. She was unemployable because her husband was deemed to have pro-Communist organization sympathy. She herself was clear and clean politically.

A little later, Bolan asked Susskind if by blacklisting he meant that practice that prevented artists from appearing on television and radio who had been identified as Communist Party members. Nizer objected to the question.

THE COURT: Overruled. I will let him answer that. He can take care of himself.

SUSSKIND: I don't know the theory of blacklisting except that it is a private vigilanteism calculated to keep people off—

BOLAN: Mr. Susskind—

SUSSKIND: —off television.

BOLAN: Mr. Susskind, I remind you to please answer my question, and yes or no would be sufficient.

SUSSKIND: I have answered, sir.

BOLAN: Yes or no would be sufficient.

SUSSKIND: I can't answer that yes or no.

BOLAN: Then you may say that you cannot answer it.

THE COURT: No. That question did not call for a yes or no answer, if the witness could not give it.

BOLAN: You stated that a whisper as to a man's political reliability would cut off his employment automatically in television. Is that correct?

SUSSKIND: I so stated.

BOLAN: Would you so state the fact that a man identified as a member of the Communist Party by sworn testimony— would that be sufficient a whisper as to cut off his employment?

SUSSKIND: A man identified as a Communist Party member?

BOLAN: Yes.

SUSSKIND: He would be dead as a duck and should be.

BOLAN: Haven't you yourself employed a number of people who have been identified by sworn testimony as members of the Communist Party?

SUSSKIND: I am not aware that I have ever employed a member of the Communist Party, and if that ever happened, I was unaware of such evidence.

BOLAN: I did not ask you whether you ever employed a member of the Communist Party, Mr. Susskind. I am asking you, did you ever employ a man who had been identified as a member of the Communist Party, identified by sworn testimony under oath?

THE COURT: You mean his sworn testimony?

BOLAN: Identified probably by sworn testimony as a member of Communist Party.

SUSSKIND: Identified by whom?

THE COURT: Wait a minute.

NIZER: I object to that, your Honor.

THE COURT: Sustained. Vague.

BOLAN: Your Honor, it is not vague. I am trying to find out—

THE COURT: That is my ruling. If you want, you can state, within the argument , your legal position.

BOLAN: My legal position is this: I am testing the credibility of this witness. He stated a short time ago—

NIZER: I object.

THE COURT: This is the argument. I want your legal position. So I will sustain the objection as put as being vague and indefinite. Put a different question.

BOLAN: Will you say the fact that a man has been identified

as a member of the Communist Party under sworn testimony would be equivalent to a whisper that you had described this morning?

NIZER: The same objection.

THE COURT: I will let him answer that. Go ahead.

SUSSKIND: If Harvey Matusow identified such a man, no. That is not a whisper, that is a lie, because he is a proven liar before a Congressional committee. It depends on who identified him, and how was that man faced with his accuser. Was he allowed to bring counsel? If they indict him, official agencies of our government, the Attorney General's office, the district attorney of New York?

Bolan seemed most eager to establish the fact that Susskind would regard it as blacklisting if an artist were barred from the air simply because he had pleaded the Fifth Amendment. They went backward and forward over that. Finally Lou questioned Bolan on the record.

NIZER: In this cross-examination, may I ask of counsel [Bolan] respectfully is it intended to justify the practice of blacklisting if somebody did testify about somebody and that person never had an opportunity to face his accuser, are you trying to justify that practice in this question?

BOLAN: I am trying to justify, Mr. Nizer, the right of a private group to advocate that people who take the Fifth when questioned on Communist Party membership need not or should not be employed on television. . . .

A moment later Bolan asked, rather sarcastically, if Susskind had not taken strenuous exception to advertising agencies who kept artists from appearing on his program for political reasons.

SUSSKIND: I took strenuous exception.

BOLAN: Fine. That's an answer.

THE COURT: Let him finish his answer.

SUSSKIND: I took strenuous exception to the whole system of blacklisting of everything decent and moral and American, and in principle I did not think that that was the advertising agency's function, or anybody's function, except

law enforcement agencies and authorized elements of our
government.

Then Bolan pressed Susskind for an answer as to whether
he would consider it blacklisting if a person who had taken
the Fifth Amendment was barred from performing or holding a job in radio and television.

SUSSKIND: Yes, I would consider that blacklisting. The Fifth
Amendment is a constitutional privilege and he was never
faced with the charge. He had no counsel, no opportunity
to answer, and the Fifth Amendment is part of our Bill of
Rights. It is not against the law. It is not a crime. It is
a constitutional privilege that I subscribe to with all my
might.

When Bolan pressed Susskind to say whether he would
consider it blacklisting if an actor who had been identified
by sworn testimony as a Communist Party member were
barred, Mr. Nizer objected and the court sustained it.

THE COURT: That was put before. The objection was sustained and sustained again. If you put the proper question,
I will permit it. Sworn testimony but of what? By whom?
An examination by whom? . . .
     Are you contending, Mr. Bolan, because somebody
comes before the House Un-American Activities Committee and swears to something about somebody, that that
establishes a fact?
BOLAN: I am not seeking to establish a fact. I am seeking to
establish the right of the advertiser to consider that a man
who has been identified under sworn testimony as a Communist Party member—that is all I'm trying. I am trying
to find out if that is part of blacklisting.
THE COURT: Put another question. If you want to put to him
questions based on judicial determination, you may put
that.

Bolan continued to press the matter of an actor or actress
identified before a committee of Congress in sworn testi-

mony as a Communist, what would Susskind do about that?
Justice Geller was becoming impatient with Bolan.

THE COURT: . . . A committee's report of Congress does not
constitute an adjudication.

Later on, in a heated exchange between the judge and
Bolan over the significance of sworn testimony before Congressional Committees, the judge said, "Somebody that is
thoroughly irresponsible can state something under oath.
Does that make it valid?"

Bolan, after trying unsuccessfully to get Susskind to testify that he really did not know too much about my professional career and had not seen me often, finally gave up and
court was adjourned for the weekend.

The second week of my direct examination started off on
the subject of my role in the union elections. Bolan strove
mightily, through objections, to keep me from testifying on
what was said at the two union meetings in the spring of
1955. They were the meetings at which the resolution to
condemn AWARE, Inc., had been discussed. He was successful, too, for much of my testimony was pure hearsay, consequently inadmissible. As will be seen later, during my cross-
examination he was eventually responsible for this very
evidence getting into the records.

My direct examination would have been completed in two
or three days, perhaps, had it not been for the interminable
arguments over the admission of evidence and exhibits. Lou
wanted me to give full and detailed accounts of each item.
He would start in on a line of questioning, for instance,
about the period when I first learned that Laurence Johnson
had come to New York and was knocking sponsors off my
show in April 1956. This involved my testifying about conversations I had with Carl Ward and Sam Slate. I would start
to relate a conversation between Ward and myself by saying,
"I went into Ward's office. He was very upset." Bolan would
object. The court would warn me not to characterize Mr.
Ward's state of mind, just to repeat his direct words to me.
Then I would undertake to explain that Ward had told me
that somebody had told him, objections again, pure hearsay.
Then a lengthy argument at the bench between Bolan and

Nizer, out of hearing of the jury, with the judge ruling that I should stick strictly to the facts. I tried to do that, but at the same time follow Nizer's instruction to get in a full account of everything.

Ben Bodne, a South Carolina gentleman, had come to New York just after the war and had purchased the Algonquin Hotel. He was a devoted friend and admirer of Nizer's and came to court nearly every day, arriving there in a chauffeur-driven Rolls-Royce that would also meet him each afternoon after court. Early in my second week of testimony, Lou had me describe what had happened after I had been blacklisted and gone broke. He urged me to describe in detail the hardships and deprivations my family and I had suffered, ending up on the note that I was still broke and heavily in debt. That day at lunch, Ben Bodne approached me and said that he wanted me to do him a favor. Since I was broke, he knew the matter of supporting myself during the trial was of great concern to me, and he wanted me to be his guest at the Algonquin for the duration of the trial. He pointed out that it would be his way of helping to fight the battle we were waging. The atmosphere of the Algonquin was genteel and literary. I loved the place. Knowing I had imposed on Chris and Merle long enough, I accepted gratefully. That afternoon after court, Ben and I sallied down to the street and prepared to climb into his waiting Rolls-Royce. George Berger came dashing up to me and said Lou wanted to see me immediately. I went over to where he was standing, some hundred feet away. "Don't get into a Rolls-Royce in front of the courthouse; some of the jurors might see you! You're supposed to be an unemployed victim of the blacklist. If you're going to ride home with Ben, walk up the street a couple of blocks and let him pick you up out of sight of the jurors." That was the procedure I followed each afternoon thereafter.

18

My direct examination lasted almost two weeks. On Thursday of the second week, Lou announced he was turning me over to Bolan for cross-examination.

Although I considered myself something of a veteran on the witness stand, by the time Bolan was ready to cross-examine me, I was uncontrollably tense and anxious. In spite of every effort, including prayer, I could not seem to calm my apprehensions.

First off, Bolan wanted to show I was never anything but a minor figure in broadcasting—a mere disc jockey.

BOLAN: Were you a disc jockey on CBS?
FAULK: I didn't regard myself as one nor did CBS regard me as one.
BOLAN: They did not?
FAULK: No.
BOLAN: Did the profession regard you as a disc jockey?
FAULK: I don't know how to answer that. Never was I included as a disc jockey in common parlance.

BOLAN: I have noticed that Mr. Nizer and yourself have not used the term disc jockey at all up to this point.
NIZER: I object to that, sir.
THE COURT: Sustained.
BOLAN: Do you have any aversion to being described as a disc jockey?
NIZER: Objection, sir.
THE COURT: Overruled.
FAULK: Not in the least, sir. I—
BOLAN: That is an answer. You said before that you were not regarded as a disc jockey in the profession.
FAULK: I was not.

BOLAN: I show you defendant's Exhibit A for identification and ask if that refreshes your recollection in any way?

FAULK: I don't know what you mean by refreshing my recollection.

BOLAN: Weren't you a member of Fresh Air Disc Jockey Committee for the Herald Tribune Fresh Air Fund at one time?

FAULK: That is perfectly correct, sir.

BOLAN: Haven't you always been referred to in reviews as a disc jockey?

FAULK: I don't remember any specific instance, but in all likelihood I have been, yes, sir.

BOLAN: You do not remember any specific instance? You are not sure you have ever been referred to as a disc jockey?

FAULK: I said I didn't remember any specific instance of being referred to.

BOLAN: But I ask you the question, have you ever been referred to as a disc jockey in the reviews?

FAULK: I say that, in all likelihood, yes.

After considerable wrangling between Nizer and Bolan over whether or not I was going to be allowed to explain what I was talking about when I said I did not regard myself a disc jockey and that CBS did not regard me as one, Judge Geller permitted me to testify.

FAULK: The reason I said that in all likelihood is at the time my contract was signed, the one to which you just referred, it was that they did not know how to describe me, describe the kind of program I was going to do, because I was employed primarily for the kind of stories and comments that I made. It was understood that I knew nothing about music. A disc jockey is an authority on music.

It was clear that Mr. Bolan wanted to derogate my abilities as a performer as much as possible. A little later he tried.

BOLAN: Did you ever hear the term "professional Texan"?

FAULK: Oh, yes indeed.

BOLAN: Did you ever hear it in reference to you?

FAULK: I think that I have, yes.

BOLAN: What does the term mean?

FAULK: I think in one instance someone writing a review of me, and I don't even recall who it was because it stung. It's very uncomplimentary as far as I'm concerned.

It means one that is pompous and inflated and goes about boasting of Texas being the biggest and best and the finest, and that the sun rises and sets there; that the first law of gravity was passed by the Texas state legislature.

THE COURT: Aren't the Texans proud of being the biggest and the best?

FAULK: I'm infinitely proud. I am trying to characterize a pompous humbug who gives Texas a black eye. By the way, it's one of the points I made quite frequently on my program, of these Texas oil men who say they could buy Russia. They would lease it back to Khrushchev, that sort of thing.

BOLAN: Isn't it a part of your act, or wasn't it a part of your act on CBS to act the part of an ignorant person rather than an intelligent one?

NIZER: Objection as incompetent, irrelevant, and immaterial.

THE COURT: I'm going to allow that.

FAULK: It certainly was not. It's far from it.

BOLAN: Did you—

THE COURT: Let him finish.

BOLAN: That is an answer.

THE COURT: I'm going to let him finish.

FAULK: I referred frequently to my lectures at Yale University. I quoted Shakespeare quite frequently, and John Milton quite frequently over the air. I do it on a folk level, that is quite true, but that's very different from conducting myself like a country bumpkin. I imagine that that is what you are suggesting I did.

I had a rather wide listening audience among university people, Princeton and Columbia universities.

Bolan finally gave up on that and wanted to know what I thought of Mr. Ward and Mr. Slate.

BOLAN: Mr. Slate was a very close friend of yours?

FAULK: Yes, I so regarded him.

BOLAN: Did you regard Mr. Slate and Mr. Ward as truthful and honest persons?

FAULK: Within the limitations of an executive in a radio and television business, I would say yes, but there are limitations, you see. . . .

BOLAN: Mr. Slate, does that statement apply to him?

THE COURT: Whether he is truthful and honest?

BOLAN: Yes.

FAULK: Mr. Slate is a truthful and honest man, but in . . . I don't want to go the whole hog there, and I'll tell you why. This is no reflection on the man's character at all, but executives, as we have heard testimony in this court, executives who are very honest men and are very good men, quite frequently are impelled to take actions and positions that could be described as less than candid, let us say.

BOLAN: They were compelled not to tell the truth?

FAULK: Let us say withhold the truth.

BOLAN: Did you just testify that because of his executive position, Mr. Slate was compelled to withhold the truth?

FAULK: I did not, and if I did, I certainly should have not said such a thing.

Mr. Bolan then turned his attention to the schedule of commercial spots on my program during the year 1956, subsequent to the attack by AWARE. This proved to be the grimmest time I had on the witness stand. For a couple of days we labored back and forth over the tedious and extremely technical matter of my rotating commercial schedule involving some two dozen sponsors. I tried desperately to remember when and under what circumstances I had which spots, and Bolan tried, with considerable success at times, to trip me up. The wonder is he did not do it more often.

When he got around to the period of my dismissal from WCBS in August 1957, he went over and over the reasons that Sam Slate had given me at the time for my firing. He was very careful to establish through my testimony that Sam Slate had never once said that I was being fired because AWARE was using pressure on him. Finally, I testified to the

several reasons that Sam Slate had given me, such as changing the programming at WCBS, my having been on the same
show too long, and several others.

BOLAN: Did you consider Mr. Slate to be a truthful man, this
   very close friend of yours, when he made these statements
   to you as to why you had lost your job?
FAULK: I considered Mr. Slate to be a man under very profound emotional stress, sir, that he had to take an action
   that he abominated.
BOLAN: Now will you answer the question? Did you consider him to be a truthful man?
FAULK: Under those circumstances, sir, Mr. Slate was neither
   truthful nor dishonest. Mr. Slate was acting at the direction of the corporation for which he worked.

Mr. Bolan had subpoenaed William B. Greene, an attorney
at WCBS, to bring down records he wanted to use in my
cross-examination. It was necessary to put Mr. Greene on
the witness stand while I stood aside for a while, to testify
that these were authentic records from CBS. To the considerable astonishment of Mr. Bolan, after Mr. Greene had identified the records as being authentic and from CBS, Mr. Nizer
asked to cross-examine him. Mr. Greene was the lawyer that
had been at CBS when Roy Cohn's office obtained the original records from them.

NIZER: Was any associate of Mr. Roy Cohn, on behalf of the
   defendants, in your office with respect to these records,
   some months ago?
GREENE: Yes sir. Mr. Lang.
NIZER: And were the original records delivered to Mr. Lang at
   that time?
GREENE: Certain of the original records were delivered to
   him, yes, sir.
NIZER: And he had those for how long, sir, in his own office?
GREENE: To the best of my knowledge, sir, I would say two
   weeks.
NIZER: And did you have a copy of these original records
   made before they were delivered to Mr. Cohn?

GREENE: A copy of those which are now in Mr. Bolan's hands, no, sir.

NIZER: So that Mr.—

THE COURT: Now, wait, let me understand that. You say "a copy of those which are now in Mr. Bolan's hand" did you not make that statement? Did you make a copy of any which were delivered to Mr. Cohn?

GREENE: No, sir, the reason I answered it that way, your Honor, there may have been copies of other papers that are in the files spread in other files within the company. I don't know that.

NIZER: I understand, in other words, sir, the records which you delivered to the defendants' counsel were the original records of CBS, of which no copy was kept in your office?

GREENE: That is correct.

Nizer turned on his heel, commenting, "That's all."

At one point, Bolan handed me an article that had appeared about a year before in *The Nation* magazine, entitled "Disc Jockey Fights the Blacklist." Nizer was on his feet at once, demanding that the entire article be admitted as evidence. The article was highly favorable to me, and it mentioned certain things about the defendants and my fight with them that could not have been put into evidence by us. However, as Bolan had presented the article in an attempt to establish that I was merely a disc jockey, the court ruled the article in its entirety be admitted into the record.

The high point of my cross-examination occurred toward its end. It happened one day when Bolan sought to prove that the anti-AWARE resolution, which had been passed by the membership of AFTRA in 1955, was actually Communist-inspired. Since my activities on the Middle-of-the-Road slate had grown directly out of this anti-AWARE resolution, Bolan wanted to connect the beginnings of the slate, at least my participation in it, with what he considered the sinister forces in the union who had promulgated the anti-AWARE resolution. His determination to do this led him, I believe, into a couple of the most costly mistakes of the entire trial.

He set out, through his questioning of me, to establish the names of those who had introduced and supported the anti-AWARE resolution. He wanted to prove that they all were of questionable patriotism; they had been charged with various Communist and pro-Communist proclivities. He also wanted to get into the record the names of prominent personalities, like Bud Collyer, Vicki Cummings, and Alan Bunce, who had supported AWARE with strong statements at the time of the voting. On my direct examination, I had testified at length (or in as much detail as possible over Bolan's objections) on what various persons had said at the two AFTRA meetings, the one in March and May 1955. I had also testified that I had received two statements in the mail with my ballot in June 1955, one statement supporting AWARE and urging me not to vote for the condemnation of same, and the other condemning AWARE and giving the reasons for it. Bolan, of course, was allowed to introduce these statements into evidence since I had testified about them. He was particularly anxious to get the pro-AWARE statement in. No sooner was it admitted in evidence than he read it with relish to the jury.

BOLAN [From the pro-AWARE statement]: "The issue is not, as the proponents of the misleading resolution would have us believe, the organization called Aware. So far, the only thing most of us know about Aware is what we are told by its enemies. But we can be sure of one thing, if what Aware said about certain AFTRA members had not been true, if it had not, if it had really been smear and inference and innuendo, these members would have challenged their exposure instead of coming crying to AFTRA. Here is the real issue. An insignificant number of AFTRAns, who have been identified under oath as Communist Party members, or who have identified themselves with Communist front organizations, have been trying for years, unsuccessfully to gain power and leadership in our union, and they have now seized upon Aware's exposure of their activities as a means of trying to gain AFTRA's sympathy and support. In this effort they have hidden behind the skirts of a few misguided AFTRAns innocently involved in left-wing affiliations hoping thereby to make themselves appear equally innocent. They tell us that an outside organization has been interfering in the internal affairs of our union, but they conveniently neglect to mention that

Aware's comments about their own unsavory outside activities were made nearly a month after AFTRA elections
were over. Furthermore, they hoped we will forget that
their Communist fronts which they do not ask us to condemn, are quite definitely outside organizations, outside
not only of our union but of our country."

Bolan had apparently forgotten all about, or had never
read, the anti-AWARE statement on the other side that had
been sent to the membership at the same time. It had now
become part of the record. Nizer reminded him of this fact.
He hesitated a moment, and then responded with noticeable
lack of enthusiasm.

BOLAN: Did you want the other side read, Mr. Nizer?
NIZER: I would like to read it, if you're not going to. I would
like to read all of it.
BOLAN: These are for the resolution: "If you read the papers
you know that the New York AFTRA membership voted
'Yes' to condemn the action of Aware, Inc. at the largest
meeting in AFTRA's history. Actors Equity membership
voted yes to condemn the actions of Aware in their last—
NIZER: May I read it please? May I have the privilege of reading the section, so that it is not read with less emphasis
than the other side?
THE COURT: That statement is stricken out. Mr. Bolan,
would you read it—maybe we're all getting hungry—read
it a little louder and a little slower.
BOLAN: "Actors Equity Council unanimously voted yes to
condemn the actions of Aware, Inc.
   "The *New York Times* said: 'Aware, Inc. condemned.
Local members of the federation have scored Aware for
promulgating smear tactics or lists in interfering in the internal affairs of the union.' *Variety* said: 'The resolution
against Aware for adopting smear methods and blacklisting was passed on Tuesday. By Friday of the week three
persons, one of whom had not acted on radio or TV for two
years, was hired by an ad agency for a network show.'"

As I listened to Bolan reading the anti-AWARE statement,
I could not for the life of me figure out why on earth he had

ever allowed such a thing to get into evidence, let alone introduce it himself and stand up and read it.

Bolan then sought to introduce portions of the minutes of the two AFTRA meetings in 1955. These minutes contained charges by pro-AWARE members against the advocates of the resolution to the effect that an anti-AWARE vote would be serving the cause of international Communism. Nizer indicated that he would not object to the admission of the minutes into the record if Mr. Bolan would agree to our looking them over during the lunch hour. During lunch we went over them and realized that the contents of the minutes would serve our interests far better than those of the defendants. Bolan had overlooked the fact that these same minutes also contained some inspired invective against AWARE. These were speeches made by anti-AWARE union members at the two meetings. When court reconvened that afternoon, Nizer, with calculated casualness so as not to arouse Bolan's suspicions, told the court that so far as he was concerned, the minutes could be admitted since it would save the court's time by avoiding an argument over them. Bolan looked downright grateful for Nizer's accommodating gesture.

Bolan started off by reading from the minutes of the March 1955 meeting of AFTRA. He read a speech by Godfrey Schmidt, at that time president of AWARE, Inc., and a member of AFTRA. Schmidt had spoken at the meeting defending AWARE and its bulletin attacking AFTRA members who had been candidates against the AWARE-supported slate the year before.

BOLAN [reading from Schmidt's speech]: ". . . There is a clear intent expressed here in the anti-Aware resolution that another type of activity should be denominated blacklisting. That is to say, to tell the truth about candidates . . . The truth, ladies and gentlemen: Every single line in this is the unchallengeable truth, and the best proof of it is that none of you will dare, if you feel aggrieved, bring it to court, as you could . . . I submit that Aware, which is also the recipient of some of these aspersions, can take care of itself. It has a fine set of principles and a good program, but it is the kind of thing that I need not bring here unless you want to. Thank you."

NIZER: May I read something from this same exhibit?
THE COURT: Yes.
BOLAN: I must finish it, your Honor. Your Honor, I will let
  Mr. Nizer read while I check my notes as to the pages.
NIZER: Thank you.

Lou then proceeded to read excerpts from the speeches of
Miss Elaine Eldridge, an actress and member of AFTRA.

NIZER [reading from Eldridge's speech]: "I had no idea that
  Mr. Schmidt was here to espouse the cause of Aware, or
  what he calls the opposition to his sentiments as being
  necessarily Communistic, which I think is most unfair la-
  beling anyone who opposes you . . . Forgive me, if I appear
  a little emotional about it, but I was one of the people
  named because I had accepted two years ago a telephone
  call which came to me from the National Committee of
  Arts, Sciences and Professions, asking me if I would be
  willing to teach on their staff. I said yes, and I went to one
  meeting at which the program was to be organized, and it
  fell through. I never heard anything further from it. That
  was two years ago, and today that organization is still not
  on the Attorney General's list. So I think it is a little pre-
  sumptuous and perhaps a little premature on the part of
  Mr. Schmidt to consider all these people as dangerous and
  menaces to our society. I assure you that I don't think I
  am. I will let you be the judge. Thank you." [Applause]

Lou then read portions of a speech by actress Lee Grant.

NIZER: [reading Miss Grant's speech]: "I think Mr. Schmidt,
  in using the sentiments of Anti-Communism which is nationally felt today, is covering the real purpose of Aware,
  Inc. It has been used by Mr. McCarthy, whom I do not
  agree with, but who Mr. Schmidt does agree with. He
  spoke at his rally in Madison Square Garden. . . . I think
  the fact that our board members [board members of
  AFTRA] are sitting with a man, Vincent Hartnett, who is
  the author of Red Channels and helped to put out lists is a
  shameful, shameful thing, and should not be tolerated in
  our union." [Applause]

Lou then read the entire statement of Leslie Barrett. It was a heart-breaking story of the punishment he received at the hands of Vincent Hartnett, who was attempting to connect him with a Communist May Day parade. Hartnett had written to Barrett saying he had a picture of Barrett marching in a May Day parade in 1951. Barrett, as it turned out, had never marched in any May Day parade at any time, but he had plenty of misery from Hartnett's charges. The jury leaned forward eagerly. Lou read on and on. Then Lou read from the speech of Mr. Harold Gary.

NIZER: ". . . he [Schmidt] frequently uses the term 'Americanism' . . . I would like to know where Mr. Schmidt has learned his Americanism. When I learned about Americanism—and I like to think of myself as a pretty good American—I learned nobody can appoint himself as a self-constituted judge and jury of his fellow man." (Applause) "I don't know how long you have been an actor, Mr. Schmidt, if you are one, but I want you to know that you're playing with dynamite, and only people who are duly authorized and licensed should be permitted to play with dynamite.

"An actor's career is very precariously perched. I have been an actor long enough to know that. The least bit of censure, whether justified or unjustified, can ruin him, whether it is on moral, political, or other grounds, and I think it is a horrendous thing, a criminal thing, for you to toy with other people's careers that they have given all their lives and emotions and study to. And the point is that not only are they involved, but also their families. This is a very dangerous business."

Bolan, of course, realized his mistake too late. I was still on the stand and he came at me.

BOLAN: Mr. Faulk, was the Lee Grant whose statement Mr. Nizer read the same Lee Grant who a few months ago took the Fifth Amendment—

NIZER: I object to that.

BOLAN: —when questioned as to whether she was a member of the Communist Party?

THE COURT: Mr. Bolan, that is sustained and in light of our discussion in the robing room, you should have understood not to put that question.

BOLAN: Your honor I take exception.

THE COURT: You cannot impute to the plaintiff the fact that somebody else took the Fifth Amendment.

BOLAN: I am not imputing to the plaintiff the fact that somebody else took the Fifth Amendment. The issue here is blacklisting, and I submit I am entitled to find out the background of the people who made the statements at the meetings.

THE COURT: No inferences are to be drawn from that question and I am now going to give the jury instructions about this Fifth Amendment business.

It has been held by our highest court that a person has the right to refuse to answer questions by pleading the Fifth Amendment, which is part of the Bill of Rights of our Constitution.

The Supreme Court of the United States has said, and I quote: "We must condemn the practice of imputing a sinister meaning to the exercise of a person's constitutional right under the Fifth Amendment."

The Supreme Court has also held that no inference of Communistic Party membership or of any subversive nature may be drawn from the exercise of the constitutional protection of the Fifth Amendment. Accordingly, no imputation may be drawn solely and in itself from the fact that a person has pleaded the Fifth Amendment and refused on that ground to answer questions by any Congressional committee, meaning the Senate or the House of Representatives, and, obviously, this question was not even put with respect to the plaintiff, but somebody else.

Mr. Bolan, in a rather futile effort to undo some of the harm done by Nizer's reading, undertook to read some more of the pro-AWARE speeches. He read one by Rex Marshall, an announcer and a defender of AWARE. Marshall made some rather astonishing statements.

BOLAN [reading Marshall's speech]: "It seems to me that we're indebted to a group [AWARE, Inc.] that gives its time freely to expose elements that are dangerous to this country and to this union. I don't think you can condemn a vigilante committee for being vigilant, but if it is accused of being a lynching committee, I think the accusation should be made properly by the persons who considered themselves in danger of lynching."

Marshall then made a breathtaking observation.

BOLAN [reading from Marshall's speech]: ". . . Until proper charges have been brought by those accused [referring to the people named and attacked by AWARE in its bulletin], we can only assume that the accusations are justified and we should thank the people who are interested enough to give their time to look for our interest."

I noticed that the jury listened with considerable interest as Mr. Bolan read Marshall's observation that an accused person should be considered guilty until he had proved himself innocent. Bolan read the speeches of several others, including one by Mr. Vinton Hayworth, who at that time had been president of AFTRA and also a member of the board of AWARE. The reading of excerpts of Hayworth's speech seemed to affect the jury somewhat the way the reading of Marshall's speech had.

There were certain areas in which Mr. Bolan was not allowed to question me. The court's rules are that a question may not be asked if it implies something discreditable to the witness, unless there is substantiation for such a question. Despite this, during the next to the last day of my crossexamination (which had already lasted nearly two weeks), Bolan suddenly backed off across the courtroom and started firing a series of questions at me, very much in the manner of a prosecuting attorney. He was anxious to establish that I had talked with an investigator for the House Un-American Activities Committee in July 1955. Nizer was objecting all over the place, lest the questions themselves imply to the jury that I had made admissions to the investigator that might be harmful to me. He made no effort to conceal his anger as Bolan persisted. Bolan's efforts backfired, though. Judge Geller interrupted with a statement that not only the jury, but the whole country needed to hear.

THE COURT: . . . As I have stated to you [the jury], the listing of any organization as an allegedly subversive or Communist front by a Congressional committee, and this applies also to any listing by the Attorney General of the United States, is simply an accusation, which is not a judicial determination and is not the result of a due process, by law.

The evidence to prove that it is a Communist front and subversive, not the mere fact that it was listed as such anywhere, must come forward here before you can find that it was a Communist-front organization. The fact that the listing is allowed into evidence for the limited purpose of the defendants' partial claim in mitigation of punitive damages, if there is such proof, that they relied on sources in making the charges against the plaintiff. Such listing does not go to the truth of the charge, but only as evidence offered by the defendants, if offered, with regard to their claim that if the charge is found to be false, they should not be found to have made it without an investigation or foundation, and that this should be taken into consideration, if you reach that point in fixing the amount, if any, of punitive damages against those defendants who are held liable by you.

So keep in mind as to the proof being offered concerning plaintiff's alleged participation in Communist front organizations, that proof satisfactory to you must be offered to show, (1) that he actually attended, entertained, or contributed material, and not merely that it was advertised that he would so participate, or was reported that he would or did so participate, and if such actual attendance by plaintiff is not shown, then no further evidence may come, of course, may be given as to the function or organization, because it is plaintiff's knowing participation which is of vital importance to inquiry; and (2) that such organization is proved by proper proof to be a Communist front or subversive organization; and (3) that you must find from all the evidence direct or circumstantial, that plaintiff at the time of such participation had knowledge of such organization being a Communist front and subversive, and intended to aid it.

All these elements would have to be established before you may consider whether the charges that plaintiff was a

pro-Communist with Communist affiliations and sympathies have been proved.

As we left the court that afternoon, Nizer commented to
me, "Bolan used McCarthy tactics today; they will cost him
dearly. He just ran the judgment up another million dollars
with that vicious gambit."

The cross-examination had begun to pall on me terribly. I
had been subjected to Bolan for nearly two weeks and had
reached the point where I did not sleep well at night; I would
lie in a semi-conscious state, fantasizing sharp questions
and feeble, vague answers. When, on Friday, May 11, Bolan
announced he had completed his cross-examination of me,
it was as though I had suddenly come to the surface after
being under water for a long time.

19

I was looking forward to getting to the courthouse now that I could sit as a spectator rather than as a witness.

I knew that we had lined up a formidable battery of witnesses who would take the stand and drive our case home. My active participation was over—or so I thought; it turned out that I was to be as involved as ever. I found out pretty soon that getting people to consent to appear as witnesses was just the first, and by far the least complicated, part of getting them on the stand. In the first place, there was the matter of preparing a witness, discovering exactly what information he could give and, just as important, what he would be allowed to say and how he would handle his cross-examination by Bolan. There was also a limit to the number of witnesses we would be allowed to call. This made it necessary to choose very carefully the ones we would use; they must be those who would lend the greatest possible weight to our cause.

When I got into court that morning, Charles Collingwood had just been sworn in. Paul Martinson and George Berger were in a sweat. Our next witness was supposed to be Tony Randall. He was flying to Greece early the following morning to work in a film. Collingwood was one of our key witnesses, and we knew his testimony would be lengthy. The problem was whether Bolan would finish his cross-examination in time for us to put Tony Randall on the stand that afternoon.

Charles Collingwood cut a fine figure on the stand. His distinguished and gentlemanly bearing, and his quiet, self-assured manner created a good impression, not only on the jury, but on everyone in the room with the possible exception of the defendants and their attorneys. I felt a surge of warm gratitude and pride as he testified in my behalf. Nizer carried him through an accounting of his days as a Rhodes scholar, a war correspondent and a serious student of international affairs. He had received countless awards for his distinguished broadcasts. He was solidly established as an expert witness qualified to estimate the damage my career had suffered. When Nizer got around to the affairs of AFTRA, the jury seemed to lean forward.

NIZER: Now, in the latter part of 1955, did you participate in the formation of what is called the Middle-of-the-Road slate of candidates of the New York local of AFTRA?
COLLINGWOOD: I certainly did.

NIZER: What was the occasion of the organization of the Middle-of-the-Road slate?
COLLINGWOOD: Well, as you may imagine, like most political processes, this didn't suddenly arise full bloom, and I think to explain that I must give a little bit of history of the union, if I may.
NIZER: Yes.
BOLAN: I object, your Honor.
THE COURT: Overruled.
COLLINGWOOD: During the 1950s the union membership became dominated by a self-perpetuating group who, among other things, made common cause with the various organizations who were interested in fighting, in their way, Communism in the entertainment industry, and this resulted in a process which is usually called blacklisting, in which the union was rather deeply involved.

Collingwood then related how the New York local of the union had in 1955 voted overwhelmingly to condemn AWARE, and that he and several others of us in the union had felt that with the election coming up in the fall, we should challenge the leadership of the union who had sided with AWARE.

COLLINGWOOD: . . . The vote of the referendum condemning Aware had strongly shown that the climate of opinion in the union was opposed not only to Aware, but to the leadership of the union and its close entanglements with the AWARE group. It was a little difficult to round up a slate because in those days the penalties visited upon those who took issue with the leadership were very strong. They amounted to blacklisting, or at least they amounted to the threat of blacklisting. People in the union were afraid to run. They were afraid and concerned, and it was, as I said earlier, with some difficulty that we secured a full slate to run against the existing leadership of the union.

Over Bolan's objection, Lou was able to get Collingwood's testimony on the practices in the industry, when rumors or accusations brought a performer's patriotism into question.

COLLINGWOOD: It was very difficult at that time for anyone who had been charged by a private organization . . . such as AWARE, or by important figures in the industry with some sort of Communist intent, however vague, it was very difficult for them to get employment, and there were many cases in which people did not know what had happened to them.

When Nizer got around to my reputation, Collingwood testified, again over Bolan's objections.

COLLINGWOOD: His reputation was very good. Although his main work had been done in radio, he had done a number of television programs, one of them was "It's News to Me," on which he was a panel member and was very good.
   I have mentioned earlier my association with him on the "Morning Show," which was presided over by Jack Paar. He told the jokes and I told the news and sometimes we would have guests. Mr. Faulk was a guest, and, indeed, he substituted for Mr. Paar for a period of at least two weeks, in which he told the jokes and I told the news, and I may say that Mr. Paar is a very difficult man to follow. Mr. Faulk followed him admirably.

He then testified that my reputation for patriotism, loyalty, and integrity was very high. He told how in April of 1956, after I had been attacked by Johnson and had begun to lose sponsors, he had asked for an appointment with Arthur

Hull Hayes, who was at the time vice-president of CBS radio
and general manager of CBS and he was presently president
of CBS radio. Judge Geller allowed Collingwood to tell of his
conversation with Mr. Hayes; but the judge first explained
to the jury that the opinion of neither Mr. Collingwood nor
Arthur Hull Hayes on what the damages done to me personally had been could be testified to.

COLLINGWOOD: There had been reports that as a result of the
AWARE bulletin, Mr. Faulk was in some trouble at CBS.
So I asked for an appointment with Mr. Hayes. I was motivated not only by my friendship with Faulk, but as president of the New York local.
I went to see him for two reasons, one, to find out
whether this was indeed the case, and, number two, to ac-
quaint him with the attitude of the union.
I said that the union would take a very dim view indeed
if, as the result of these allegations in the AWARE bulletin, Faulk was severed from his employment with CBS.
As far as I could see, the only reason that this might have
happened was that he ran for and was elected an officer of
the union, brought down AWARE on his head, and if that
were to happen to the first vice-president of the union, we
would take a very strong view on it, that I would have to
hold hearings because this would be a clear-cut case of
blacklisting, to which the leadership of the union was opposed. . . . Mr. Hayes said that he was not about to be influenced by this kind of statement, that he felt that he was
qualified to run his station and pick his performers without outside advice, and as long as Mr. Faulk's programs
were good and as long as his sponsors stayed on, he would
continue him in the capacity in which he was employed.

Nizer later asked him if Ed Murrow of CBS had conversations with executives of CBS in respect to my continued
employment. Over violent objections, the court ruled that
Charles could testify.

COLLINGWOOD: Mr. Murrow was active in Mr. Faulk's behalf,
and I remember a conversation with Mr. Slate, who was the

program manager of WCBS at the time, in which both Mr.
Murrow and I urged that Mr. Faulk not be victimized because of these allegations in the AWARE bulletin.

One of Collingwood's strongest bits of testimony came
when Lou asked him:

NIZER: What is the employment practice with respect to an
artist who becomes involved in a controversy with respect
to his loyalty?
BOLAN: I object.
THE COURT: Overruled.
COLLINGWOOD: Well, it really depends, Mr. Nizer, on how
much guts the sponsor has, the network and the station,
whether they have got enough guts to stand up to the pressures which are brought against them, or whether they
don't. The time of which we are speaking, in most cases
they didn't have very much guts.

Collingwood's testimony on the relationships between
sponsors, advertising agencies, and performers was particularly persuasive.

COLLINGWOOD: Quite often performers were denied employment when it later turned out that the charges against
them were unfounded. Therefore, it would appear to be
pretty clear that actual guilt or innocence was not the con-
trolling factor in the decisions that were made. . . . There
were instances in which an actor, either because he was
well connected or for some other reasons, was brought before one of these persons charged by the organizations for
whom he worked for clearing of people. He was brought
before them to explain. This was by no means, however,
the universal practice. . . .
    He [the accused actor] was not usually informed of the
source of the charges, if they had not been made public.

By the time Collingwood's direct examination was completed, it was apparent from the faces of the jurors that he
had scored heavily for us.
After lunch, in Bolan's cross-examination of Charles, he

turned to the subject of organizations other than AWARE which had been engaged in blacklisting in the industry.

COLLINGWOOD: I am not aware of the whole spectrum, but there were people who organized themselves and presented information. There were letters from the American Legion and other groups referring to performers. There was an apparatus of pressure upon the network and the stations relating to their performers.

Bolan continued to press him to name other organizations aside from the American Legion. He did this, obviously, to discredit Collingwood's rather broad statement. This brought forth the following.

COLLINGWOOD: The principal one [blacklisting organization] from the point of view of the union, which was my immediate concern, was Aware, which had become an issue within the union. That there were others I had reason to believe, although I can't identify them for you, due to the inadequacy of my recollection.

Bolan then turned to the matter of Collingwood's testimony that morning on the subject of artists who had been discharged on unsubstantiated charges of disloyalty. He asked Collingwood if he could name one such artist.

COLLINGWOOD: I can certainly name one.
BOLAN: What was the name of the performer involved?
COLLINGWOOD: The performer was Mr. Leslie Barrett.
BOLAN: And is it your testimony that Mr. Barrett was discharged by reason of charges brought by the defendant AWARE?
COLLINGWOOD: Discharged or had difficulty in gaining employment as a result.

And so it was that all the testimony on Barrett, which certainly was not flattering to the defendants, was reintroduced into the record. Bolan then sought to establish through Collingwood's testimony that actually the main purpose of the Middle-of-the-Road slate had been to oppose AWARE.

COLLINGWOOD: Mr. Bolan, the union had been torn asunder. This local union of performers in radio and television had been torn asunder by a controversy over AWARE, about issues involving the blacklisting, the supposed blacklisting, the fear of blacklisting, the union wasn't getting work done, it wasn't performing the functions which we felt a union should perform. We hoped that by this Middle-of-the-Road slate, a plague on both your houses, we would be able to clear the air for the resumption of normal trade union activities.

Late in Collingwood's cross-examination, Bolan took the AWARE bulletin which had attacked me, Collingwood, and Bean, and read what it said about Collingwood.

BOLAN [reading]: "Will middler Charles Collingwood, new president of AFTRA New York, discharge his responsibility to enforce AFTRA's Constitution and National Rule? In a public statement of January 22, 1956, Collingwood did not show any knowledge that twelve members of his local had been identified as Communist Party members, and that fifteen, in all, had refused to answer when asked by the House Committee on Un-American Activities that they were Communists, Collingwood belittled the document findings of the House Committee, 1955 Annual Report, that there was a 'militant Communist faction in the New York local of AFTRA.'

"He stated, 'The blacklist is dying and the present officers of the majority of the New York local Board of AFTRA intend to do everything they can to assist the process.'"
BOLAN: Now, Mr. Collingwood, did you make a public statement on January 22, 1956?
COLLINGWOOD: Yes.

It will be remembered that back in January 1956, shortly after the Middle-of-the-Road slate had taken over as officers of the New York local, the House Un-American Activities Committee, in its annual report, attacked our slate, and that Collingwood, on January 22, 1956, wrote a letter to the Committee repudiating its statements. For some reason or other, Bolan wanted to get this letter into the evidence. I still don't know why in the world he wanted to do this. The letter could certainly do no harm to our side. If anything, it would increase Collingwood's stature in the eyes of the jury. I watched the jurors' faces as Mr. Bolan read the letter. Several of them were gazing at Collingwood on the witness stand with admiration.

BOLAN [reading Collingwood's letter of January 22, 1956]: "I have read with amazement the quotations from the Annual Report of the House Committee on Un-American Activities which deal with alleged Communism in the radio and television industry, with special reference to conditions within the New York Local of the American Federation of Television and Radio Artists.

"With the air of omniscience which has become traditional with such documents, the report states that 'An investigation uncovered a militant faction within the local, New York City, affiliate of the American Federation of Television and Radio Artists.'

"It is possible, of course, that the Committee has sources not available to the union. In that case it would seem to be the Committee's duty to communicate to the union information that it 'uncovered.' It is curious that, to the best of my knowledge, the Committee in its researches made no attempt to seek information from the officers or paid executives of the New York Local of AFTRA. In its annual report the Committee on Un-American Activities further states that 'The principal activity of Communists within AFTRA was against so-called blacklisting. Through their campaign these Communists have falsely convinced many fellow artists that they are denied employment if they at one time innocently supported a cause supported by the Communist Party.'

"Now if the Committee on Un-American Activities really thinks that the only people in the entertainment industry who are disturbed by the excesses of blacklisting system are Communists or their dupes, then it is laboring under a misapprehension.

"Concern over the manifest inequities of the black-list—"

NIZER: Iniquities.

BOLAN: "Inequities." Oh excuse me. "Iniquities of the black-

list is shared by the overwhelming majority of the performers and by, one suspects, a large proportion of the employers as well.

"No one in the industry wishes to have the Communist
Party derive benefits from the employment in radio and
television of actual dues-paying Communists, or desires
to aid it or defend anyone who has been duly proven to
be subversive. The New York Local of AFTRA has just
elected, with the largest vote in its history, a slate of
twenty-seven officers and twenty-seven board members,
who ran as unequivocally opposed to the indiscriminate
blacklisting as it now exists. There were no Communists
among these elected, nor any dupes, either, and surely the
electorate which swept them into office with an unprecedented large vote cannot be exclusively composed of Communists or deluded pawns, either.

"The Committee's report deplores indications that the
blacklisting machinery of the industry is losing some of
its force.

"It is my belief and fervent hope that this is indeed the
case. The climate of opinion within the industry is changing. Perspective is returning. The blacklist is dying, and
the present officers and the majority of the New York Local Board of AFTRA intend to do everything that they can
do to assist the process.

"Now that people are beginning to look at these matters
dispassionately, it is clear that the degree of Communist
infiltration in radio and television was exaggerated from
the beginning. This is not to say that the problem was not
a real problem and may not be again.

"The safeguards which exist in our union's constitution
in the normal management practices are more than sufficient to deal with the situation. It is regrettable that the
Committee on Un-American Activities has painted a picture of the industry which is not only inaccurate, but
tends to perpetuate rather than eliminate the abuses of the
recent past."

BOLAN: Now, Mr. Collingwood, were you severely rebuked
by the National Board of AFTRA for making such a
statement?

NIZER: Objection, sir, both as to the characterization—

THE COURT: Reframe your question.
NIZER: And also because it is irrelevant.

After much wrangling between the lawyers, Bolan finally got a chance to read into the record for the jury's benefit the statement in the AWARE bulletin.

BOLAN [reading]: "In public reply January 31, 1956, House Committee Un-American Activities Counsel Frank S. Tavenner told Collingwood the Committee's New York City hearings had 'established beyond any doubt the scope and the nature of concerted Communist activities in the entertainment industry and within the professional union.' He [Tavenner] continued:
   " 'The hearings leave no doubt as to the existence of such Communist Party faction and the recent election battle within your local further corroborates these findings.'
   "Tavenner further states that 'There's no blacklisting at all . . .' " 'It is significant to note that the election of the so-called anti-blacklist candidates in the recent AFTRA election (the middlers) has been greeted enthusiastically by the Communist front.' "
THE COURT: All right, now. The jury will also recall my extended remarks with respect to the Fifth Amendment and with respect to the accusations before the House Un-American Activities Committee. I don't have to go into it extensively at this point.

Luck was with us. Collingwood was dismissed from the stand in plenty of time for Tony Randall to testify. Tony was enjoying the success of a multitalented star of stage, screen, and television. However, despite his considerable experience before audiences, it was quite obvious that he was nervous. He told how he had been an active member of AFTRA, until AWARE became so dominant in its affairs that he was afraid to attend meetings. As he put it, he "crawled under a rock and stayed there" until AFTRA voted to condemn AWARE in 1955. After that he helped us organize the Middle-of-the-Road slate. His powerful voice impressed the jurors as he testified. They liked him. Bolan, after a vain attempt to ridicule his "crawling under a rock," wisely dropped the cross-examination.

We spent that entire evening with Kim Hunter at Nizer's apartment. She said she was extremely nervous and looked on her forthcoming session on the stand with dread. All the same, she was determined to go through with it. Her anxiety seemed to stem, in good part, from the fact that she would be publicly testifying to having given way under Hartnett's threats, which placed her in an embarrassing position. Nizer assured her that the great courage and integrity she would display by her willingness to testify would win the warm approval of both the jury and the public.

When I arrived at the courthouse the next morning, the corridors were full of photographers waiting for Kim to appear; apparently it had leaked out that she would take the stand that day. As Nizer and Kim came down the hall, Lou refused firmly the photographers' requests for them to pose for pictures.

Our first witness that day obviously caught the defendants off guard. He was Tom Murray, the account executive at the Grey advertising agency. He had vital testimony to give. Throughout the trial, Mr. Bolan had been maintaining that Laurence Johnson had nothing to do with my being blacklisted and that we had no evidence connecting him directly with my case. Tom Murray was prepared to establish that connecting link. Murray had placed his career in the advertising industry at stake by coming forward as a witness. He was a gentle and quiet man, with a deep conviction, which became evident as he testified.

He gave his background and told of his placing of Coca-Cola advertising on my program. Then he continued.

MURRAY: Mr. Faulk got more laudatory mail from listeners to the program than all other performers combined.
THE COURT: When you say Mr. Faulk got that, did he get it directly, or did you and Coca-Cola, the vice-president, get it, or both, or what?
MURRAY: It came to me, but it referred to Mr. Faulk.

Murray then told how he listened to my broadcasts regularly. Later, when he became an account executive in charge of the Hoffman Beverage account at the Grey advertising agency, he discovered that I was advertising Hoffman beverages too. Nizer asked whether my performance for Hoffman beverages account was satisfactory.

MURRAY: It was more than satisfactory. It was as good for Hoffman as it had been for Coca-Cola.
NIZER: Now in March 1956 did you receive a communication from one Laurence Johnson?
MURRAY: Yes, I did.
NIZER: Tell us about it.

This was crucial testimony that was about to be given, and Bolan recognized it as such. He effectively and persistently objected as Nizer questioned Murray about the important facts of his conversations with Laurence Johnson. Murray testified that his conversations had taken place by telephone and in person. The court refused to allow Murray to testify as to the telephone conversation until Nizer elicited from him the fact that he could positively identify the voice on the telephone as Mr. Johnson's.

MURRAY: First Mr. Johnson identified himself as Larry Johnson of Syracuse. He said that he owned several supermarkets and had influence over a number of others in central New York State. He gave me an indication of the total gross volume of food business that was done in the area and it was most impressive. It ran into the millions. I believe the figure was $18 to $20 million annually.

He then said, Mr. Johnson then said, that he felt that it was a disgrace that our company was using a Communist, John Henry Faulk, to advertise its products.

I replied that I had no such knowledge about Mr. Faulk. And he said, "Well you had better get in line because a lot of people along Madison Avenue are getting in line and the display space which the Pabst Brewing Company has in the stores that I either own or control" is what he called "hard-won space."
THE COURT: What do you mean by "hard-won"—w-o-n, or o-n-e?
MURRAY: W-o-n. In other words, it had been difficult to

achieve status that Pabst Brewing Company had, in a display sense, within his stores. That happens to be a very accurate statement, by the way.

NIZER: Now we will come back to what hard-won space is, but would you be good enough to finish the conversation for us.

MURRAY: I will. I said that I could not accept a telephone implication of this kind. I felt that there were legal ways of establishing whether or not Mr. Faulk—Mr. Faulk or for that matter, anyone else—was a Communist, and that I had no intention of firing or recommending the firing of a man who was a first-rate salesman for our product. Then he (Johnson) said, "How would you like it if your client were to receive a letter from an American Legion Post up here?"

And I said that I was a veteran myself and that I could not believe that the American Legion would lend itself to what I considered to be an obvious blackmail attempt, and he said, "Well, you will find out."

NIZER: Now, what did you do immediately after you received this telephone call?

MURRAY: I went to my superior, Mr. Dalsimer. And I told him of this conversation. Mr. Dalsimer said to me, "This could be very serious. You had better get on it fast and do something about it."

NIZER: What did you do then?

MURRAY: I called the hotel again and asked to talk to Mr. Johnson. There was no answer in his room. Then, because of the fact that it had been stated to me that this was indeed a serious matter, I think Mr. Dalsimer's phrase was . . . "This could be dynamite," and that was my cue to get on it and try to solve it. I got into a cab. I went to Mr. Johnson's hotel. I picked up the house phone in the lobby and asked to speak to him.

Again, no answer in Mr. Johnson's room. Then because, frankly I was very upset, I ran over to the desk clerk and said, "Can you help me find Mr. Larry Johnson. I have to find him." Then the clerk said, "He is standing right over there in the lobby with that other gentleman."

So I went over and I introduced myself to Mr. Johnson. I said, "I am the Tom Murray you talked to on the phone a while ago, Mr. Johnson, and I would like to discuss the matter with you further, the one that we talked about on the phone."

And Mr. Johnson said, "After the way you spoke to me, I want nothing further to do with you" and he turned and with his companion left the hotel.

NIZER: After your conversation with Mr. Johnson did your client, to your knowledge, the Pabst Brewing Company, receive a letter from an American Legion post in Syracuse?

MURRAY: It did.

NIZER: Was there attached to that letter a bulletin from AWARE, Inc., which in this case has been marked Exhibit 41, but I show it to you to ask whether this is the original document that was received?

THE COURT: This very one? This is the original?

NIZER: This very one. This is the original.

THE COURT: All right.

NIZER: The letter of the American Legion and the annexed document as it was received, is this the original document that your client Pabst Blue Ribbon Company got?

MURRAY: Yes, it is.

NIZER: Did you show this letter to Mr. Dalsimer?

MURRAY: I most certainly did. As a matter of fact, we discussed it at some length.

NIZER: What did your superior Mr. Dalsimer tell you to do?

BOLAN: I object your Honor.

THE COURT: Overruled.

MURRAY: He said that this was now even more serious than the situation had been before and that we would have to get an answer.

NIZER: An answer to?

MURRAY: An answer to the charges contained in the attached material.

NIZER: And did you take this letter to CBS?

MURRAY: I did.

NIZER: Did you personally deliver this original document, Exhibit 35, with the annexed AWARE bulletin to anyone in CBS?

MURRAY: Yes, I did, to Mr. Sam Slate, who was manager of WCBS Radio.

Bolan, in his cross-examination, was most anxious to minimize the effect that Johnson had had on my loss of sponsors.

BOLAN: When Mr. Johnson said to you that Mr. Faulk was a Communist, didn't you ask him what the basis of his statement was?

MURRAY: I said I had no knowledge myself of Mr. Faulk being a Communist.

BOLAN: But you didn't ask Mr. Johnson what the basis—

MURRAY: Mr. Johnson had not qualified himself as an authority on such subjects. I thought he should be back wherever he comes from, selling baked beans, to tell you the truth. By what right does a grocer call me up and tell me so and so is a Communist, "get rid of him." I don't mind admitting I was kind of sore.

After several more attempts to shake Murray's testimony, Bolan gave up, and Tom was dismissed from the stand.

Lou called another witness that the defendants did not expect, Samuel Dalsimer, executive vice-president of the Grey advertising agency. He verified everything that Murray had said concerning Johnson's attempt to get the Hoffman Beverage account knocked off my show. It seemed that Dalsimer also had had a previous experience with Johnson, in 1952, when he was an account executive on the Block Drug Company account. Lou managed to introduce a letter that had been written in 1952 by Johnson to the Block Drug Company, and had Mr. Dalsimer identify it as the one that he had read at that time. In the letter Johnson had threatened the Block Drug Company, producers of Ammident tooth paste, which was advertised over a television program called "Danger." The program had employed persons that Mr. Johnson described as "Stalin's little creatures." In the letter, Mr.

Johnson suggested that perhaps he would get the veterans groups in Syracuse to conduct a poll in his supermarkets by placing a sign over the Ammident display in the stores, asking the public if they wanted to buy products whose purchase price went to the international Communist conspiracy.

Lou then called Kim Hunter to the stand. She was so nervous that I became nervous myself. However, Judge Geller was very sympathetic. He understood that she was under a strain, and he said to her, "Miss Hunter, even though you are in a courtroom you can relax. Just assume that we are all in the living room. Just take it easy." Kim flashed him a gracious smile and somewhat more calmly testified to the innumerable Broadway plays, television shows, and movies she had been in. She testified that she had appeared in the Broadway play *A Streetcar Named Desire*, which later earned her an Oscar for her performance in the screen version. This was in 1949. Nizer then asked her if she began to find that she was unable to obtain television appearances thereafter.

MISS HUNTER: It was a gradual awareness. It started in 1950.

BOLAN: Your Honor, I'm going to object to any testimony in this case long before any of the defendants were on the scene at all.

THE COURT: I am going to receive subject to connection and as indicated, subject to connection with defendants or a defendant with the same admonition that I made before with respect to the background material. I don't have to repeat it, but I made it just before when we had some other testimony through the last witness.

NIZER: You may finish your answer. You were saying there was a gradual awareness?

MISS HUNTER: Awareness of difficulties in getting employment from 1950 until 1953. There was, as I recall, a firm bit of awareness during 1952 when I was on a television program. I think it was the Celanese Theatre. I know the name of the play. It was *Petrified Forest*. There were objections. From what? Where? How? I don't know. I was never told. All I know is that my agent came to me and said—

BOLAN: I object, your Honor.

THE COURT: Sustained.

NIZER: Did your former employers report to you why they did not employ you during this period?

Kim did not want to discuss her former employer, or tell his name in open court. Bolan wanted the name. The court ruled that Nizer could not pursue the line of questioning unless Miss Hunter stated the name, and so that line of questioning was dropped.

The next day, however, Nizer asked the same question again, for during the evening Kim had had an opportunity to consult someone and she readily gave the name of the gentleman to whom she had talked about her being blacklisted—William Dolger, at that time a top executive at CBS. Lou then elicited from her that she had gone to Dolger about getting work, and the court allowed her to tell about the conversation.

MISS HUNTER: I went to Mr. Dolger's office at CBS and talked to him. I can't remember the exact conversation but the substance of it was this, I am having difficulty getting employed, are you aware of that? And he said, "Yes, I am." And I said, because I didn't know who to go to—I wanted to know whether it was possible in any way for him to help me or advise me what I might do to clear away this fog.

THE COURT: What was his position at WCBS?

MISS HUNTER: At CBS he was an executive producer. I cannot remember the exact position.

NIZER: Producer of television shows?

MISS HUNTER: Yes.

NIZER: Go ahead, finish your answer.

MISS HUNTER: He said, "I am not sure that there is anything I can do, but if I possibly can do something, I will."

She then related how some months later Mr. Dolger had called her and given her one spot on a television drama. That was the only television work she had for the entire year of 1954. Lou then had her testify how, in 1953, her position against blacklisting had been well known, and further, that she had contributed to the fight against blacklisting. Then, after she had been completely blacklisted, her public-relations man, Arthur P. Jacobs, had written to Vincent Hartnett on May 12, 1953, trying to make some arrangement with Hartnett to let up on Miss Hunter, and as it turned out, Mr. Hartnett wrote back to Mr. Jacobs saying that he would investigate Miss Hunter, but there would be a fee of $200 connected with the investigation.

NIZER: Was Mr. Hartnett's request for $200 conveyed to you, Miss Hunter, at any time?
MISS HUNTER: Yes, sir, it was.

NIZER: What did you do with respect to that request?

MISS HUNTER: May I explain that Mr. Jacobs called me on the telephone. We had a phone conversation in which he explained to me about the correspondence . . . and asked if I were willing to pay the $200 for information from Mr. Hartnett. I said that I would not, that my life is absolutely an open book, and I did not feel I needed Mr. Hartnett's information or investigation and I certainly wasn't going to pay $200 for it.
NIZER: And you did not?
MISS HUNTER: And I did not. However, Mr. Jacobs said "Please—"

Lou managed to get permission to read to the jury a letter that Mr. Hartnett had written to a Miss Geraldine B. Zorbaugh, general counsel for the American Broadcasting Company, on October 7, 1953.

NIZER [reading]: "Dear Gerry, On October 2 (1953), I received from you the enclosed list of names for the purpose of evaluation. To keep my own records straight I note that on the list appeared the following names . . . and one of these names is Kim Hunter. . . . In my opinion, finally, you would run a serious risk of adverse public opinion by featuring on your network Kim Hunter."
NIZER: Miss Hunter, had you known that Mr. Hartnett had written to the American Broadcasting Company to this

effect? That they would have a serious risk if they ran you on their show?

MISS HUNTER: No sir, I did not know it.

Kim later testified that when the resolution to condemn AWARE had come up before the membership of AFTRA, Mr. Hartnett had called her and she had called him back late at night.

NIZER: Will you give us the substance as well as you recall and take it easy, Miss Hunter. Give us the substance of that conversation.

MISS HUNTER: The substance of it was that he said to show— kind of show my good faith, that I was truly a loyal American and not pro-Communist, that affidavits were not sufficient, that I should by all rights do something actively anti-Communist and did I object to do any such thing, and I said, "No, certainly not."

He asked me then if I knew about the AWARE resolution, the resolution to condemn AWARE that was pending within our television union at AFTRA, and I said yes, I know about it.

And he said, well one way that I could show a strong anti-Communist stand would be to go to that meeting and speak up in support of AWARE, publicly, in front of everybody.

I said, "Mr. Hartnett, it would be very difficult for me to speak in support of AWARE because I am not in support of AWARE, Incorporated."

He said, "Well, it wouldn't be necessary to support AWARE, Incorporated, as such, and, in fact it wouldn't even really be necessary for you to go to the meeting, if you would be willing to send a telegram that could be read before the meeting publicly, speaking, saying in so many words that you are against this resolution to condemn AWARE."

I said, "Mr. Hartnett, I will do my best to form a telegram."

NIZER: This was the time that you were having these difficulties getting employment?

BOLAN: I object, your Honor.

THE COURT: Sustained.

NIZER: I read from Mr. Hartnett's deposition [opening examination before trial] page 362, this question to Mr. Hartnett on the examination before trial. "Q: Did you ever ask an actor who was trying to clear himself from an accusation of pro-Communist affiliation and you were guiding him, did you ever ask him to demonstrate . . . his patriotism by voting a certain way in AFTRA, in other words for an AWARE group in AFTRA?"

BOLAN: I object, your Honor.

NIZER: [reading from EBT] "Q: Did you ever ask him to vote a certain way in AFTRA, in other words, voting for an AWARE group in AFTRA? A. Yes I did. Q: Did you ever ask him to make certain speeches for the AWARE group in AFTRA? A: On at least one occasion I did. Q: Who was that one occasion? A: Kim Hunter. Q: Did you do so as making that one of the tests of their clearing themselves, in other words, seeing the light of anti-Communism? A: I did."

Now, Miss Hunter, did you thereafter send a telegram to the union?

MISS HUNTER: Yes, sir.

NIZER: Was there annexed, did you annex to a copy of that telegram a note to Mr. Hartnett?

This was objected to. However, Lou managed to get into the record a copy of the telegram Kim had sent to the membership of AFTRA. He read it aloud to the jury.

NIZER [reading]: "To the membership: For your union to condemn AWARE, Inc. shouldn't it also bring suit against AWARE for libel and defamation of character? Is AFTRA prepared to follow this through to its logical conclusion? And what earthly good do we hope to accomplish for the union or its members by passing this resolution?

"I'm neither a member of AWARE, Inc. nor a friend, nor am I in sympathy with any of its methods, but I urge you all to think very carefully indeed before voting for this resolution. The individuals hurt by Bulletin No. 12 have recourse to right any wrong that may have been committed, but AFTRA will have no recourse whatsoever if it places itself on record as protesting and aiding the Communist conspiracy, even if this action is taken in the noble desire to aid and protect the innocent. Signed, Kim Hunter."

And annexed to it, this is from Mr. Hartnett's files, May 25, 1955: "Dear Mr. Hartnett. Enclosed is a copy of the wire I sent to the AFTRA membership meeting last night. I was unable to attend the meeting so I have no idea whether it was read or not. Signed, Kim Hunter."

NIZER: After this date, did you get television appearances?

BOLAN: I object, your Honor.

THE COURT: Overruled.

MISS HUNTER: Yes, Mr. Nizer, I worked.

THE COURT: I didn't hear that. Did you finish your answer?

MISS HUNTER: I worked quite frequently after that and to the present date.

Kim's voice trembled as she gave this last testimony. The entire courtroom, including the jury, gasped. Lou then followed this by reading a letter from Hartnett to Laurence Johnson dated May 23, 1955.

NIZER [reading]: "Dear Larry, Confidentially, I had a good telephone conversation this morning with Kim Hunter who just returned to New York from the Bucks County Playhouse. I stressed to Kim Hunter that she had [and "had" is underlined] to take a public stand against Communism. She assured me that she would do so and if she comes through tomorrow night at the AFTRA meeting as she promised she would do, you will hear the comrades shrieking all the way from New York to Syracuse.

"The Kraft situation seems to me to be very much improved, thanks to you know who! Keep up the fight, Larry. You and your associates have done wonders. Sincerely, Hartnett."

After reading this, Nizer turned to Bolan and said, "Your witness."

Bolan, realizing what harm Kim's testimony had done in reference to the telegram Hartnett had forced her to send to the union, started his cross-examination of her on that subject.

BOLAN: Did Mr. Hartnett ask you to do anything you did not
  wish to do?
MISS HUNTER: Yes.
BOLAN: What was that?
MISS HUNTER: I did not really wish to go on record in my
  union as opposing the resolution.

Bolan then wanted to introduce an affidavit that Miss
Hunter had given to Mr. Hartnett in 1955. Nizer objected to
this unless a whole series of affidavits, the first in 1952 made
by Miss Hunter, could be introduced in the evidence. Bolan
had not anticipated this. A Mr. Roy Brewer (whom Mr. Nizer
described as "another Hartnett on the West Coast; he does
the clearance and he tries to pass people, and he worked with
Hartnett") and Hartnett had gotten together and obtained
from Miss Hunter the series of affidavits. As Lou explained
to Judge Geller outside the hearing of the jury: "In the endeavor to get Miss Hunter to comply with what they demanded as a clearance for her, she had to make a whole series of affidavits. I have them here, all sworn to. They have
tried to present the last one that they accepted from her. I
say that it is incomplete under the context of the circumstances, and that either they offer all of them to show how
she was squeezed, otherwise I object to the whole thing."
  Kim testified that back in 1953 a Roy Brewer out in Hollywood had suggested that she work with him on an affidavit
that would meet Mr. Hartnett's specification and remove
her from the blacklist.
  Bolan read her affidavit to the jury. It was a lengthy, grim
recital, obviously written under great stress. In it she protested her patriotism and stated her loathing of Communism. She told how she had lent her name to several causes,
back in 1949 through 1952, which were of dubious nature in
the eyes of AWARE and like folk. She had endorsed a couple
of peace conferences and had signed a petition asking clem-
ency for a condemned Negro in Mississippi, Willie McGee.
She told how she had committed the grievous error of not
realizing how sinister the Communist influence was and
that she hoped that she could be forgiven and thenceforth
would never again be duped. During Bolan's reading of the
long, long affidavit, Kim dropped her eyes and seemingly had
to restrain herself to keep from weeping. When Bolan had

finished cross-examining Kim, Lou took over her redirect examination. He went directly to the matter of the series of written statements that Kim had given under pressure, starting back in 1953. She testified that Roy Brewer of Hollywood had assisted her in these statements. He would consult with Hartnett and then advise her on what she would have to say in each succeeding statement to meet Hartnett's requirements. The affidavits were not introduced, but Kim's testimony about each revealed how, in each succeeding one, she had to bow a little lower to Brewer and Hartnett's demands.

During her entire ordeal upon the witness stand, Kim had fought back tears as her testimony and the documents introduced revealed how she had been punished in the past years. She was excused from the witness stand late in the afternoon and came over to me at the counsel table, and embraced me warmly.

20

The newspaper accounts of the trial were stirring up widespread interest in the case. Nizer's office began to get calls from people volunteering information, many anxious to come as witnesses. But each had to be able to contribute something new and important. So, for the most part, Lou concentrated on those witnesses we had already lined up.

One caller was Harvey Matusow, who suggested that while he would not be a suitable witness—he had been jailed on a perjury charge—he could direct us to a witness who would be very valuable. In the early 1950s, he had been an informer for the F.B.I.; later a professional witness for the HUAC and for cases involving persons charged with subversive activities. He had worked closely with Senator McCarthy and with Roy Cohn, and he had later become a close friend of Laurence Johnson. Johnson had insisted that a certain advertising agency employ Matusow for the purpose of checking on the patriotism of performers before they were employed on its radio and television shows. Matusow had long since repented his part as an informer. As part of his recantation, he alleged that Roy Cohn, while an assistant United States Attorney, had suborned him to testify falsely in a pending criminal action. Matusow was charged with perjury and convicted, and he spent three years in prison. Now he told us of one particular case involving a Frank Barton, of the Lennen & Newell advertising agency, and he gave a detailed account of a luncheon meeting at which he and Barton and Johnson came to an agreement on a procedure for dealing with performers whom Johnson found undesirable. If Matusow's account of the meeting with Johnson was accurate, Barton certainly could be an important witness. We reached him at his agency. He was a vice-president, a conservative gentleman, and a man of unimpeachable integrity. But he did not want to become involved; it seemed unlikely that we could get him to testify.

While Lou was trying to persuade Mr. Barton, he put other witnesses on the stand who had had experience with Johnson and blacklisting. One was Himan Brown, a very successful producer and director and packager of shows. He had produced or directed such shows as "Inner Sanctum," "The Thin Man," "Bulldog Drummond," and many more. He testified that back in 1952 he was producing and directing a radio series called "The Private Files of Matthew Bell." The series was sponsored by the Seabrook Farms, and the advertising agency that represented Seabrook Farms was Hilton & Riggio. Brown told how in 1952 he had received a telephone call from Harvey Matusow, who invited him to a conference with Mr. Johnson to discuss some important business. Brown met Johnson and Matusow at a midtown hotel.

BROWN: Mr. Johnson told me that I was using the wrong people, actors who were Communist-fronters, actors with Communist affiliations, and that unless I used the right actors by his lights, meaning people with other affiliations, as he described them, I would be very much in danger of losing sponsorship and losing my position with this particular client.

NIZER: Which client is this?

BROWN: The Seabrook Farms people. He had already written to them and threatened them to take all of their display of his merchandise out of his markets.

NIZER: What markets are you referring to?

BROWN: In Syracuse, he [Johnson] had several supermarkets in Syracuse. He further went ahead to tell me that there are other supermarkets because there were some affiliations and associations where he carried a great deal of weight, that these people would listen to him, and the third thing which he stressed to me was that the American Legion Post in Syracuse would also flood the sponsor with letters to let them know that I was out of line or that I was doing the wrong thing using Communist front actors.

Brown testified that Laurence Johnson was not only against certain people, he was for some people too. For instance, he suggested that Brown should hire actors like Frank Pulaski, Vinton Hayworth, and Ned Weaver. On his cross-examination, Bolan asked Brown if he had been listed by Hartnett in *Red Channels*. Brown said that he had, that one of the charges that had been listed against him was that he had sponsored a dinner for Governor Lehman and Senator Mead of New York of 1947.

BOLAN: Well, do you have a personal hatred for Mr. Hartnett?
BROWN: I have.

Peter Hilton, president of the advertising agency Kastor-Hilton, was then called to the stand. He testified that he had been an advertising man for thirty-one years on Madison Avenue and that he had been the Hilton of Hilton & Riggio, the agency that had the Seabrook Farms account in 1952. Mr. Hilton was a personable and handsome advertising executive, and he seemed to be at ease on the witness stand. One felt that he was almost eager to give the testimony that Nizer was asking him to give. He too had met Laurence Johnson in connection with the Seabrook Farms.

HILTON: After the program was on the air for three weeks I received a telephone call from C. F. Seabrook, who was the President of Seabrook Farms, advising me that he had received a letter from Laurence Johnson on the letterhead of the American Legion Post in Syracuse, raising the question as to whether or not Seabrook was aware that it was sponsoring a program featuring Joe Cotton [Joseph Cotten] and produced by Himan Brown. They were advancing the cause of Stalin's little creatures, as he quoted.

Johnson indicated that if Seabrook was aware of what it was doing that he, operating supermarkets in Syracuse, would see fit to boycott Seabrook Farm products and, furthermore, would make other supermarket operators aware of what he was doing and the reasons for doing it. This, naturally perturbed Seabrook very much and he looked to me, since I had recommended the program, to determine what it was all about.

Mr. Hilton then testified that he had gone to M.C.A., who had booked the program and who represented Joseph Cotten.

Mr. Cotten had come to New York and, with Mr. Hilton, Mr. Seabrook, and an attorney for Seabrook, flew up to Syracuse to see Mr. Johnson in a Seabrook Farms plane.

HILTON: We proceeded from the airport in Syracuse to Johnson's office, which was in the rear of one of his supermarkets. When we arrived, after some very stiff formalities, since it was almost noon we adjourned to a nearby restaurant, and at that time Mr. Seabrook took the initiative and indicated to Mr. Johnson that he, personally, was very much against anything that might be tinged with Communism. He cited the record of Seabrook Farms throughout the war and indicated that he would not knowingly support anything that might foster or help a known Communist. On that occasion, as a peace offering and as an indication of good faith I suggested that one of the commercials of the three commercials we had on our Sunday afternoon program be devoted to an institutional message indicating the bounty of America, the need for protecting its free institutions.

Mr. Johnson felt that that was a very good idea and it lessened the tension.

NIZER: Now, before you made this suggestion, this compromise or resolution, did Mr. Johnson indicate that he would let up in his boycott, as you call it, against Mr. Cotten?

Hilton said that Johnson had not been so easily persuaded about Cotten, saying that Mr. Cotten's record spoke for itself.

NIZER: Did Mr. Cotten speak up in his defense, as to his Americanism?

HILTON: Mr. Cotten protested vehemently.

Cotten went on at length to cite the work he had done during the war, and he had come prepared for that meeting with letters attesting to that fact and detailing trips that he had made entertaining the troops and engaging in war bond drives and the like.

He also related—there was an organization in California—the name of which I didn't remember, which he had been identified with some years before and it was this organization that was cited by the Un-American Activities Committee and with which he was identified. He explained his membership in that as long predating the period when it was cited.

NIZER: Did Mr. Johnson when he referred to the record testify anything particularly?

HILTON: No he did not.

NIZER: He just referred to the record?

HILTON: That is right.

NIZER: After he [Cotten] made his reply, did Mr. Johnson make any statement accepting that reply or rejecting it?

HILTON: Again, in the same spirit, he said that he had only the record to go by and he had to make his judgment as to who was American and who was not American by the record.

NIZER: Did you leave immediately for the airport to go back?

HILTON: We left shortly after lunch and on the way to the airport passed a Johnson supermarket. Mr. Johnson asked if we would be interested in seeing it. We did. We stopped. We toured the supermarket, met his managers, and Joseph Cotten autographed some, gave some signatures to customers.

Johnson had agreed to let the program stay on as long as it included the patriotic commercial. Nizer now asked Hilton how the program fared after the attack.

NIZER: Did you have any conversations with the sponsor concerning the continuation of the program?

HILTON: Yes.

NIZER: What were they?

HILTON: In view of the problems that had arisen with it, the sponsor indicated very clearly that he had no interest in continuing beyond the thirteen weeks that we were committed to.

Mr. Hilton testified then that somewhat later the series was canceled, and his agency lost the Seabrook Farms account. He attributed this to the attack by Laurence Johnson.

Mark Goodson was one of our star witnesses. He was one of the most distinguished producers in TV, and he had employed me a number of times over the years. Mark testified that he was the president of Goodson-Todman Productions, and told of his long-time experience in the field of quiz and panel shows: his company had produced such TV landmarks as "What's My Line," "I've Got a Secret," "The Price Is Right," and "To Tell the Truth." After getting from Mark some of the dozens of awards he had received, Nizer started on Mark's experience as an employer of performers.

Mark testified that he had possibly hired more performers in his years as a producer than had Susskind. He confirmed Susskind's testimony by describing the system of "clearance" in greater detail. Lou asked him to elaborate on the television industry's practice of having producers submit, for approval, or clearance, names of performers to be used. Mark explained that the names of everyone he used had to be submitted to the network upon which his show was appearing or to the agency that represented the sponsor.

GOODSON: . . . Actually, no one ever went into the specific details and openly called it what it was, but before people were used they would be called on the phone, either to the network or the advertising agency, or a general list would be submitted, and then if there were objections to any of the people on the list there would come back either a phone call, more often a phone call, or another list written, and a notation would be made that these people are unacceptable. No great conversation was gone into as to why they were unacceptable, but it was understood that it was because of political reasons.

Let me give you a couple of examples of how it might be done. I will not mention names but assume that a certain week was coming up on a program and a new panelist or a mystery guest was going to be put on. A phone call would be made by one of the [Goodson-Todman] staff and say, "Is this person all right?" And the answer might come back, "Yes, fine," or "We will have to check into it further," and, perhaps, an answer would come back in a couple of days, "Forget it. Don't use that person."

In certain instances we found this was very difficult to

work with, and so a long list might be submitted and say "Just go down this list and let us know who we can work with or not," and back would come four or five checks and perhaps on the phone they would say, "The following five people should be eliminated from your consideration."

It was well known to the jurors, as well as to everyone else in the courtroom, that most of the Goodson-Todman shows were on CBS network, so there could be little doubt that Mark was making a rather vital point for us. CBS had engaged in the practice of blacklisting artists. Mark then made another important point.

NIZER: Was it the general practice for the producer or packager to be informed as to the specific grounds on which an artist was not passed?
GOODSON: It was not.

Nizer then produced a letter written by Laurence Johnson to Gilbert Swanson, of C. A. Swanson and Company, dated December 26, 1953. The Swanson company was at that time sponsor of the Goodson-Todman television panel show "The Name's the Same." The letter from Johnson protested the appearance of Miss Judy Holliday on the program as a guest celebrity.

GOODSON: After Miss Holliday was used we were rebuked for the use of Miss Holliday by the advertising agency, who thought that we had made a serious mistake.

NIZER: Mr. Goodson, was Miss Holliday used again on this program?
BOLAN: I object.
THE COURT: Overruled.
GOODSON: She was not.

Lou then turned his attention to the unemployability of an uncleared performer.

NIZER: Can you state with reasonable certainty whether, if a performer becomes controversial in the sense of his or her patriotism being involved, such performer—can you state with reasonable certainty the general practice as to whether such performer can obtain employment in the television and radio industry, generally, as a trade practice.

GOODSON: Yes, I would say in general that nonclearability meant unemployability.

NIZER: Does it matter, in giving your answer--can you state with reasonable certainty what the practice was whether the innocence or guilt of that performer were established or not?

GOODSON: Well, the innocence or guilt was never brought up, Mr. Nizer, because the facts of the matter were never discussed. When a name was not cleared, it was difficult to get further information. We tried on occasions and in certain instances were able by virtue—

BOLAN: I object.

THE COURT: Overruled.

BOLAN: Not responsive.

NIZER: I submit he should finish his answer.

THE COURT: Let him answer.

GOODSON: And in certain instances were able by virtue of pressure and argument to convince the network or agency that the person should be permitted to go on.

Nizer then had Mark testify as to the difficulties they had had with Abe Burrows when he was a panelist on "The Name's the Same."

GOODSON: Starting in December 1951 we began to get mail protesting his appearance and it seemed to us to be what I would call organized mail, that is, you could tell by the quality of the postcards addressed to you that the phrasing is generally similar, so it looks as if the mail is organized as opposed to individuals writing on their own. As this mail grew I talked to our people about this and I brought Abe in.

NIZER: Abe Burrows?

GOODSON: Abe Burrows in, and I said, "We're getting a lot of mail on you. What does this mean? What is the story on it?"

Mark told how Abe had answered all his questions to his own satisfaction and that they had put up a battle for him. However, the mail continued to pour in.

GOODSON: Mr. Swanson then called me on the phone and said, "I would like to come into New York and see you about this Abe Burrows matter because we are getting mail here too." So I met with Clark Swanson. He came to see me, and Clark Swanson, who was the president of the company, discussed this with me. The advertising agency was not present, and we agreed together—as a matter of fact he said, "I think that Abe—I have to say—I think that Burrows is O.K. as far as I am concerned, and I think I'm going to ignore this mail. I think he is all right. Let's continue to use him."

About three months after that, he called me from Omaha and he said, "I have just received a call from a Laurence Johnson, Syracuse, New York. Do you know him?" I said, "No, I don't. I have heard about him." And he said—

At this point Judge Geller cut Mark off, saying that he could not testify as to what Johnson had told Clark Swanson, nor what Clark Swanson had said to Johnson. However, he was allowed to continue with his first-hand testimony.

GOODSON: I will only say then, if I have to eliminate what he told me, what Mr. Johnson told him, that the net result was that Clark Swanson regrettably felt that he had now to accede to the pressure, and we would have to drop Abe Burrows, and I came to Burrows and I told him the full facts and he agreed that in the light of the pressure which was being threatened that I agreed with Swanson, who had been very decent up to this point, could not stand up under it.

NIZER: And did Mr. Burrows still state that he was innocent of any Communist affiliations?

GOODSON: Yes he did.

NIZER: Was the pressure, without giving us the conversation, did it involve the taking off of the goods of the Swanson products?

GOODSON: It was precisely the same you read in your letter about Judy Holliday.

Mark then testified as to the sensitivity of the networks and agencies to protest mail and to pressures generally. He summed the whole thing up for the jury and the court.

GOODSON: A sponsor is in business to sell his goods. He has no interest in being involved in causes. He does not want controversy.
NIZER: He does not want what?
GOODSON: Controversy. The favorite slogan along Madison Avenue is "Why buy yourself a headache?" The advertising agency's job is to see to it that the products are sold but that the sponsor keeps out of trouble, and an advertising agency can lose a great deal, it can lose the account. The sponsor can lose a little bit of business, but he still can recoup it. The agency can lose the account and I would say that a great portion of an agency's job is concerned with the pleasing and taking care and serving a client.

So I think in many instances, the clients were perhaps even less aware of all this than the advertising agency, which considered one of its principal jobs keeping out of trouble, just keep out of trouble. I don't think that they took a political position. I think it was apolitical. It was just anti-controversial.

Given the choice between performer A who is non-controversial, and performer B, about whom there is any kind of a cloud whatsoever, the natural instinct on a common-sense business basis is to use the non-controversial personality. Again, a favorite saying is, "There are a lot of other actors, a lot of other performers. Why bother with this one? Why buy this headache?"

Mark was now at ease, speaking as an expert, and Nizer took advantage of the favorable impression he was making on the jury to drive home a strong point as to my capabilities as a panelist. Bolan had, of course, been playing down my television performances. Mark told the jury how I had been a regular panelist along with Quentin Reynolds, Anna Lee,

Kitty Carlisle, and at times Nina Foch, Moss Hart, Russel Crouse, on a Goodson-Todman show "It's News to Me," which had been on CBS network from 1951 to 1954, with John Daly as the moderator.

GOODSON: I think that Johnny Faulk was a very good performer. He falls into the classification of what I would call a talker. There are actors and there are singers and there are what Fred Allen once called "pointers" like Ed Sullivan, and there are talkers.

Now the talker was a type of personality who developed in the early fifties in television, who could play games, who could ad-lib, and who had a definite personality, and Faulk's capabilities were in all these areas. He was a good talker. He had a capacity to play our games and he was what I would call a country-style personality. He was a Will Rogers, Herb Shriner, rural-boy type. He was like a country boy lost in New York, surrounded by the city folks and with it a certain kind of urbanity that came through because Johnny had been a teacher and knew what he was talking about, and this is what made up the particular things that Faulk delivered.

Nizer then established that a panelist on a network show was receiving several times as much today as he was in the early fifties. Moreover, a panelist on a network show usually had many other sources of income. Mark testified, for instance, that Tom Poston, who was on "To Tell the Truth," made much larger amounts of money making pictures and acting in summer stock; Arlene Francis made a movie in Munich; and most of the Goodson-Todman panelists were engaged in many other activities, which brought them huge incomes. Then Nizer asked him a question that elicited an effective answer, but that somewhat chilled my blood.

NIZER: You have told us about marquee value. Suppose a performer like John Faulk ceases to appear on television, beginning on February 10, 1956, and hasn't had any television appearances, assume this, with the exception of one Jack Paar appearance at night, between 1956 and this date, and assume further, sir, that—

THE COURT: 1956 and this date?

NIZER: To this date—leave out other assumptions for a moment and assume that he wanted to or could pick up, assume that whatever difficulty there existed was cleared away and that he could pick up his employment again, that he could be employed in television, could he start where he left off—

BOLAN: I object.

NIZER: Or can you state with reasonable certainty on that assumption whether the general practice in the industry is that having been off for these years there is an effect upon him?

BOLAN: I object.

THE COURT: Overruled.

GOODSON: You will agree, Mr. Nizer, that that is a difficult question, but I would be able to state that if a person has not been exposed for any substantial period of time, his value is definitely diminished. He becomes, in effect, an unknown all over again, and it is harder today to start an unknown than it was back in the 1950s when prices were lower, how he would be able to start again, he would certainly not be able to pick up where he left off. Possibly he could pick up—No, I can't even say he could pick up with the original salary, because those payments would not be appropriate today, but he would certainly have lost because of the lack of exposure over the years.

This testimony was helping to establish my damages, of course, but it was something of an emotional bump for me to sit there and hear stated aloud from an authority what I had secretly been fearing to face myself. The next was a key question.

NIZER: At the present time, and limiting yourself for the purposes of this question, to television performers who were talkers, as you put it, the same kind of talent, can you state with reasonable certainty, based upon your knowledge and experience in the industry, what the earning capacities, men similar to these talents, what they earn in television work?

BOLAN: I object.

THE COURT: Overruled. Talking generally now, talkers. We are not talking of anyone in particular.

GOODSON: Yes, I am not giving away any trade secrets about any particular performer, although the figures I will talk about are actually earned by various people. I would say that somebody in Faulk's—

THE COURT: No, no, that is not the question.

GOODSON: You don't want that?

THE COURT: We want areas of earnings.

NIZER: Areas of earnings for similar kind of performers in television.

GOODSON: $100,000 up to $1 million a year if you're talking areas.

NIZER: In your opinion does Mr. John Henry Faulk fall into the category which you have generally described with these wide limits of potential earnings?

BOLAN: I object.

THE COURT: Overruled.

GOODSON: I would say that, if I can say it, that Faulk would have fallen probably between the $150,000 and $500,000 mark if he had continued as he was.

NIZER: A year?

GOODSON: A year.

NIZER: Annual earnings?

GOODSON: A year.

NIZER: Your witness.

In his cross-examination, Bolan ventured into the area of blacklisting, and at this point Mark came back with some stinging answers. It seemed to me that Bolan was getting the worst of the exchange, for his questions were eliciting answers from Mark that re-emphasized our position. Bolan asked again about the practice in the radio and television industry.

GOODSON (sharply): The practice in the industry, sir, was that people were not cleared and that nobody ever said why. Now, if you asked what the general understanding was as to why this was going on—it was because we knew that there were organizations that were listing these people as being left-wing or, if you will, left-wing and Communist associations.

Bolan continued to press Mark for his direct knowledge of actors blacklisted from shows at the insistence of any of the defendants.

GOODSON: Every actor including every extra was cleared with CBS.
BOLAN: CBS cleared them?
GOODSON: CBS did, yes.
BOLAN: When CBS cleared a person, was that a guarantee that there would be no complaint?
GOODSON: We never found a situation, with one exception, where the network cleared somebody and we later got a complaint from another organization.
BOLAN: What was the exception?
GOODSON: That was the situation where CBS cleared Judy Holliday for an appearance on "What's My Line." We used her and then used her in a subsequent week on "The Name's the Same," and Mr. Swanson was called by Mr. Johnson and told that if he didn't get her off they would boycott his goods.

Bolan then made the mistake of asking Mark what problem he had had with "The Name's the Same," which appeared on the ABC network.

GOODSON: Yes, "The Name's the Same" did not have a clearance system, although I pretty much followed the CBS policy. So if somebody were not cleared by CBS I would tend to avoid using that person on "The Name's the Same" on ABC, just because I wanted to keep our company out of trouble, I suppose.
     In the case of Judy Holliday, which was the incident that we discussed, I had tried for some time to persuade CBS that Judy Holliday should be used. They said their list indicated that she had a questionable background and that they would not go into it. Then we were approached by her agent, William Morris, and were told that George Sokolsky, a political writer, had been meeting with Miss Holliday and had determined in his judgment that she was

a good American and had done some other behind-the-scenes business of which I was not aware, and they asked whether we would be willing to use Miss Holliday on "What's My Line." I said we would be very happy to, but they had to check with CBS. They went to CBS. CBS looked at the various documents and they said "Go ahead and use her," which we did.

So, just a few weeks later—we had no reaction from that at all from Mr. Johnson or from anybody. A few weeks later we decided to use Miss Holliday on "The Name's the Same," but in that particular show we billboarded it in advance. The guest star on "What's My Line," as you know, because of the fact that it is a mystery, the person comes on as a surprise. If there is going to be any protest, it is after the fact. In this particular case we announced Miss Holliday in advance and we began to get mail very quickly and after this performance of Miss Holliday, which was practically a duplicate of what she had done on CBS, we got a call from Clark Swanson who said we could never use Miss Holliday again because "we have been threatened by the Laurence Johnson organization."

Now, since they [CBS] had also rejected Oscar Hammerstein, Richard Rodgers, Moss Hart, Jerome Robbins, and an entire list of other famous people, we figured we ought to come back and find out why—

So Mark proceeded to explain why people were on the network blacklist.

GOODSON: Mr. Bolan, all I can say is there were no differentiations made between Communists, Communist sympathizers, those who had lunch with Communist sympathizers, those who knew somebody who had lunch with Communist sympathizers, and so forth, but there was one over-all list and the differentiation was not made for us.

At a later point Mark summed up the prevailing attitude among the network, agency, and sponsor people.

GOODSON: Sponsors and their agencies wanted to keep out of trouble with the public and, therefore, wanted to eliminate anybody that might be accused of anything which could involve the sponsor in controversy, including things that you mention, but also those lists could easily also include someone who had nothing to do with it.

It [the reasons for blacklisting] also included various forms of associations that were much narrower, much further apart than that. It included general controversy of any kind and in certain cases it even—I'm ashamed to say—included the elimination of people from shows because they had the same name as members of the Communist Party.

BOLAN: Can you give us an illustration of this situation where you said it included some form of association further apart than association with the Communist Party?

GOODSON: John Henry Faulk.

BOLAN: Apart from that illustration, Mr. Goodson, can you give us another illustration?

GOODSON: Bennett Cerf.

BOLAN: And Bennett Cerf was kept off a program?

GOODSON: No, but he was put on a list.

BOLAN: Whose list, you never saw a list, did you?

GOODSON: Yes, I saw this particular list.

BOLAN: You did, you remember now that you saw a list?

GOODSON: Yes.

BOLAN: Where did you see this list or is this one in your head?

GOODSON: No, this is not in my head, this was very tiny pamphlet and I am not sure who put it out, but it was sort—I think it was called—I think he was put on that list because he attended some kind of a meeting, I am not sure what it was, to make some sort of protest about something, and I'm not even sure what that was.

BOLAN: Let's get what you are sure of.

GOODSON: I can assure you that I am sure about Mr. Cerf. He is not a Communist—

BOLAN: I know Mr. Cerf.

GOODSON:—or a Communist sympathizer, and he was on a list.

BOLAN: Has anyone said he was Communist?

GOODSON: He didn't have to be, because if I hadn't stood up and fought for him, he might have been thrown off.

BOLAN: Who made the objection to Mr. Cerf's appearance?

GOODSON: A certain amount of mail that came in together with the little pamphlet.

BOLAN: Aren't there a lot of crank letters received, Mr. Goodson?

GOODSON: I can't define what a crank is any more, Mr. Bolan.

BOLAN: Didn't you say?

GOODSON: Yes, there was a group of people listed on this and I think, by the way, in this list there were such names as Leopold Stokowski, Leonard Bernstein, possibly Dwight Eisenhower, and he was listed on this list.

Several jurors commented, after the case was completed, that Mark Goodson's testimony had been the most effective heard on the subject of my damages, the activities of AWARE and Johnson, and the CBS policy of forbidding certain performers to appear.

Everett Sloan, who is considered one of the finest character actors in the profession, was willing and able to give testimony. As he sat on the stand testifying, he would frequently glance with contempt toward Mr. Hartnett at the counsel table. He told how his career as an actor had gone steadily forward from 1930. He listed the motion pictures that he had been in, the radio work that he had done, and how he had gotten into television in the late 1940s. Then suddenly, after 1952, he could not find any work. Prior to that time, he had not been able to take all of the jobs that had been offered him. He looked frantically for work, and then one day in early 1953, he ran into a man he knew, a writer, who told him that he had submitted Sloan's name for a part in a play that he had just written for television.

SLOAN: He [the friend] said, "I recommended you yesterday for a part in the Ford Theatre that I just wrote," and he said, "They turned you down." I said, "Why?" He said, "Because you are in *Red Channels*." I said, "I am not in *Red Channels*," He said, "I wasn't aware of that. They told me you were." I said, "You'd better go back and tell them that I am not." And so I called him the following day, he gave me his phone number. I called him the following day and he said, "You were right," which of course I knew I was, "you are not in *Red Channels*, but they say they must have confused you with Alan Sloane."

NIZER: What is your first name?

SLOAN: Everett.

Clearing up this matter did not help Sloan. He still could not get work, and Lou produced a letter that Sloan had never seen and did not know existed until that moment. It was a letter that Hartnett had written to Johnson in November 1952.

NIZER [reading]: "Dear Larry: Enclosed is data on Everett Sloan. You will have to be careful about the item from the Hubert Diary, as it is not privileged. If Sloan challenged it, it would be his word against Hubert's."

Lou then asked Sloan what he had done about getting himself cleared so that he could work in television again.

SLOAN: I found out by inquiring that if you work for the UN Radio more than twice, that the third time you work for them you are required to obtain the same status as a permanent employee, and that included submitting to an F.B.I. check.

NIZER: What did you do then?

SLOAN: And so, having already worked for the UN Radio twice, I sought a third employment from them, which I received.

NIZER: Was there an F.B.I. check made of your record because of that third employment for the UN?

BOLAN: I object.

THE COURT: Overruled.

SLOAN: Yes there was.

NIZER: And did you thereafter receive a writing from the United States Civil Service Commission of Washington, D.C., concerning your status?

SLOAN: Yes I did.

Then an odd thing happened in a case that was full of odd things. Bolan revealed how little he knew of his own client's connections.

NIZER: Did you thereafter meet one Paul Milton, whom you now know as a director of AWARE, Incorporated?

BOLAN: Your Honor, I object to such statements. Mr. Milton is not a director of AWARE and I object to such statement.

THE COURT: Sustained, assuming—I don't have to state the reason.

BOLAN: He may have been at one time. I'm not sure of that.

NIZER: We will read it from the deposition.

Lou then took Milton's examination before trial and read Milton's testimony to the effect that he was a member of the board of directors of AWARE, Incorporated. Mr. Bolan admitted that he had not known this fact. Lou asked Sloan what he had done with the document that he had received giving him a clean bill of political health. Sloan said that a friend of his, a writer, Stanley Niss, suggested that he should see Mr. Milton. Sloan met with Milton and told him that he had the clearance from the F.B.I. as to his loyalty and asked Milton what was the best procedure to follow to re-establish himself in television. Milton read the document.

SLOAN: [Milton said] "Well, I take this with a grain of salt." Then I said, "What do you mean by that?" He said, "Well, we don't put much stock in it." And I said, "Who is we?" He said, "AWARE, Incorporated." And that was the first time that he represented AWARE in any way. I said, "I wasn't aware of the fact you were a member or a director of AWARE or represented them in any way." I said, "If I had known that, I certainly wouldn't have come to see you." I said, "But aside from that, what is your objection to this document, now that you have seen it?" He said, "Well, we at AWARE had different standards of clearance than the United States Government's agencies. We are a little more stringent. We feel they are a little too lenient." And I said, "You mean to say that you set yourselves up as opposed to the United States Government in the matter of loyalty, which is, indeed, I would say, their province?" He said, "Yes, we do." I said, "Well, what would AWARE, Inc.

suggest that I do, then, in view of the fact that this document doesn't seem to mean much to them?"

And he said, "I suggest that you let me arrange a meeting for you with Mr. Hartnett, at which meeting perhaps you and he can evolve some statement that you can make that will be satisfactory to Mr. Hartnett and will also prove satisfactory to, perhaps, the people who are not presently hiring you."

NIZER: What did you say to that?

SLOAN: I said, "Go fly a kite." I told Mr. Milton that as far as I was concerned I was much more interested in the opinion of the United States Government than of Mr. Milton of AWARE or of Vincent Hartnett, and that as far as I was concerned both their purpose and methods as I could gather were immoral and illegal and that I would have nothing to do with them whatsoever, and I hoped that soon that this, my feeling about their—

BOLAN: Your Honor—

NIZER: This is conversation.

THE COURT: This is part of the conversation. He may finish it.

SLOAN: I hoped that very soon the fact that they were conducting their business in a way that I considered immoral and illegal would be proven and come to light, and I walked out of the restaurant.

21

As I sat there listening to witness after witness tell of the weird, punishing effects of blacklisting, I thought of the leadership of AFTRA, the performers' union. It had been charged with protecting the members from such abuses; yet the leadership had turned a deaf ear and looked the other way. In fact, when an attempt had been made to censure AWARE, Inc., the officers of the union had violently opposed it. Later, when the Middle-of-the-Road slate had attempted to take action against blacklisting, the opposition had been solid and violent. How, I thought, could the officers have been so callous, so indifferent, to the suffering of the members? But, as I reflected on this, I realized that the union leadership had not been alone; the responsible persons in the industry had capitulated with equal indifference. Carrying the thought further, I had to admit that the citizens of the country had been equally susceptible to fear and the dread disease of passive indifference to injustice.

Lou wanted to use Gerald Dickler as a witness in a dual capacity—as my business manager who could give first-hand testimony about what exactly had happened to me at WCBS and afterward; and as an expert in the television and radio industry. This would enable Gerry to testify as to what my probable earnings might have been had I not been blacklisted.

Having testified and retestified to his experience in the field of radio and television, Gerry proceeded to describe what an enormous success I would have been had I not been blacklisted.

Gerry testified in some detail about how Sam Slate had called him in April 1956 and reported that Laurence Johnson was in New York, knocking sponsors off my show. Slate had asked Gerry to help him stop Johnson. Then Gerry told how he and Collingwood had gone to a meeting with Arthur Hull Hayes, manager of the CBS radio network.

DICKLER: Mr. Collingwood said he had known Johnny for a long time and felt completely confident of Mr. Faulk's patriotism and his loyalty to the country, and Mr. Hayes brushed that aside and said, "Of course, we have never had any doubt of that ourselves, but this thing came along and we have to deal with it. It is a damn nuisance and it is a kind of blackmail, and this man Johnson has done it before and he is probably going to do it again, but nobody seems to have figured out how to stop him."

Gerry testified that while I was away on vacation in July 1957, Sam Slate had called him to tell him that I was being fired. They had a meeting about it.

DICKLER: . . . He said, "We are going to have to let [Faulk] go and I am sending you a letter, it has already been prepared. I haven't sent it out yet. I wanted to talk to you first. I am sending you a letter of termination."

I said to Sam, "Before Johnny went away, you told him that he had nothing to worry about except that there was a possibility, a probability that the Godfrey Show for Ford was likely to come in and pick up a half hour of this time, but that would not affect his relationship with the network, and he could go away with a perfectly free mind." And I said, "Why the sudden switch?" "Well," said Sam, "his ratings have been dropping and his share has been off," meaning share of audience, as used in the trade.

And I said to him at that point, "It is not worse than it was at the time that you renewed his contract," and indeed, the whole network was off considerably, and if he was off . . . and I really don't think it was off . . . I said, "Sam, this doesn't make sense." He said, "Well, there is nothing I can do about it. The decision has been made. I have had it up with the people upstairs and Johnny is through. I feel terrible about it, but he is through."

And I said, "He is through in more ways than one. He is through in the game if this gets around."

Gerry then testified to the details of my efforts to find a job and his efforts to help me during 1957. Lou asked him to give, as an expert, his estimate of what I would be earning per year now. Gerry put the figure at somewhere between $250,000 and $500,000. He and Nizer then went over the total earnings of my show for WCBS from the time it first went on the air in 1951 until I left the show in 1957. They went through all sorts of mathematical gymnastics, and Gerry ended up with an estimate that I had earned during that period for WCBS in the vicinity of $1 million.

No other performer in the country has an off-stage personality that so nearly parallels his on-stage personality as Garry Moore. He is a sincere, affable soul at all times. His interest in me and my struggle had not diminished a bit since he joined me in my AFTRA fight. He now willingly came forward as a witness in my behalf.

Garry gave his background in radio and television, which dated back to the mid-1930s. He testified that since 1950 he had been an actor-producer. His eminence in the field made it unnecessary to qualify him further as an expert; it was accepted as a fact by judge, jury, and Mr. Bolan. Asked to tell how he came to join our Middle-of-the-Road slate, he said it was because he felt our union deserved a change in leadership and that something should be done about blacklisting. Lou then produced and read aloud into evidence a statement that Garry had made on November 23, 1955, while we were running for office in AFTRA. It was a statement made to Joe Coppola, who was writing a column at that time.

NIZER [reading]: "Garry Moore, when asked what a victory for the Middle-of-the-Road slate would mean in eliminating blacklisting, had this to say: 'I don't think anything revolutionary is going to happen, but the greatest thing in the world is human dignity. We have all been scattered in fear. I had the occasion to hire an aerialist whose name was on the blacklist. I was told he was unacceptable. I accepted the precept that if you pay a Communist it is a bad deal because while he doesn't editorialize on the air the money may go back to the Communist Party. But I insisted that they check on the aerialist. It turned out that he had the same name as a blacklisted performer, but he wasn't the same man. When a patently unproven case arises you must force it to be proved. This [Middle-of-the-Road slate] is the first thing I have ever joined.'"

NIZER: Did you engage this aerialist for one of your shows?
MOORE: Yes, sir, I did.
NIZER: And you submitted his name, as you did all other performers [to the network for clearance]?
MOORE: And all other performers, yes.

NIZER: Were you familiar with Mr. Faulk's reputation for loyalty and patriotism in the industry?
MOORE: Certainly, I would never have joined the slate had I not been aware of his reputation.
NIZER: What was it?
MOORE: The reputation for being a fine man, fine citizen, absolutely anti-Communist.

Lou then had him testify as to the extent of his experience as a producer of television shows, the hundreds of artists that he had hired, and his complete familiarity with the radio and television industry. Garry stated that he knew the general salary range of artists in various categories, such as dancers, singers, emcees, etc. It was his business to know them well, since he produced shows.

NIZER: In what category of performer would you place John Henry Faulk?
BOLAN: I object, your Honor.
THE COURT: Well then you object to the witness's qualifications?
BOLAN: No, your Honor. I object to the question, to its form particularly.
MOORE: John Henry Faulk has a rare sort of talent. There are only a handful of people in the business who function the way John Henry Faulk is capable of functioning. These are

generally referred to, I suppose, as personalities, because it is hard to pinpoint the kind of talent, as opposed to dancer, or singer, or acrobat. It is a kind of talent which has a great sustaining quality, because you may have a different singer each week or a different dancer, a different actor, but the host, master of ceremonies personality is a continuing job. He is there every week. His employment is far steadier than that of people in other categories. It is a talent that is very hard to duplicate. As I say, there are a handful, Arthur Godfrey, Art Linkletter, Dave Garroway.

THE COURT: How about Garry Moore?

MOORE: No opinion, sir. (laughter)

NIZER: Can you state, with reasonable certainty, the range of earnings that Mr. Faulk would have earned in the years I have indicated [1956 to 1962]?

MOORE: I can state with reasonable certainty that Mr. Faulk would have fallen within the category of a performer that I have discussed. . . . His earnings would have, of course, been commensurate anywhere between $200,000 and upward to conceivably $1 million.

NIZER: That testimony is, with reasonable certainty, limited to earnings from general television performance, is that not your testimony?

MOORE: Yes sir.

From his very first question on cross-examination of Garry Moore, it was obvious that Bolan wanted to discredit the million-dollar estimate.

BOLAN: Mr. Moore, you have testified, have you not, that you can state with reasonable certainty that Mr. Faulk's income from television between the years of 1956 and 1962 would have been in the range of $200,000 . . . up to $1 million a year?

MOORE: Yes sir.

THE COURT: Keep your voice up, Mr. Bolan.

BOLAN: Isn't it a fact that you are not able to state with reasonable certainty what your own income might be next year?

MOORE: No, my contract's all signed up for next year. I know exactly what it's going to be.

Garry seemed to be actually enjoying his session with Mr. Bolan. He answered each question quickly and brightly, often to the amusement of the jurors as well as the judge. For instance, Bolan asked him about his programs.

BOLAN: Has Mr. Faulk appeared on any of these with you?
MOORE: John Henry Faulk is not the type of talent that I would hire to be on a show that I am on because he does the same thing that I do and there isn't room for the two of us on one show.

Then Garry answered a question about why he had participated in the Middle-of-the-Road slate's campaign for officers.

MOORE: . . . I was terribly frightened by what was happening to people, being blacklisted, suddenly becoming unemployable, for what reason they knew not, not even being confronted or told why they were unemployable. It was a little bit like fighting with six men in a closet with the light out, and you can't tell who is hitting you.

As Bolan pressed him harder for his definition of blacklisting, Garry was very explicit in his answers.

MOORE: . . . I am speaking of cases where I hired people for jobs because they were good, because they were fine performers, gave their names to the network [CBS], as I was required to do, and the message would come back to me that such and such person is "unacceptable," and if you would say, "Why?" they would not say "It is incompetence," they would say, "He is unacceptable."

Then Bolan wanted to know whether it was the sponsors or the network who blacklisted people.

MOORE: It could come from almost any direction. The networks had a clearance board which functioned. Sponsors, too, would come to you and say, "So and so is unacceptable because he is in *Red Channels*," or something of that nature. But most of the time the word came 'way round about, you never quite knew who was making the decision about this man's livelihood.

Lou had at last succeeded in persuading Frank Barton to appear and testify on the Johnson-Matusow episode. He testified that he was vice-president and general manager of the Lennen & Newell advertising agency and went on to tell how in 1952 his agency had handled the Schlitz Beer account and produced a television show "The Schlitz Playhouse of Stars." At this point Lou read a portion of the examination before trial of Laurence Johnson, wherein Johnson admitted sending a telegram to E. C. Eihlein of the Schlitz Brewing Company protesting the use of Frank Silvera on the program. The matter had been passed from the brewery executives on to the executives of the agency to look into. A short time later Johnson called Barton and asked that they have a meeting to discuss the matter. Barton met with Johnson and Harvey Matusow, and Barton described what happened at the meeting.

BARTON: . . . Mr. Johnson made a long patriotic speech about Communists and what they were doing and how we should fight them and they shouldn't be appearing on programs where they were before the public.

I assured him that we were just as patriotic as he was, and that we and our client had no more desire to have Communists on our show than he did, or any other good American did, but the question was, who were Communists? We had no knowledge in this field. He claimed that he did have knowledge and that a lot of other people had knowledge, and if we would take the trouble, make the effort, we could gain such knowledge and know who was and who wasn't.

Then he raised the specific issue with regard to certain programs that he knew about, he said, where he had gotten the cast lists somehow, and claimed certain people were Communists, and he wanted those programs off the air.

Barton then went on to describe his discussion of the matter at lunch with Johnson.

BARTON: He [Johnson] got fairly angry with me and started to pound the table and raise his voice sufficiently to attract attention around the dining room, then he calmed down.

The matter was resolved by an agreement, suggested by Mr. Johnson, that in the future Mr. Barton's agency would use the services of Mr. Matusow to discover who was Communist or pro-Communist and who was not, so far as the programs were concerned. Lou then probed further.

NIZER: Was there any discussion with respect to what Mr. Matusow would be and any financial arrangements?
BOLAN: I object.
THE COURT: Overruled.
BARTON: Yes, we agreed to pay Mr. Matusow the sum of $150, I think it was, in return for which he supplied us with two years' back issues of a publication called *Counterattack*, which listed information, or reported information, about a great many people many of which were in our field of entertainment, of the entertainment business, and from these lists Mr. Matusow showed us how to set up a card index where we could find references.

Lou then called up Harry J. Blackburn, an executive in the Rheingold Brewery, who testified that Laurence Johnson had phoned him in 1956 and told him that I was a Communist. After that, Lou called up Lester Wolff, an advertising executive and television program operator, who testified that I came to him, sometime in late 1957 or early 1958, looking for work. He wanted to use me on a program, but on investigation he discovered that there was too much controversy raging around me, and consequently he didn't use me.

Ed Murrow had suggested that J. Frank Dobie should be brought up as a character witness for me. Murrow was so anxious to have Dobie's strong personality come before the jury in the case that he offered to pay Dobie's expenses to New York from Texas. Mr. Dobie had told me that he would gladly come and pay his own way if it would help our case.

At the time of the trial, however, he was in poor health and I was afraid that the trip would tax his waning strength too much.

However, after several character witnesses, Justice Geller ruled that he was calling a halt to our parade of witnesses.

Thus, just before noon on Friday, May 25, more than a month after the trial had begun, Lou announced: "The plaintiff rests."

22

We had presented our side of the case. Now the time had come for the defendants to present theirs.

We had speculated at length on what witness Bolan would put on the stand first. This was not idle speculation. It was of utmost importance that we know, in order to be prepared to cross-examine him. Lou prepared for four or five different possible witnesses, just in case they led off with someone other than Hartnett. One of these was Paul Milton, who had been in on the founding of AWARE, Inc., was long associated with Mr. Hartnett, and did most of the writing on the bulletins that AWARE circulated. His fame as a hyperactive, self-appointed guardian of other writers' political morals and his tireless activities as an informer before Congressional committees had earned him quite a reputation. It was Mr. Milton who took the stand as the first major witness for the defense, and Nizer was well prepared.

As Milton settled into the witness chair he looked as calm and as composed as a dignified businessman taking his place in a church pew on Sunday. He was balding and gray, with a neatly trimmed gray mustache. His expression was that of a pleasant but serious, responsible citizen performing a civic duty which neither pleased nor displeased him.

Answering Bolan's questions with apparent candor and diffidence, he was the very picture of respectable cooperation. His expression was almost pious as he raised his eyes toward the ceiling during the frequent and heated wrangles between Bolan and Nizer over objections. I was uneasy at seeing him making such a fine impression on the jury. As a matter of fact, he was making a pretty good impression on me, as his answers came, even and direct, without a hint of guile. His testimony revealed that he had been graduated from Cornell in 1926, had become a writer, then an editor, and then had moved into the field of script-writing for radio and television. He described in detail the origins of AWARE in the early 1950s and how he had participated actively in that organization. For some years he had been chairman of AWARE's Information Committee. As such he was responsible for the preparation of the bulletins and other written information that AWARE put out.

At several points in Milton's direct testimony that day, he said things that rather amazed me.

BOLAN: You stated that AWARE's membership at one point was 350 members, is that correct?

MILTON: Yes.

BOLAN: Were there some members of AWARE who were also members of the American Federation of Radio and Television Artists?

MILTON: Yes, there were.

BOLAN: And at its peak of 350 members, approximately how many members were members of AFTRA?

MILTON: I would say from seventy-five to one hundred.

THE COURT: Were you a member of AFTRA at that time?

MILTON: No, sir, never.

Bolan got testimony from Milton to the effect that he and other members of the board of directors of AWARE had relied on Vincent Hartnett for their information, which went into bulletin 16, the one libeling me, and to build this up, he wanted Milton to testify as to Hartnett's reputation as a researcher. Nizer objected to this, and the court sustained Nizer's objection. A very interesting colloquy took place outside the hearing of the jury but on the record, before Judge Geller.

BOLAN: I'm entitled to show that the board of directors of AWARE had considered Hartnett's reputation to be one of the finest as a researcher, and that they were confidently relying on the material which he supplied for the publication of their bulletins. It is a pure question of reliance. . . . They relied on Hartnett and I have a right to show, I submit, why they relied and placed so much reliance upon Hartnett.

NIZER: In other words, Milton can say that he relied on
    Hartnett, and Hartnett can say that he relied on Milton,
    and this is internal reliance testimony on reputation, and
    Milton is going to say Hartnett had a good reputation as a
    researcher. Do you think that is the reliance proof that is
    submitted by courts with respect to libels?

Judge Geller sustained Lou's position. Bolan continued his
questioning of Milton.

BOLAN: Well, with respect to the allegations of bulletin 16
    concerning Mr. Faulk, did you have any personal knowl-
    edge on which you relied with respect to the allegations
    concerning Mr. Faulk? . . .
MILTON: As an individual, no.

The next day Milton began testifying under cross-examination by Nizer. Within a matter of minutes, his pious self-
composure evaporated. He began to look shopworn and gray.
He was clearly shaken by the turn his life as a witness had
taken. His work with AWARE and Hartnett did not seem as
selfless and noble under Nizer's questions as it had appeared
under Bolan's.

Nizer was allowed to ask Milton if he had relied on a citation in the House Un-American Activities Committee report on People's Songs when he described the organization
as a Communist-front organization in the AWARE bulletin.
Milton replied that he had indeed relied on the HUAC
report.

NIZER: You have just testified, Mr. Milton, that you relied
    on this paragraph in the House Un-American Activities
    Committee Guide which has a quote, "All of the produc-
    tions of People's Songs follow the Communist party line
    as assiduously as do the people behind the organization,"
    and at the end of the quote, the source of that quote is
    given as the "California Committee on Un-American Ac-
    tivities report 1948, page 302." You so testified a moment
    ago, did you?
MILTON: Yes.

NIZER: And the California Committee on Un-American Activities is also called the Tenney Committee?

MILTON: It was, yes.

NIZER: Have you not testified that the Tenney Committee, the California Committee, was unreliable?

MILTON: I don't think I said that, sir.

NIZER: You don't? Page 162, were you asked the following question on your examination before trial under oath?

"Q: You knew that the citations by the California Committee are not reliable necessarily? A: That's right."

Did you make that answer to that question [in 1960]?

MILTON: Yes.

Nizer established on cross-examination once and for all that it was the purpose of AWARE, Inc. bulletins to influence AFTRA's affairs.

NIZER: And have you also testified that, broadly speaking, you intended to influence the AFTRA member's conduct even in their own elections?

MILTON: Broadly speaking, yes.

NIZER: At the very time that exhibit was published by you
. . .

THE COURT: "You," meaning AWARE.

NIZER: AWARE, Inc. You knew, did you not, there was going to be a national election a few months later?

MILTON: Yes.

NIZER: And Exhibit 41 [AWARE bulletin attacking the Middle-of-the-Road slate], of course, is not a private publication, that is the one that went out to thousands, right?

MILTON: About 2,000.

NIZER: You knew that there was a national election coming up that year, in 1956, didn't you?

MILTON: I think in the summer.

NIZER: And you also knew that there would be another annual local election in the fall of 1956, didn't you?

MILTON: Yes.

NIZER: And you also knew that AWARE members who were officers of AFTRA ran repeatedly, that is, they ran in succession for re-election—you knew that, too, didn't you?

MILTON: That's my impression. I'd have to look at the names to see exactly who did what . . .

NIZER: And those same AWARE members who were members of AFTRA were active in election disputes in AFTRA, weren't they?

MILTON: I assume they were, yes.

Lou then took the libelous bulletin 16 and turned to a statement in it that Milton admitted having written— namely, "The Middle-of-the-Road ticket was first reported by the *Daily Worker* on November 15, 1955."

NIZER: Now I ask you isn't it a fact that in addition to the *Times* and the *Tribune* there were other publications which, prior to the *Daily Worker*, discussed the Middle-of-the-Road slate?

MILTON: All that our files show now is *Variety* and straight news reports.

NIZER: And *Variety* is the trade publication for the entertainment industry; isn't it a leading one, right?

MILTON: Yes.

NIZER: And a reliable one?

MILTON: Yes, sir.

NIZER: You didn't mention the fact that there was one report prior to the *Daily Worker*; you said the first one was the *Daily Worker*, didn't you, at that point?

MILTON: Yes, there are some other references, however.

NIZER: And you knew that was incorrect at the time you wrote this, didn't you?

MILTON: Yes.

NIZER: As a matter of fact, as far back as July 11, 1955, not November, I show you Exhibit 52 in evidence, the *New York Times*, "More about AWARE" and refers to the Middle—

MILTON: This dealt with the previous condemnation, had

nothing to do with the Middle-of-the-Road slate, which didn't even exist then, as far as the public knew.

NIZER: I call your attention to Exhibit 52 . . . and ask you if this language didn't mean to you that the *New York Times* article as far back as July 1955 was suggesting a middle position between the AWARE blacklisting and the Communist issue? Doesn't that mean that to you?

MILTON: That was Mr. Gould's [Jack Gould of the *New York Times*] opinion.

NIZER: Yes. I am not asking you—

MILTON: I do not recognize the use of the word "blacklisting" in connection with AWARE.

THE COURT: That isn't the question.

MILTON: I don't recognize that statement to mean anything whatsoever except Mr. Gould's opinion.

Lou then took each one of the specifications in bulletin 16 that Milton had written against me and went down them one by one. He established that Milton did not even know what organization it was that I was supposed to have appeared before at Club 65 back in 1946. It turned out to be the Newspaper Guild unit from the *Amsterdam News*, a Harlem newspaper.

NIZER: Do you consider the *Amsterdam News* in any way a pro-Communist newspaper?

MILTON: Not to my knowledge, no, sir.

NIZER: Do you consider the *Amsterdam News* unit of the Newspaper Guild of New York a pro-Communist organization?

MILTON: I don't know anything about it.

NIZER: . . . Have you not testified that the only thing was the *Daily Worker* that you relied upon?

MILTON: As you read my statement, yes.

NIZER: And you never inquired of Mr. Hartnett as to what organization was meeting at Club 65?

MILTON: I don't recall that I did. I hope that I did.

NIZER: Now that you see that it is the Newspaper Guild function which took place at Club 65, you should know that that organization and that meeting so far as that function was concerned, was a legitimate, non-Communist function of professional newspapermen, wouldn't you?

BOLAN: I object, your Honor.

THE COURT: Overruled.

MILTON: I don't know what kind of meeting it was.

NIZER: I am asking you now. I just read to you what was in the bulletin. I am asking you, didn't you know at the time that you published this that Club 65 was a site for non-Communist affairs.

MILTON: It may have been.

NIZER: And didn't you also testify that Club 65 was not subversive?

MILTON: The place itself may well not have been subversive.

Lou then elicited from Milton a rather fascinating statement.

NIZER: And as a writer, did you consider this item, which omitted the meeting that took place, omitted the Newspaper Guild that was supposed to meet there, you have stated that this is a favorite pro-Communist site, did you consider this a fair report based upon a full investigation?

MILTON: In the light of what we were doing, yes.

NIZER: In the light of what you were doing, which was to injure Mr. Faulk, you mean, don't you?

MILTON: No, the bulletin says what we were doing.

NIZER: Haven't you testified that what you were doing was trying to bring out everything adverse to Mr. Faulk that you could in this bulletin?

MILTON: That was an incidental purpose. The main purpose was the union question.

Milton had been mighty chary about using the term "blacklisting" in connection with his or any of the other defendants' activities. He preferred to call it "screening." On the last day of his cross-examination, I suppose, Nizer had punched so hard that Milton didn't have his wits about him. Nizer asked about the days immediately before AWARE was organized.

NIZER: Haven't you testified that Johnson, Laurence Johnson, and his Syracuse friends were active in the work of, as you put it, "screening" or blacklisting performers, before AWARE, Inc. was organized? Haven't you so testified?

MILTON: That's right.

Milton was at great pains to explain, however, that he had never intended to charge any individual with pro-Communism. It was simply, the groups to which they belonged that were pro-Communist.

Milton had belonged to a faction of the Radio Writers Guild called We, the Undersigned, which Milton admitted, was the forerunner of AWARE, Inc. The faction had charged that some of the Guild members were pro-Communists.

Nizer brought out that Milton had corresponded with Matusow to obtain information about these "pro-Communists" Guild members. It was these people who opposed We, The Undersigned that Milton took pains to investigate.

NIZER: In other words, as I understand you, Mr. Milton, if a person belongs to an organization that is pro-Communist, that does not make him pro-Communist, is that right?

MILTON: Not automatically.

NIZER: Certainly, if he doesn't belong to it but he just attends a function, even of a pro-Communist organization, that doesn't make him pro-Communist, does it?

MILTON: I said the other day, not automatically.

THE COURT: That, in and of itself, does not make him a pro-Communist?

MILTON: I said no, not automatically.

THE COURT: I don't know what you mean, not automatically, to that question. Will you explain?

MILTON: I do not deduce personal pro-Communism from—

THE COURT: Mere attendance in an organization?

MILTON: Or even membership, depending of course what the organization is. . . .

NIZER: Some of these writers [of the Radio Writers Guild]
lost their jobs, didn't they?

MILTON: I suppose so. All writers lose jobs.

NIZER: No, after your criticism under the We, The Undersigned statement I am talking about, some of these writers
lost their jobs, didn't they?

MILTON: One man told us he was in danger of losing his job.

NIZER: Some of them actually did lose their jobs, didn't they,
as a result of this?

MILTON: I don't know.

NIZER: You don't know. Was there a man by the name of
Sheldon Stark who, prior to your criticism and testimony
about him, was employed in "Treasury Men in Action"?

MILTON: He was employed at the producing office. I can't
tell you whether it was that program or another they produced. I am not certain now.

NIZER: Was it Mr. Hartnett, the gentleman who acted as a
consultant, as you call it, through that program, "Treasury
Men in Action"?

MILTON: I am not sure.

NIZER: Didn't you obtain a job on "Treasury Men in Action"
after Mr. Stark lost his job?

MILTON: Yes.

NIZER: Wasn't this program sponsored by the Borden Milk
Company?

MILTON: I think so, yes.

Nizer read aloud one of the allegations which Milton had
written against me in the AWARE bulletin; "According to
the *Daily Worker*, of April 17, 1947, 'Johnny Faulk' was to
appear as an entertainer at the opening of 'Headline Cabaret,' sponsored by Stage for Action (officially designated
a Communist front). The late Philip Loeb was billed as
emcee."

NIZER: Had you ever heard of Headline Cabaret at the time
you wrote this?

MILTON: Prior to—no, I think it was a one-time show or
something.

NIZER: Did you know at that time that that particular show,

"Headline Cabaret" show, had been approved by the Theatre Authority?

MILTON: No, I don't think so.

He gave this answer in spite of the fact that the "Approved
by Theatre Authority" was clearly printed on the exhibit or
advertisement from which he had taken his information
about me. It turned out that Milton was not even sure of
what the Theatre Authority was. He asked Nizer what it
was. Nizer said it was an agency set up by four unions in
the entertainment field—Equity, AFTRA, AGVA, and the
Screen Actors Guild—to protect the interests of the unions
and their members in relation to performances at benefit
shows. Members of these unions are forbidden to perform at
any benefit production that has not been approved by the
Authority. Milton expressed some surprise to learn this.
Also, he was surprised to learn that the Theatre Authority
had approved the entertainment that I was said to have
attended.

NIZER: Did you deliberately and purposefully omit that statement ("approved by the Theatre Authority") from your
paragraph in Exhibit 41?

MILTON: Yes, we omitted it.

NIZER: Is the answer to my question, "Yes, you deliberately
and purposefully omitted it?"

MILTON: Yes.

NIZER: Did you put in the fact that the late Philip Loeb was
billed as emcee? Did you also notice that Art Carney was
one of the entertainers at this function?

MILTON: Yes.

NIZER: Did you deliberately and purposefully omit the name
of Art Carney from this item?

MILTON: Yes. . . .

NIZER: You were the head of what committee? What was it
called, your committee [in AWARE]?

MILTON: Information.

NIZER: Did you ask for information about a program of this
event before you wrote this charge in Exhibit 41? Did you
or did you not?

MILTON: I said I don't recall specifically the same program.

NIZER: I would like a direct answer, Mr. Milton. I don't mean specifically in any way. Did you make any inquiries to see the document of the printed program for this occasion before you made this charge?

MILTON: I have to say no as you phrased it . . .

NIZER: To this day, have you any information that John Henry Faulk appeared at the "Headline Cabaret"?

MILTON: In my possession, no.

Lou took up the matter of Milton's charge that I had entertained for a Henry A. Wallace benefit under the auspices of the Progressive Citizens of America. He asked Milton if he wrote the paragraph charging me with doing so. Milton answered, "Yes, sir." He then elicited from Milton that he had relied on the House Un-American Activities Committee's guide as a source for the allegation that the Progressive Citizens of America was pro-Communist. Nizer then got him to admit that any mention of any organization whatever before the House Un-American Activities Committee ended up in the guide. There was a House Un-American Activities Committee Guide and a House Un-American Activities Committee Cumulative Index that just contained every name that was ever mentioned before it.

NIZER: Take the cumulative index of names. You know that President Eisenhower's name appears in that cumulative index, don't you, from our own experience?

MILTON: The index, as I understand it, lists everyone who testified regardless of the nature of their testimony.

NIZER: It also lists anybody who was mentioned by some witness as having, say, sent greetings to the Russian Relief or something like that; you would have President Eisenhower on that if he were mentioned? . . . The index would mention the name of any individual who was mentioned by some witness in connection with any activity that he claimed was pro-Communist, right?

MILTON: I'd have to look at that again. I haven't seen that publication for some time. I am not sure. My impression was that it lists only witnesses. Whether it also mentions people who were mentioned by other witnesses I couldn't say now.

NIZER: You don't know that?

MILTON: Not without looking at the publication again.

NIZER: Going back to organizations now, if, for example, Harvey Matusow testified that a certain organization in his opinion was questionable, that organization would appear on this guide index, wouldn't it?

MILTON: Some, yes.

NIZER: And individuals that you have mentioned have appeared on the cumulative index, haven't they?

MILTON: I believe so, yes.

NIZER: Did the House Un-American Activities Guide that you referred to cite solely this California Un-American Activities Committee item, their citation, as a sole basis for calling the Progressive Citizens of America pro-Communists?

MILTON: Talking from recollection, yes.

NIZER: And you have already testified that the California Un-American Activities Committee was unreliable in many respects?

MILTON: In some, yes. I don't know if I said many.

Lou continued to take up, one by one, each of the charges that Milton had made against me in the AWARE bulletin. Under Lou's merciless cross-examination, Milton admitted that he had no knowledge of the truth of a single one of the charges. But Lou went further. He had Milton admit that he did not even believe in the reliability of any of the sources he had used.

NIZER: My question is, haven't you testified that you had heard, before you wrote Exhibit 41, that the Progressive Citizens of America was simply a liberal organization, not a Communist-front organization, that you had heard that and you had no reason to disbelieve that?

MILTON: The record shows that I did.

NIZER: Nevertheless, you still wrote in Exhibit 41, "Progressive Citizens of America officially designated as a Communist front," didn't you?

MILTON: Yes.

Lou then made Milton admit in each case where he had used the term "officially designated Communist front," it was a calculated misuse of such term. Actually, it had no meaning whatever, since there had been no official finding on any of the so-called Communist-front groups. After getting from Milton an admission that he knew before he wrote the bulletin that I was not a member of any one of the organizations that he mentioned in the bulletin and for which I allegedly entertained, Milton admitted one of the principal points of our charges against the defendant, namely, that the entire problem grew out of my activity in the union. AWARE had attacked me only because I had taken part in the union election.

MILTON: The entire purpose of the entire bulletin was to illuminate a controversy in AFTRA, and another purpose was to draw attention to Mr. Faulk and several other individuals in relation to that question.

Then Lou drove the point home even more strongly:

NIZER: Isn't it a fact that at this time in July of 1955, the chief officers of AFTRA were either members of AWARE or strong supporters of AWARE?
MILTON: I have to see the list of officers.

Lou then read off a number of names of AFTRA officers who had opposed us most violently: Ned Weaver, Vinton Hayworth, Alan Bunce, Bud Collyer. Milton admitted that they were all either active members or former members of AWARE. He further got Milton to admit that AWARE had become interested in the Middle-of-the-Road slate shortly after we had announced we were running for office in the fall of 1955.

Lou then read from the minutes of a board meeting of AWARE in December 1955, in which the officers of AWARE had discussed preparing a run-down of those who had won on the Middle-of-the-Road slate, with particular emphasis on what they called the "worst people on that slate."

NIZER: And the special people that were singled out in Exhibit 41, a Mr. Collingwood, a Mr. Faulk, and a Mr. Bean right, those three?
MILTON: Of the slate, that's right.

It was actually on the fourth item that had been alleged against me in the AWARE bulletin that Mr. Nizer made his strongest case against Milton.

NIZER: The fourth item that you alleged against Mr. Faulk reads as follows: "A program dated April 25, 1946, named 'John Faulk' as a scheduled entertainer (with identified Communist Earl Robinson and two non-Communists) under the auspices of the Independent Citizens Committee of the Arts, Sciences and Professions (officially designated a Communist front, and predecessor of the Progressive Citizens of America)."
Did you write that item, sir?

MILTON: I wrote it or rewrote it.

NIZER: Did you see that program before you wrote Exhibit 41?

MILTON: I believe I did.

NIZER: And you read it, did you not?

MILTON: Yes.

NIZER: You know, therefore, you knew before you wrote Exhibit 41, this charge, that this event was a first-year salute to the United Nations; you knew that, didn't you?

MILTON: Yes, sir. . . .

NIZER: And you deliberately and purposefully omitted the fact that this occasion was a United Nations' salute on the first-year anniversary of the United Nations when you wrote this article that I have read to you from Exhibit 41, didn't you?

MILTON: Yes. . . .

NIZER: You also knew before you wrote Exhibit 41, this item in which you referred to simply Mr. Faulk as an entertainer "with identified Communist Earl Robinson," you also knew at that time that on this occasion the secretary of State of the United States at that time, Edward Stettinius, was a speaker? You knew that too didn't you?

MILTON: Yes.

NIZER: And you deliberately and purposefully omitted that from this item, didn't you?

MILTON: That's right. . . .

NIZER: You observed from looking at Exhibit 53 that the Columbia Broadcasting System broadcast this event on a network? Do you see that? Not only do you see it, didn't you notice that before you wrote your item in Exhibit 41?

MILTON: Yes, yes. . . .

NIZER: You also saw by looking at Exhibit 53, which you say you read before you published this, that Trygve Lie of the United Nations also was there and presided in a way over that part of the program? You noticed that, didn't you?

MILTON: Yes, sir.

NIZER: And you purposefully and deliberately omitted that fact in describing the occasion which you said Mr. Faulk attended, didn't you?

MILTON: That's right. . . .

NIZER: And you noticed and knew before you wrote Exhibit 41 that among the sponsors of this event which you accused Mr. Faulk of attending was the American Association of the United Nations, right? You noticed that?

MILTON: Yes.

NIZER: And the American Association of University Women?

MILTON: Yes, the whole list.

NIZER: And the American Bar Association?

MILTON: Yes.

NIZER: And the Young Men's Christian Association?

MILTON: Yes.

And then Nizer moved up close to Milton and sternly looked him in the eye.

NIZER: . . . Wasn't it your purpose when you wrote this item in the way you did to give the impression to the sponsors, the advertising agency, the newspapers to whom you mailed this Exhibit 41, that Mr. Faulk had attended a pro-Communist function? Wasn't that your purpose?

MILTON: I said so, didn't I?

Every now and then I would glance back into the spectators' section during the grilling that Lou was giving Milton. Bob Cenedella, Philo Higley and their wives and several other writers who had had unhappy experiences as a result of Mr. Milton's maneuverings in the years past sat with expressions of grim satisfaction as he squirmed and floundered before Lou's relentless cross-examination. It was interesting to note that none of the writers wore expressions of vengeance. They were not unkind men. Rather, they seemed to be feeling that at long last the world was being told something that they had known for many years—a shabby hoax had been perpetrated on the television industry and the American public. Now, it was being revealed for what it really was.

23

On June 6, the day Vincent Hartnett followed Paul Milton to
the witness stand, a heat wave was settling over New York.
The court room was getting uncomfortably warm and Justice Geller directed attendants to put up tall electric fans
near the jury to keep jurors as comfortable as possible.

As I watched Hartnett being sworn in and taking his seat
in the witness chair, I had the feeling that had it been swel-
tering hot or icy cold in the courtroom, Hartnett's precise,
proper manner would have been the same, unaffected by any
outside influence.

Sitting there neat and prim, his mouth a thin straight line,
his eyes straight ahead, he gave the appearance of a well-
disciplined little soldier, awaiting orders, which he would
carry out to the minutest detail. It touched me somehow, to
see that he wore a military decoration in the lapel of his neat
blue jacket. For some reason I felt terribly sorry for him at
that moment. My own direct testimony had taken a week,
two full days of which had been spent reciting my virtues
and accomplishments in open court. I assumed that Hartnett would take at least that much time, perhaps more, so I
settled back into my chair as Bolan began Hartnett's direct
examination. As a matter of fact I was eager to hear about
Hartnett's background. I knew very little about it, since our
researches and examinations of him had been confined to
his activities, subsequent to 1950. Bolan seemed to be just as
eager to have Hartnett go into his background as I was to
hear about it. Mr. Hartnett, it turned out, was even born on a
patriotic note.

BOLAN: Mr. Hartnett, when and where were you born?
HARTNETT: I was born in St. Louis, Missouri, on July 4, 1916.

BOLAN: In connection with obtaining your Master's degree

at Notre Dame, did you take any courses dealing with Communism?

HARTNETT: Yes. . . .

BOLAN: What were those courses?

NIZER: Objection.

THE COURT: Sustained.

BOLAN: I am trying to line up a foundation to establish Mr. Hartnett as an expert in the field of Communism and Communist infiltration of the radio and television industry.

THE COURT: I will let you—on the question of Communism, I don't understand the concept of an expert on Communism. An expert has to be an expert on a scientific subject or something of that character. You may qualify him, if you intend to use him as an expert, in the practices of the radio and television industry. That you may do, but on the question of Communism, you may elicit any facts that he has, but the jury is the one that will have to judge that, Mr. Bolan.

Bolan followed what I considered a rather odd course in his direct examination of Hartnett. It seemed to me that he was having Hartnett describe his occupation exactly as we had described it—that of a private vigilante.

BOLAN: Mr. Hartnett, beginning in August 1952, what was your occupation?

HARTNETT: A professional consultant on the Communist and/or Communist-front records of persons working in the entertainment industry, particularly radio and television.

BOLAN: Did you continue in that occupation through and until 1956?

HARTNETT: I did.

BOLAN: Was that a full-time job?

HARTNETT: Yes.

BOLAN: Mr. Hartnett, you testified that you began accumulating files [reports on entertainers] particularly in 1949, you started to build up files concerning the Communist infiltration of the radio and television industry. Did you use those files in connection with your work as a researcher?

HARTNETT: Yes.

BOLAN: Will you tell us briefly what your files consisted of?

HARTNETT: First, a virtually complete file of all the published hearings and reports of the Special Committee on Un-American Activities of the United States House of Representatives and of the successor committee, the Standing House Committee on Un-American Activities of the House of Representatives.

Secondly, all the relevant published hearings and reports of the Senate Internal Security Subcommittee.

Thirdly, all the relevant published hearings and reports of the Senate Permanent Subcommittee on Government Operations, some incidental reports and other Congressional investigating committees.

A file of Communist publications, particularly of the *Daily Worker*, official organ of the Communist Party. A file of *Masses and Mainstream*, monthly Communist magazine, and its successor, *Mainstream*. A file of *Sing Out*, a publication of People's Artists, successor to *People's Songs*. Some early Communist theatrical literature as *Tack Magazine*, *Theatre Arts Committee Magazine*, *New Theatre Magazine*, a Communist monthly publication in the theatre. A file of the *Daily Compass*, a party-line newspaper, a daily newspaper. A file of show business, *Actor's Cues*, which at a certain period contained a good many items about Communist-front activities in entertainment.

NIZER: I object to these conclusions as to what these publications contained. He was asked to give the names of the publications.

HARTNETT: A collection of what we term primary source material, that is, letterheads, circulars, programs, and announcements of various Communist-front organizations.

NIZER: I object to that phrase, "Communist-front organizations" as a conclusion of this witness.

THE COURT: Yes, strike that out.

Hartnett testified that what he didn't have in his own files he could usually find over in the theatre collection at the

New York Public Library, the place he frequently went to for further information on artists.

BOLAN: Mr. Hartnett, after you went into this research business in 1952, did you obtain any clients on a regular basis?

HARTNETT: Yes.

BOLAN: Who was your first client?

HARTNETT: The Borden Company.

BOLAN: When did you obtain that client?

HARTNETT: In August 1952.

BOLAN: Did you have any discussion with any official of Borden's prior to your being engaged?

HARTNETT: Yes.

BOLAN: With whom?

HARTNETT: Stuart Peabody.

BOLAN: What was his position with Borden's?

HARTNETT: In general, over-all charge of their advertising program.

BOLAN: What duties did you perform for Borden's after you were retained?

NIZER: Objection, your Honor.

THE COURT: I will allow it. You may answer. Don't give us conversations. Just indicate the services and duties you performed.

HARTNETT: I checked the names of prospective employees on their television program for any known Communist Party or Communist-front records.

NIZER: I object to the word "known" as a characterization.

THE COURT: Right, strike it out. Bear in mind what I said before, Mr. Hartnett. It is for the jury to make determinations, so that if you refer to them, don't characterize it as "known." That is for the jury to determine, not your conclusion. . . .

BOLAN: What is your financial arrangement with Borden's, Mr. Hartnett?

HARTNETT: Initially, a fee of $20 for each name checked.

BOLAN: Did the arrangement change subsequent to that?

HARTNETT: Yes, as the volume of names increased, by mutual agreement, we set a fee of $5 per name checked, and later, of $2 if a name was repeated, came back a second or third time.

BOLAN: Were you later paid a flat fee by Borden's?
HARTNETT: I was.

He continued—proudly, I thought—to list the names of clients he had. There were: Lever Brothers, the American Broadcasting Company, Young & Rubicam advertising agency, the Kudner Agency. Hartnett sought to relate how he had furnished information to various government agencies including the F.B.I., but this was not permitted by Judge Geller, who said, "Obviously, anybody can supply information to any governmental authority, if they ask for it, or voluntarily they can appear before it. That doesn't add anything to the issues in this case."

I was somehow impressed with the sincerity with which Hartnett was testifying. I was convinced that he really didn't know what his testimony sounded like to a nonbeliever. There I sat listening—I who had been unemployed for the last five years, largely through the doings of Mr. Hartnett—scarcely able to keep from laughing out loud at his testimony.

BOLAN: Did you, when you rendered any reports, indicate whether the performer, artist, or who it may be, should or should not be employed?
HARTNETT: In my reports? My reports were always strictly objective, sir.

Hartnett also testified as to the methods he followed in giving his reports to his clients.

HARTNETT: Well, the initial report would be almost always by telephone, and then there would be a written report where there was information to be reported. However, I want to make this point, that I was generally—such a volume that I could often be behind in the written reports.

Bolan and Hartnett ran into a real problem. For years, Hartnett, AWARE and others had been citing the House Un-American Activities Committee as their authority for allegations of Communism or pro-Communism. For years Mr. Hartnett had been selling such information to sponsors, networks, agencies, and the general public. Now Mr. Hartnett was in a court of law; and each time he applied the term "Communist or pro-Communist" to an individual or an organization, Judge Geller informed him that in a court of law such characterizations are not admissible unless their truth is established. Hartnett would fall back on the citations of the House Un-American Activities Committee. Repeatedly, Judge Geller would state that these citations of the House Un-American Activities Committee had no legal standing as truth:

THE COURT: . . . those citations, as I have already told the jury, are not binding and do not constitute a finding—a proper finding. It must be a judicial finding, and those statements of citations by the House Committee and the Attorney General's list do not constitute truth, or that this organization is such a Communist-character organization.

Mr. Bolan seemed somewhat surprised by the judge's ruling.

BOLAN: Your Honor, unless I misunderstand, and I would like some clarification, in other words, unless it can be established that this organization by judicial process was designated and found to be a Communist-front, no testimony on that area is permitted.

THE COURT: No, I didn't say that, Mr. Bolan. I did not say it. I said that the jury will make the determination based on the evidence that you offered. I did say that the House Un-American Activities Committee citation, the Attorney General's list citation, do not constitute proof that these organizations—that this organization—is a Communist-front or a Communist or a pro-Communist organization; and I elaborated on that fully. Such citations or listings by the House Committee or Attorney General do not constitute a judicial finding that an organization is a Communistic or pro-Communistic front organization.

So it came about that the only thing that Mr. Hartnett could do was to attempt, by testifying that he had relied on the House Un-American Activities Committee reports in good faith, to mitigate the damages that might be assessed. That was at least a partial defense, but it had nothing whatever to do with *truth*, which would have been a complete defense.

By the end of the second day of Hartnett's direct testimony, when I was beginning to be terribly bored with it, Bolan announced that he had completed his direct examination. Word went out from spectators to friends outside that Nizer was about to start his cross-examination. As Lou stood up, I knew that my prolonged experience with the defendants had reached a stage that was in a way the most dramatic of the whole affair. But it was about three-thirty in the afternoon, and I supposed that Lou wouldn't get really warmed up on Hartnett in the short time before court adjourned. I was mistaken. Lou plunged right in, hitting Hartnett where he lived—in the House Un-American Activities Committee reports.

NIZER: Now, sir, we have had all these booklets and citations offered on the subject of reliance all day today. You realize that citations of the House Un-American Activities Committee are not official designations; isn't that so? . . .

HARTNETT: Yes, in the legal sense. . . .

NIZER: None of the people who employed you to give them data about professional artists who are going to appear on radio and television, none of those ever made an inquiry to you about Mr. John Henry Faulk, did they?

HARTNETT: No.

NIZER: Did you ever, in the case of John Henry Faulk, write to employers of John Henry Faulk citing anything against his record so far as patriotism and loyalty are concerned even though you weren't employed by that sponsor agency?

HARTNETT: Not to my knowledge, sir.

NIZER: Is it not a fact, Mr. Hartnett, that on your own, without anybody asking you for any information, you wrote to employers of John Henry Faulk complaining about his background of Communist affiliation? That is a fact, isn't it?

HARTNETT: No, not to my knowledge, it is not a fact.

NIZER: I show you Exhibit 58-A. Are you the writer of this letter to Young & Rubicam, the agency? In 1955?

HARTNETT: Yes.

NIZER: I read to you from your letter of November 27, 1955: "Since the name of Louise Allbritton was proposed, she has been announced as a candidate for the Independent ticket of AFTRA, New York Local board. I find no Communist or Communist-front record on her, however, and therefore conclude that she is just a liberal. The coleader of this ticket is John Henry Faulk. He has a significant Communist-front record." Did you write that to Young & Rubicam?

HARTNETT: Yes.

NIZER: At that time, had Young & Rubicam asked you for any opinion about John Henry Faulk?

HARTNETT: No.

Hartnett had justified his collecting of fees for clearing performers on the grounds that he was an expert, and that he investigated with great care and accuracy. He had stated time and again that he knew that any mistakes he made could result in serious harm to the artist. It was in this area of his activities that Nizer began his cross-examination. Just how much care had Mr. Hartnett taken in the case of me, for instance, how well had he checked my background, what had he omitted and what had he made up?

There had been a rather laudatory article about me in *Newsweek* magazine back in 1952. A careful researcher could certainly have found it. Lou held in his hand a file card that Hartnett had kept on me in his files. He stood in front of Hartnett and continued.

NIZER: There is a reference in your file card, is there not, to *Newsweek*, December 29, 1952; is that correct?

HARTNETT: I believe that's the date there was a reference to *Newsweek*.

NIZER: And there was an article you found out in *Newsweek* about Mr. Faulk, correct?

HARTNETT: That's correct.

NIZER: Did you look at that article before you published Exhibit 41 [the libelous bulletin]?

HARTNETT: No.

NIZER: You say you didn't look for the *Newsweek* article at all, even though you knew there was one?

HARTNETT: I did not know there was one prior to the publication.

NIZER: You did not?

HARTNETT: No sir. . . .

NIZER: Mr. Hartnett, you have a stamp, have you not, which you plant on these file cards on which you keep your records. A stamp?

HARTNETT: A rubber stamp.

NIZER: And that rubber stamp has about thirteen sources that you check off; is that correct?

HARTNETT: I wouldn't be sure there were thirteen, sir, without looking. It varied as more publications were issued.

NIZER: And when you made this card for John Henry Faulk, among the items on the rubber stamp were N.Y.P.L., what does that stand for?

HARTNETT: New York Public Library.

NIZER: Before you wrote Exhibit 41, did you go through all of these rubber stamp sources for information?

HARTNETT: I'd have to look at that, sir, just to make sure. It would be marked if I had.

NIZER: You mean that you would occasionally not even check at all? . . . on those sources which are listed on the rubber stamp?

HARTNETT: I would not always check on all those sources.

NIZER: Then you would never know whether you had turned up everything that was either for or against the man, would you?

BOLAN: I object.

THE COURT: Sustained.

NIZER: You have told us how thoroughly you checked in your practice of checking on a person's record, that you were very thorough and careful, have you not?

HARTNETT: Yes, I would say that I was thorough and careful.

NIZER: And even though you were thorough and careful, you tell us that there were occasions when you would send in a report about the people that you were reporting about, without checking all of the items which you had for sources on this card?

HARTNETT: Yes. . . .

NIZER: Did you go through all the sources which you had placed on your rubber stamp for checking?

HARTNETT: No, not in every case.

NIZER: Therefore, isn't it true that when you handed in these reports, in those instances where you didn't check all, you couldn't be sure that you had given a complete report, could you? That's correct, isn't it?

HARTNETT: As complete as was asked for.

NIZER: As asked for?

HARTNETT: Yes.

NIZER: Do you mean to say, Mr. Hartnett, that when your so-called client asked for a name, that he told you what sources to check?

HARTNETT: No, he didn't tell me.

NIZER: Then he didn't ask you for specific information. He asked you for your report on this man's alleged affiliation, didn't he? Wasn't that the meaning of it?

HARTNETT: Yes, if there were any alleged Communist or Communist-front affiliations.

NIZER: And unless you checked all the sources, you couldn't be sure either that you had all of the alleged Communist-front affiliations or things which were favorable to the man which would negate that. Isn't that so?

HARTNETT: No, I could not be 100 percent sure.

NIZER: But you knew at the time you submitted the report that the man might lose his job, didn't you?

HARTNETT: No, not necessarily at all.

NIZER: You knew that in many instances in which you submitted reports the people lost their jobs, didn't you?

HARTNETT: I don't think that's precisely correct, because they didn't already have a job.

NIZER: You mean they didn't already have a job? Didn't you submit reports on many occasions where the man was trying to get a job and you were giving a report about him? That's right, isn't it?

HARTNETT: No, that's not right.

NIZER: Well, either the man was working or he was trying to get work. One of those two alternatives applied?

HARTNETT: No, I don't think that is correct.

NIZER: When you submitted your report about these people, if the report was adverse, you knew that there was a real likelihood that these people would not get that job on that television show, didn't you?

HARTNETT: If it was really adverse, yes.

NIZER: Yes, and yet when you submitted that report there were occasions when you hadn't even looked all the sources up with respect to these people, did you? Isn't that so? Yes or no to that.

HARTNETT: That's correct.

NIZER: Did you consider it important to find the affirmative things, the good parts of a man's record, as well as any meeting he might have attended, let's say, of a Wallace rally? Didn't you want to know whether he had served in the Army and other things that might be helpful to the patriotic record?

HARTNETT: I certainly did, so much that I spent over 750 hours in the public library checking for such information.

NIZER: Did you go to the New York Public Library with respect to John Faulk before you published Exhibit 41?

HARTNETT: I most certainly did.

NIZER: Did you look up in the public library any publications such as *Newsweek* that had been published about him?

HARTNETT: I initially found no references whatever to *Newsweek*.

NIZER: You say that you found out about *Newsweek* four months after Exhibit 41 was published on February 10, 1956; approximately four months?

HARTNETT: That's my best recollection, four or five months.

NIZER: So that would make it what—March, April, May, June, or July of 1956?

HARTNETT: I would say so.

NIZER: Haven't you testified that the first time you found out about *Newsweek* was in December of 1957?

HARTNETT: I don't recall that, sir.

Lou then read from Hartnett's examination before trial a clear and unequivocal statement that he had first learned about the *Newsweek* article on December 5, 1957. Then he turned back to Hartnett.

NIZER: Did you make that answer?

HARTNETT: Apparently I did, yes.

NIZER: Was it correct when you made it?

HARTNETT: It must have been. I apparently had the document in my hand.

NIZER: Do you take back your answer that you found out
about it four or five months—
BOLAN: Objection.
THE COURT: Sustained.
NIZER: Were you correct when you testified a few moments
ago that you found out about *Newsweek* in June or July
1956?
HARTNETT: Apparently not, no.

Lou then got from Hartnett the admission that he had
checked all the indexes of the House Un-American Activities Committee hearings. He had found my name in only
one place, the sixth edition of the cumulative index of the
HUAC hearings, and it appeared there as John B. Faulk,
which Hartnett characterized as a typographical error or a
garbled version.

NIZER: This reference was to the item of those several hundred names that were supposed to be sponsors of what was
called the United States Sponsors of American Continental Congress for Peace; is that the reference?
HARTNETT: Yes.
NIZER: Did you ever check with any of those several hundred
names as to whether Faulk had attended that Peace
Congress?
HARTNETT: No.
NIZER: Had you ever lifted the telephone or personally talked
to Mr. Faulk and asked him whether he had authorized his
name or attended that conference? Did you do that as a
check?
HARTNETT: No, I did not.

Nizer then got a very interesting admission from Mr.
Hartnett.

NIZER: Weren't you a member of the American Civil Liber-
ties Union under your own name?
HARTNETT: Yes, I had a membership card in the American
Civil Liberties Union.
NIZER: Was that union at a later time cited by the very Cal-
ifornia committee you have been citing in this case a
Communist front?

HARTNETT: Yes, it was cited by the California committee [the Tenney Committee]. . . .

NIZER: . . . Therefore, if you were still publishing *Red Channels*, you would have listed yourself, if you were following regular procedure?

HARTNETT: I would never list anybody for membership in the American Civil Liberties Union. . . .

NIZER: One of the charges, one of the facts, one of the flags you would wave to warn a sponsor is that this man appeared, was a member of a committee condemned by the Un-American Activities Committee, the investigating committee of California called the Tenney Committee?

HARTNETT: I would list it, sir.

NIZER: Therefore, if you prepared such a list, you would list yourself, wouldn't you?

HARTNETT: I was never called upon to bring a report home on myself.

NIZER: If you were preparing such a list, you would list yourself if you were consistent?

HARTNETT: No, because I never listed anyone solely for that one thing. I differ with the Tenney Committee. I don't know if it has characterized the National A.C.L.U., but I wouldn't list anybody merely because of that.

NIZER: If you had only one listing against somebody else, you wouldn't list it at all?

HARTNETT: I don't think I ever did in publication, but I would so state in a report to a client.

Nizer elicited from Hartnett some of the standards he used in listing people.

NIZER: Now, being listed in the index of the House Un-American Activities Committee can be of no significance whatsoever, isn't that so?

HARTNETT: It can be of no significance.

NIZER: As a matter of fact, you testified that President Eisenhower's name is listed, haven't you?

HARTNETT: Former President Eisenhower's name is, I believe, listed in the cumulative index.

NIZER: Isn't it a fact that the House Un-American Activities Committee Index will list the name of anybody that any-

body has testified to, or any letterhead that has been offered with all the names is put into the index; isn't that a
general practice?

HARTNETT: Yes, the general practice is that there is included
in the cumulative index of the House Un-American Ac—
the House Committee on Un-American Activities any reference in published testimony to persons or organizations,
and to names listed on exhibits entered in evidence.

NIZER: Have you not testified that if President Eisenhower
wanted to go on radio or television, since he has become
ex-President, that you would list him on your citation,
that you would list in your report these citations in the
House Un-American Activities Committee?

HARTNETT: Yes.

If we could show and prove that the defendants had attacked my patriotism and loyalty without even believing
their own allegations against me, it would go a long way toward proving malice and establishing the chances of our re-
covering punitive damages from them. Lou set out to do
this.

NIZER: You have testified on direct examination that you
were the author of *Red Channels*, is that correct?

HARTNETT: Co-author.

NIZER: What year was that published in?

HARTNETT: 1950.

NIZER: All of the seven specifications against Mr. John Henry
Faulk are with respect to occasions—right or wrong they
are with respect to occasions that took place before 1950,
aren't they, every one of them?

HARTNETT: Yes, we all know that.

NIZER: And in *Red Channels* you listed the names of a number of television and radio entertainers who you charged
had pro-Communist affiliations, didn't you?

HARTNETT: That's a generally accurate characterization.

NIZER: And nevertheless, you never mentioned John Henry
Faulk in *Red Channels*, did you?

HARTNETT: I did not.

NIZER: In addition to *Red Channels*, you prepared, as you
claimed, a far more comprehensive summary of the al-

leged Communist-front affiliations of actors and entertainers which you called File 13; right?

HARTNETT: . . . I did.

NIZER: Again, prior to that publication of File 13, all the alleged seven specifications against Mr. John Henry Faulk, true or not, all of them preceded File No. 13, that first volume; right?

HARTNETT: That's right.

NIZER: And you never included the name of John Henry Faulk in your comprehensive File 13, did you?

HARTNETT: No. . . .

NIZER: In addition to that File 13, you kept personal notes from your personal file in which you intended to include virtually every entertainer with Communist-front affiliations according to you, didn't you keep such a file?

HARTNETT: Yes.

NIZER: And prior to Exhibit 41, had you ever included Mr. Faulk's name in that file?

HARTNETT: Yes.

NIZER: In your File 13?

HARTNETT: Yes.

BOLAN: I object.

NIZER: All right, let's see if you testify to that [p. 605, Hartnett's examination before trial]. At the bottom: "Q: I believe at one time during this examination, you defined File 13 to include not only the publications you released but your own personal file? A: Yes, I used it as a cover term for all that. Q: Did you have any reference to Mr. Faulk in File 13 which you published in 1951? A: No."
Did you make that answer?

HARTNETT: Yes, I have just so testified.

NIZER: Was it correct when you made it?

HARTNETT: Surely.

NIZER: And you have stated that *Red Channels* was the most comprehensive listing of persons with alleged Communist-front affiliations that had ever been published by a private organization, haven't you?

HARTNETT: . . . Yes.

NIZER: Then you prepared Volume 2 of your File 13, didn't you?

HARTNETT: Yes.

NIZER: And that again listed any actor with an alleged Communist-front affiliation, didn't it? . . .

HARTNETT: No, not any actor.

NIZER: Only some actors?

HARTNETT: I think about ninety in all, performers, directors, producers, writers.

NIZER: And together between Volume 1 of File 13 and Volume 2 of File 13, you were intending to cover all of those that you could file who had, according to you, Communist-front affiliations?

HARTNETT: Oh, no, no.

NIZER: Did the volume have two hundred names in it?

HARTNETT: Give or take ten or twenty, it had two hundred names.

NIZER: Was Mr. Faulk's name listed in that at all?

HARTNETT: No.

NIZER: You have testified that you read at least a large majority of the government's publications having any relation to Communist-front participations, haven't you?

HARTNETT: Of people in the entertainment industry and the literary field, not all fields of endeavor.

NIZER: Mr. Faulk is in that field, of course?

HARTNETT: Yes.

NIZER: You have not seen Mr. Faulk's name mentioned by any witness in those publications, did you?

HARTNETT: Yes, he was mentioned by a witness.

NIZER: The only time he was mentioned after Exhibit 41 was by Mr. Milton who testified that John Henry Faulk brought a suit which you are testifying in now; isn't that the only other reference?

HARTNETT: Yes, that is the reference I had in mind.

NIZER: After the period between 1949 and 1955, six years preceding your writing of Exhibit 41, you yourself attended a number of Communist-front meetings, didn't you?

HARTNETT: Yes.

NIZER: Those meetings were attended by persons in groups who were connected with the radio and television industry, weren't they?

HARTNETT: Yes.

NIZER: The subject matter of some of those meetings was in connection with the radio and television industry?

HARTNETT: Yes.

NIZER: You never saw Mr. Faulk at a single one of those meetings, did you?

HARTNETT: I don't recall that I did. I never knew him.

NIZER: You never heard his name mentioned at any of those meetings, did you?

HARTNETT: I can't recall that I did.

NIZER: Even if Mr. Faulk had attended any of the functions which you referred to in Exhibit 41, he could have done so without the slightest knowledge of the alleged Communist-front nature of the event and been there innocently, correct?

HARTNETT: Well, that would be difficult to concede to the Jefferson School of Social Science.

NIZER: So as to make progress, let us for the moment leave out the Jefferson School, which Mr. Faulk, you know, denies he ever heard of or went to. With the exception of that, take the other six affiliations, affiliated fronts that you say he attended even though there is a dispute about it. Have you not testified that he could have done so without the slightest knowledge of the alleged Communist-front nature of the events that had been there innocently?

HARTNETT: There is so much testimony, Mr. Nizer, I don't recall. I really don't recall it.

NIZER: Which one of the seven items do you say are those that he could have attended innocently even if he had been there? Just give us the ones that you would say, even assuming he had attended, that could have been very innocent, a loyal American going there.

HARTNETT: Club 65. . . . The Independent Citizens Committee of Arts, Sciences and Professions, Year One Salute to the United Nations, Stage for Action, Headline Cabaret. Sending greetings to People's Song on its second anniversary. . . . Showtime for Wallace, contributed cabaret material.

NIZER: The Jefferson School you excluded, that is fixed?

HARTNETT: Yes.

NIZER: And the possible sponsorship, his name on some kind of document of the American Continental Congress for

Peace, or the claim that it was, would you include that as an innocent one possibly?

HARTNETT: It could possibly be.

NIZER: So you have mentioned six out of the seven as being innocent.

HARTNETT: No no, possibly.

NIZER: Possibly innocent. And have you not testified not merely that those were possibly innocent, but that they could have been attended in good faith?

HARTNETT: I can't—

NIZER: Let me read it [Hartnett's examination before trial] so you don't trouble yourself.

HARTNETT: Would you please?

Lou then read from Hartnett's EBT a direct quote of Hartnett saying, "I had no knowledge, I had no evidence to back up a charge that he [Faulk] was a pro-Communist. He might have attended those things in good faith."

NIZER: Did you make that answer?

HARTNETT: Yes.

NIZER: At the time you signed and swore to this testimony, was that still a correct answer?

HARTNETT: Yes. . . .

NIZER: Let me ask you, during the entire time prior to Exhibit 41 and when you wrote it, did you have any authority from any governmental agency to do this kind of work . . . of checking records of alleged Communists affiliations of any artist?

HARTNETT: Was I authorized by any government body? No.

NIZER: You were acting entirely as a private citizen in doing this checking, weren't you?

HARTNETT: In doing this checking, yes.

NIZER: Did you have any authority from the F.B.I. to do the checking that you were doing for these sponsors, associations, television companies, or advertising agencies?

HARTNETT: No.

I was impressed by Hartnett's ability to keep up a front as Nizer carried him through his embarrassing testimony. In spite of the fact that he admitted that he had not found my name in any of the favorite spots in which he looked for subversives, he answered each question precisely and confidently.

I had noticed that, from his first day on the stand, Hartnett would occasionally take a card from his inside pocket and jot down a note on it after looking at the clock on the wall. Eventually it became clear that he was noting the arrival or departure of certain spectators. He continued doing it when Nizer was cross-examining him; yet he did it so unobtrusively that Nizer, who might have been preoccupied with his notes or arguing a point before the judge, didn't notice it. It became obvious, however, that Hartnett was plying his trade right in the witness box—he was writing down the names of actors and actresses who were attending the trial, and he was recording the times at which they came or went. What possible use he could make of this information could only be surmised.

I mentioned this behavior of Hartnett's to Nizer at lunch that day. Later in the afternoon, he began the cross-examination by asking Hartnett about the notes he was making. He asked the question in a tone of voice that would not have been inappropriate had the notes been an execution list. Hartnett's admission that he was writing people's names on his cards brought a gasp from the judge and the jury, who leaned forward and peered at Hartnett as though he had admitted to a monstrous crime. Lou asked no further questions about the cards.

There were times when Hartnett's testimony caused me to become so tense with anger that I would have to take a walk in the corridor to calm myself enough to sit and listen to any more of it. I don't believe my anger was personal; that is, it stemmed not from the fact that I had been the target of Hartnett's calculated plan, but rather from the fact that Hartnett symbolized the poison that had seeped through the entire country from Hollywood to New York. I had had the good luck to be able to do something about him. I knew that there were many hundreds of honorable citizens who had not been so fortunate, and I felt deeply for them.

Lou kept Hartnett's testimony to the matter of whether he had been motivated by malice.

NIZER: Was it your policy, in making these reports or in writing bulletins, to limit yourself to charges which were supported by documents?

HARTNETT: Yes.

NIZER: In how many of these seven charges did you not have in your physical possession the document which is referred to in the charges at the time you wrote Exhibit 41?

HARTNETT: I did not have in my physical possession four or five of the supporting documents.

NIZER: And I call your attention to the middle of that paragraph, "Faulk was reported to have stated that the victorious slate's principal platform was opposition to AWARE and to have said: 'The first interest of a union's officers should be employment of members, not blacklisting them.'"

The only newspaper which is referred to in that item by name is the *Daily Worker*, correct?

HARTNETT: By name, yes.

NIZER: This quote appears there under the beginning of a paragraph which says: "On December 15, the Communist organ," meaning the *Daily Worker*—this quote comes from the *Herald Tribune*, doesn't it?

HARTNETT: Yes it does.

NIZER: And you had the New York *Herald Tribune* in front of you when you wrote those words, didn't you?

HARTNETT: I most likely did, yes.

NIZER: You didn't mention the name of the *Herald Tribune* as a source of that quote, did you?

HARTNETT: No I didn't.

NIZER: And it was your purpose, wasn't it, to give to the reader the impression, when he read in Exhibit 41, that it was the *Daily Worker* to whom Mr. Faulk had said these things which you were quoting, wasn't it?

HARTNETT: Yes.

Paul Martinson had extracted from Hartnett back in 1958, testimony to the effect that he had prepared an original draft of the AWARE bulletin which was much longer than the one mailed out. Paul had managed to get hold of one page of this original draft; it had far more pernicious things to say about me than the one which was actually mailed out, and he had questioned Hartnett about it extensively. Hartnett could only produce the one page at the time of his EBT, claiming that he had destroyed the rest of it.

NIZER: You knew when this suit was instituted, by talking to your attorneys, that one of the questions that would be involved in litigation would be any malice on your part or AWARE's part in preparation of this document; didn't you know that?

HARTNETT: I would say so, yes.

NIZER: You knew that this first draft, which was, and you so testified, about 50 percent longer than the final Exhibit 41, would be an important document in this case, didn't you?

HARTNETT: No I didn't.

NIZER: Did you destroy it because you didn't have any file space?

HARTNETT: I had file space, certainly.

NIZER: Do you testify, sir, no, do I understand you to say that at the time that you destroyed Exhibit 41's first draft, you had no idea that that document might be of importance in this case?

HARTNETT: I didn't think this case would ever even come to trial, sir. I thought it was a publicity stunt.

NIZER: You heard your attorney state that there were many sessions, you tell me, of this examination at which you were examined?

HARTNETT: I believe twenty-three.

NIZER: Twenty-three times that you came down to be examined under oath, is that right?

HARTNETT: That is correct.

NIZER: And you said you didn't think that this case would come to trial?

An objection to this question was sustained, but Nizer pursued the matter.

NIZER: You knew that Mr. Faulk was charging in this suit that he had not one cent from television or radio after the time he left CBS as the result of the Exhibit 41 that you published; that was his position in this suit was it not?

HARTNETT: No, he remained at CBS for over a year after the publication. A year and a half.

NIZER: With the exception of that, didn't you know that his position was that he had been deprived of work in his profession which he had been in for all those years? You knew that was his position in this suit, didn't you?

HARTNETT: I knew that that was—yes, that was his testimony.

NIZER: Yet you testified now that you felt that this suit was a publicity stunt?

HARTNETT: At the time originally filed, yes sir. . . .

NIZER: Did you search on the *Daily Worker* to find out if Faulk was mentioned after 1949 and before 1956?

HARTNETT: No.

NIZER: Didn't you think it was important to find out whether there was any record, according to you, in the *Daily Worker* which would make reference to him during the seven-year period between 1949 and at the time you published Exhibit 41? Didn't you think that was important?

HARTNETT: Yes, but I myself had read the *Daily Worker* for that period.

NIZER: You mean without looking again, just from reading it for seven years, you knew he wasn't in it; is that it?

HARTNETT: At least I had no recollection of any reference to him in it from 1949 to 1956. . . .

NIZER: Did you ever make this statement about Mr. Faulk any place in writing or orally, "that it is no wonder the *Daily Worker* refers to John Henry Faulk because the readers are so familiar with his name." Did you say that in 1955?

HARTNETT: In 1956 . . . I did.

NIZER: And even though his name had not appeared, according to your search, from 1948 to 1956 you thought the readers would recognize his name instantly because they were so familiar with it in the *Daily Worker*, is that it?

HARTNETT: It must have been if I said that before. . . .

NIZER: Even though for eight years, approximately eight years, his name had not appeared in any way according to your search, you think that eight years later readers would have recognized Faulk's name, it would be familiar to them in the *Daily Worker*? Is that right?

HARTNETT: Yes, I got that impression. . . .

NIZER: Did you ever write that AWARE, Inc., had solid control of AFTRA union?

HARTNETT: I don't recollect such a writing, no.

Lou then produced a letter written in the fifties by Vincent Hartnett to a John Dungey. Mr. Dungey was the head of the Onondaga County American Legion; he also was a close friend of Laurence Johnson and a Mr. Neuser, the fruit and vegetable buyer for Johnson supermarket. Mr. Neuser headed the Veteran's Action Committee of Syracuse, which was composed of the veterans in Mr. Johnson's supermarkets. The letter was read by Nizer to the jury.

NIZER [reading]: "Those of us who are on the spot and in a position to know the facts realize that Equity is virtually lost, and that we may well lose our solid control of AFTRA. . . . "That Equity is virtually lost and we may well lose our solid control of AFTRA," and you were writing this to Mr. Dungey of the Syracuse Post in Syracuse, right?

HARTNETT: Yes.

NIZER: And when you said "our solid control," none of the Syracuse groups were members of AFTRA, were they?

HARTNETT: Not to my knowledge, no.

NIZER: And AWARE wasn't, of course, a member of AFTRA was it?

HARTNETT: No. . . .

NIZER: And you weren't a member of AFTRA, were you?

HARTNETT: No.

Hartnett testified that the problem AFTRA had in enforcing its constitutional amendment against Communists was that there were no persons in the union who were proved to be Communists without certain "procedures." He explained what he meant by that:

HARTNETT: The establishment of the Communist Party membership through certain court procedures are by identification by the State Department or by the F.B.I.:

and therefore there had been no such procedure by the government resulting in such an identification of party members. . . .

NIZER: You, of course, approve of those proper procedures to establish that a person is a Communist or a pro-Communist, don't you? . . .

HARTNETT: I think—no, I think they are entirely unrealistic. They don't conform to realities.

NIZER: You think that instead of leaving it to the government and the F.B.I. and the government authorities, that to do that would be very unrealistic; correct?

HARTNETT: Absolutely.

NIZER: And you think that the realistic approach is not to depend upon the government authorities but to have you, for an example, as a so-called consultant, determine who is a Communist; right?

HARTNETT: No, sir, that is not correct.

NIZER: Or to have AWARE, Inc., decide and make recommendations as to who is a Communist?

HARTNETT: No, that's not correct, either.

But Nizer would not let him stop there. He proved that that was exactly what Mr. Hartnett indeed did believe.

NIZER: Did you write to the American Broadcasting Company "in my opinion, finally, you would run a serious risk of adverse public opinion of featuring on your network James Thurber, Kim Hunter, Olive Deering?"

HARTNETT: Yes.

NIZER: When you said to the American Broadcasting Company "you would run a serious risk," did you mean to suggest that they better not hire Mr. James Thurber to appear on the air?

HARTNETT: Yes, I obviously did.

NIZER: Had you gotten in touch with Mr. James Thurber before you wrote this?

BOLAN: I object, your Honor.

THE COURT: Sustained.

NIZER: Did you also know that the general practice of the advertising agencies when they got a report from you was not to tell the artist about that report? You knew that was the general practice in the industry, didn't you?

HARTNETT: Yes, I would say that was the general legal practice . . .

NIZER: Did you not volunteer information to various companies with respect to the alleged record of Mr. Faulk, even though they didn't ask you about Mr. Faulk?

HARTNETT: No, indirectly they did ask me about Mr. Faulk. They asked me about performers who had been on the slate.

NIZER: The sponsor, the company asked you for performers who had been in the Middle-of-the-Road slate? That is not right, is it Mr. Hartnett?

HARTNETT: Yes, as shown by the exhibits. They asked me about performers who in fact had been in the Faulk slate, which was certainly relevant to mention Faulk's record.

NIZER: You show me a letter. Please call for any letter in which the company, Borden's, or Young & Rubicam, or the Kudner Agency, asked for the record of the people who were in the Middle-of-the-Road slate. Please show me that document. Have you got such a one?

Hartnett stirred up three exhibits, letters which he had written to the Young & Rubicam agency and the Kudner Agency and said they were the letters he referred to.

NIZER: You point, and you can read it out loud, to the language that indicates that any one of those companies asked you for a report on anyone who ran in the Middle-of-the-Road slate of AFTRA. Point to any such sentence that would so indicate.

HARTNETT: Yes, my letter of November 27, 1955, to Mr. William D. Thompson of Young & Rubicam. "Since the name of Louise Allbritton was proposed, she has been announced as a candidate on the Independent Ticket of AFTRA, New York Local 4."

NIZER: You were writing that. They didn't ask you whether she was running on any union slate, did they?

HARTNETT: No, they asked me what information I had on her.

NIZER: On Louise Allbritton?

HARTNETT: Yes.

NIZER: And you, giving what you thought was pertinent information, referred to the fact that she was running on the Middle-of-the-Road slate, as a pro-Communist allegation?

HARTNETT: No, not pro-Communist.

NIZER: This you volunteered?

HARTNETT: No, as a matter of fact, she was on the Middle-of-the-Road slate. I can't make it any plainer. . . . That's all I can say. He asked me for any record on Louise Allbritton and this was part of the record.

NIZER: Is it not a fact that no "client" of yours ever said, "Will you please give me the record of some people who ran on the Middle-of-the-Road slate." That is correct, they never did that, did they?

HARTNETT: Put in that form, that is correct, yes. . . .

NIZER: Read the reference to Mr. Faulk that you wrote.

HARTNETT: Yes. "The . . . leader of this ticket, John Henry Faulk, had a significant Communist-front record. I am afraid he is using the liberals."

NIZER: Did they ask you about Mr. Faulk at all in the list of names that they gave you a check? Did they mention the name of Faulk at all?

HARTNETT: Not to my recollection, no. . . .

NIZER: Nevertheless, when you wrote a report as to the people they did ask you to write about, you added the words "John Henry Faulk" and said he had a serious record, didn't you?

HARTNETT: Yes. . . .

NIZER: For each of the names that you submitted these reports on, you received an amount of money, $5, $20, $25, is that right?

HARTNETT: $5, sometimes $20, yes.

NIZER: But in the case of John Henry Faulk, in this case, you volunteered that without any compensation didn't you?

HARTNETT: No, I was compensated for the report on the person who was elected from the Middle-of-the-Road slate. . . .

NIZER: For each name, you were accustomed to receive a separate payment that you made a report on, right?

HARTNETT: Yes.

NIZER: But you did not get any payment for John Henry Faulk that you mentioned in that letter, did you?

HARTNETT: No I wasn't paid for any report on Faulk.

NIZER: You volunteered and threw that in free?

HARTNETT: Mr. Nizer, I can't make it any plainer. That was part of the information on the given subject whose name was proposed to me and for which names I received compensation.

NIZER: My last question is: You volunteered the name of John Henry Faulk and your evaluation of him free; you threw that in free, didn't you?

HARTNETT: I can't say yes to that, Mr. Nizer.

NIZER: Well, you didn't get paid for it did you?

BOLAN: I object.

THE COURT: Overruled.

HARTNETT: I did get paid for information about Faulk.

Lou then had Hartnett testify about a letter that he had written to the Kudner Agency in which he had volunteered the information about me.

NIZER: Did anybody in the Kudner Agency ask you for any opinion or any report about John Henry Faulk?

HARTNETT: Not directly.

NIZER: Did they ask you for it indirectly?

HARTNETT: Yes.

NIZER: How, by asking you about Luis Van Rooten?

HARTNETT: Yes.

NIZER: Did you make a report on Collingwood because they asked you about Van Rooten?

HARTNETT: No that would be extending it a little bit.

NIZER: The only place you would extend it was to John Henry Faulk; correct?

HARTNETT: Yes, he is obviously—he was the only one mentioned. . . .

NIZER: Did you in substance ever write to Mr. Larry Johnson of Syracuse asking him to help in your effort to see that certain artists did not appear on air in view of their records?

HARTNETT: None come to mind, sir.

NIZER: Let me see if I can refresh your recollection. Did you ever ask Mr. Larry Johnson to take action against Franchot Tone?

HARTNETT: I don't know whether I asked him to take action. I remember writing to him about Franchot Tone.

NIZER: Mr. Johnson is not in the theatrical profession, is he?

HARTNETT: No.

NIZER: He was in the grocery business, supermarkets; right?

HARTNETT: Yes.

NIZER: What were you writing to Mr. Laurence Johnson with respect to Mr. Franchot Tone? Will you reconstruct that for us?

HARTNETT: As best I recall, he had probably asked me for a report on Franchot Tone, which I furnished him; and I believe I had made inquiry to see if Franchot Tone had offset his past record, and had been told he had not done so, at least my source of information. Yet, as best I recall, I expressed an opinion that Franchot Tone should do more than—

NIZER: Before he could appear on television?

BOLAN: I object.

NIZER: He should do more before he could appear—he should appear or be allowed to appear on television? Isn't that the substance of it?

HARTNETT: Before he was allowed to appear on television?

NIZER: Yes.

HARTNETT: Could be. I am not sure of that.

NIZER: Could be. Did you ever write to him, "if he refused to take a public stand, then we can take the necessary measures?" Did you ever write that to Laurence Johnson?

HARTNETT: Yes, that sounds right.

NIZER: "We" in that case is you and Laurence Johnson, right?

HARTNETT: It would seem so. . . .

NIZER: So you asked groups, various individuals to write protests to try to get people off the air that in your opinion had pro-Communist affiliation; right?

HARTNETT: Yes, I did.

Lou then took Hartnett's examination before trial from the session of June 17, 1958, when Godfrey Schmidt was still acting as attorney for the defendants. Schmidt had stated that AWARE never intended to charge me with subversion.

NIZER: I read to you from page 553 of your examination before trial "Q: Mr. Hartnett, so you don't think I misunderstand, let me repeat what your counsel has said and I will put it in the form of a question to you so you can state it on the record. As I understand your position, you never charged Mr. Faulk with being a Communist; is that right? That is what your counsel is saying. A: Yes. Q: You adopt that, don't you? A: Yes. Q: And you had never charged him with being pro-Communist sympathizer; you never charged him with that? A: I was once sold a barrel of false information."
Did you make those statements to those questions?

HARTNETT: Yes, later corrected.

NIZER: What was that?

HARTNETT: Later, I believe later there was a correction on that.

NIZER: When you testified on June 17, 1958, you made those answers under oath, didn't you?

HARTNETT: I did.

NIZER: And when you said that you were once sold a barrel of misinformation, whom were you referring to as having sold you the barrel of misinformation?

HARTNETT: The anonymous informer, Mr. Adams.

NIZER: You are, of course, an investigator, aren't you?

HARTNETT: A researcher, research consultant.

NIZER: You consider yourself a competent researcher, don't you?

HARTNETT: I have made—language to that effect, yes. . . .

Nizer then took Hartnett's EBT and read further from his testimony of June 17, 1958.

NIZER [reading from Hartnett's EBT]: "Q: Aside from the fact that you say you were sold false information about him, you don't charge him with being a Communist today? A: No sir."

If there ever was such a charge, you would know it was false?

HARTNETT: I do.

NIZER: Did you make that answer?

HARTNETT: I did, later corrected.

NIZER: Did you make that answer—first answer my question—in 1958?

HARTNETT: Yes.

NIZER: At the time you gave these answers in 1958, did you feel that John Henry Faulk should be free to obtain employment?

HARTNETT: Yes, I did.

NIZER: Did you in answer to a question by me agree to send out a letter stating that he was a good and loyal American, had no pro-Communist affiliation at all, and therefore, that you had been in error in asserting these things in Exhibit 41? Had you agreed to that in substance?

HARTNETT: In substance, yes, without the addition of the phrase "in error."

NIZER: And had Mr. Schmidt, before Roy Cohn replaced him, had Mr. Schmidt agreed as the president of AWARE, Inc., to send out on behalf of AWARE, Inc., a letter to any sponsor or advertising agency or anyone else that I would select stating that this had all been a barrel of false information?

HARTNETT: No, there is no reference again to any false information. He agreed—Mr. Schmidt did agree to send out some—to the issuance of letters of that nature.

THE COURT: Issuance of letters of that nature without this expression of—

HARTNETT: Yes, without acknowledging any false information.

NIZER: But acknowledging that, so far as you and AWARE were concerned, he was a good and loyal American and ought to be employed without any besmirching of his loyalty by reference to alleged pro-Communist affiliations; that in substance was agreed to?

HARTNETT: Well, again you are adding language to it which I don't believe was there, but it was in substance.

NIZER: Yes, and then it was a short time—how long after that was Mr. Schmidt replaced by Mr. Roy Cohn as counsel?

HARTNETT: Well, somewhere between one and three months.

. . .

NIZER: It was after Mr. Roy Cohn was substituted as counsel for Mr. Schmidt that you changed your position that you have given us in substance; is that right?

HARTNETT: I don't recall whether it was after that or not, sir. I may have changed it personally before.

Hartnett never testified as to why he had changed his mind and withdrawn his offer.

I was aware, back in 1958, when I received a subpoena from the House Un-American Activities Committee, that Hartnett consulted with members of their staff frequently. But I did not know that he had sought to interest the House Un-American Activities Committee in me long before that.

NIZER: . . . didn't you in November 1955, about two months before you published Exhibit 41, write to the chief clerk of the House Committee on Un-American Activities about Mr. Faulk?

HARTNETT: I did.

NIZER: You wrote that letter when you knew that Mr. Faulk was running on the Middle-of-the-Road slate and the campaign for the election was going on, didn't you?

HARTNETT: Yes, I did. . . .

NIZER: Mr. Beal didn't ask you for information about Mr. Faulk, did he?

HARTNETT: He did not.

NIZER: He didn't ask you for information concerning the candidates running in the AFTRA union, did he?

HARTNETT: He did not. . . .

NIZER: You stated to Mr. Beal that Mr. Faulk was listed as— and I am quoting—"was listed as a member of the Radio Division of the Progressive Citizens of America." You wrote that to the House Un-American Activities Committee in November 1955, didn't you?

HARTNETT: I did.

NIZER: That was an incorrect statement, wasn't it? Mr. Faulk was not listed as a member of the radio Division of the Progressive Citizens of America, was he, to your knowledge?

HARTNETT: I believe it was my information that he was.

Lou then took Hartnett's EBT in 1958 and read the questions and answers from it:

NIZER [reading EBT]: "Q: Did you make any inquiry as to whether he was a member of the Radio Division of the Progressive Citizens of America? A: I don't believe so. . . . Q: But you just made no attempt either way to verify that, is that right? A: It is one of those things that would be almost impossible to verify. I don't have access to the membership list of either organization. Both of them are defunct long since. . . . Q: Did you at any time know any other people who were members of the Radio Division of either of those organizations? A: Yes I think I have. Q: I take it you made no attempt to ask them whether Mr. Faulk had been affiliated. A: No I don't believe I did."

Then I heard for the first time, from Hartnett's lips, what had happened when I had been called for a job at the Mutual Broadcasting Company, late in 1957.

NIZER: After Mr. Faulk was let out of Columbia Broadcasting System, you knew he was trying to get other jobs, didn't you?

HARTNETT: The only one that comes to mind is I knew that someone had made application to Mutual Broadcasting System of offering a job there or seeking a job for him.

NIZER: And you talked to an executive of the Mutual Broadcasting System then, didn't you?

HARTNETT: Call him an executive. It amounts to that, yes.

NIZER: Did you discuss Mr. Faulk's background . . . with that gentleman? What was his name, incidentally?

HARTNETT: Mr. Pat Winkler.

NIZER: Yes, of WOR Mutual Broadcasting Company, . . . and he told you that they were considering Mr. Faulk for a job on their network; correct in substance?

HARTNETT: No. . . . Where, he said that, as I recall, someone was trying to sell Mr. Faulk to the network, not that they were considering him.

NIZER: By someone, you mean an agent of some kind?

HARTNETT: That's right, yes.

NIZER: And that they were considering him for that job?

HARTNETT: Words to that effect, yes.

NIZER: Then do you recall that the statement by Mr. Winkler was: "We are considering hiring him;" is that right?

HARTNETT: I don't recall, but it would amount to that.

NIZER: . . . did you tell him that he had a pro-Communist affiliation record?

HARTNETT: A record of affiliation with pro-Communist groups, yes.

NIZER: You said that some agent or somebody was trying to sell him. I read to you from your testimony on your examination before trial, page 1337: Q: What did Mr. Winkler say to you? A: He said that somebody from the network proposed hiring Mr. Faulk."

NIZER: Do you recall making that answer?

HARTNETT: Yes, I do now, yes.

NIZER: Do you want to correct the impression that it was somebody trying to sell him; it was the network that was proposing to Mr. Winkler that he be hired; right?

HARTNETT: Probably both, probably both an agent and the network, yes.

The newspapers followed the case very closely. However, there was a significant bit of testimony which the newspapers never reported; it concerned Hartnett's relations with the New York City Police Department. As far as I know, no one ever followed through on it. It came about during Hartnett's cross-examination.

NIZER: In January 1956, did you advise any member of the police department about the charges that you had made in Exhibit 41 against Mr. Faulk?

HARTNETT: At about that period of time I did convey information I had about Mr. Faulk to the police department.

NIZER: Did you call up a member of the Police Department

of the City of New York to tell him you had information for him about Mr. Faulk?

HARTNETT: To my best recollection . . . it's not too clear, but I think I did tell him certain information I had about Mr. Faulk, yes.

NIZER: They hadn't asked you for any information about Mr. Faulk, had they?

HARTNETT: No.

NIZER: You are not a member of the police department?

HARTNETT: No.

NIZER: You have no association of any official kind with the city of New York, have you?

HARTNETT: No.

NIZER: Or did you have at that time, in January of 1956, any association with the police department or any other department in any official capacity?

HARTNETT: Not official; unofficial.

NIZER: Unofficial?

HARTNETT: Surely.

NIZER: With the Police Department of the City of New York?

HARTNETT: Yes.

NIZER: What was your capacity?

HARTNETT: Well, I furnished—frequently furnished them with information, the F.B.I., many agencies.

NIZER: I didn't ask you about the F.B.I. I move to strike that out.

THE COURT: Strike that out. And do I understand by furnishing information, you feel that you were unofficially connected with the police department?

HARTNETT: I think that's a connection, your Honor, yes.

THE COURT: That is a connection, but it is unofficial, you would say?

HARTNETT: Yes, I mean it was no official relationship.

THE COURT: You mean anybody that gives information to the police department is unofficially connected with the police department? Is that what you are saying?

HARTNETT: I would suppose it is a connection your Honor. I am trying to answer that the best I can.

NIZER: Did you have any crime report with respect to Mr. Faulk?

HARTNETT: No.

NIZER: Did you ask the police department if they had anything about Mr. Faulk and to tell you?

HARTNETT: Yes.

NIZER: You did?

HARTNETT: Yes.

NIZER: Whom did you talk to?

HARTNETT: Lieutenant Crain.

NIZER: What is the full name, please?

HARTNETT: Thomas F. Crain.

NIZER: And when you called Lieutenant Crain, you told him
of what you claimed were the past Communist-front affiliations of Mr. Faulk; is that right?

HARTNETT: As best I recall, yes.

NIZER: Did you tell Lieutenant Crain anything about the
AFTRA election in the union and the Middle-of-the-Road
slate? Did you tell him about that controversy?

HARTNETT: I believe I did make reference to that, yes, to the
election in AFTRA.

NIZER: You thought the fact that Mr. Faulk had been elected
on the Middle-of-the-Road slate of the union was a subject
for you to advise the Police Department of the City of
New York; is that right?

[Objection sustained]

NIZER: Did you ask him for any information that he might
have against . . . about Mr. Faulk so that you could use it
in connection with the AFTRA controversy?

HARTNETT: Well, I asked him about it, and I did intend to use
it in connection with the AFTRA controversy, yes. . . .

NIZER: You told Lieutenant Crain of the Police Department
of the City of New York that the Middle-of-the-Road slate
was helping Communism, didn't you?

HARTNETT: I don't recall saying that they were helping Communism. Did I so testify? I don't recall it, sir.

Nizer then read the following question and answer from
Hartnett's examination before trial.

NIZER: "Q: Did you say anything to the effect that the Middle-of-the-Road slate was helping Communism? A: Yes I
think I did."

So that was what you told Lieutenant Crain, that the

Middle-of-the-Road slate was helping Communism, right. You explained that to him?

HARTNETT: Apparently so, yes. . . .

NIZER: You have claimed, have you not, that Inspector Robb of the police department gave an authorization to give or receive information of the pertinent public nature to and from AWARE?

HARTNETT: Yes, that was my understanding.

NIZER: And was it your understanding that the Police Department of the City of New York had the right or duty to give this information if it had any?

HARTNETT: They had the right.

NIZER: They had the right?

HARTNETT: Yes.

NIZER: On what did you base that understanding that they had such a right?

HARTNETT: I can't say on what I based it. I just felt that they had.

NIZER: You claimed that such an understanding was had with Mr. Milton who testified here previously, of AWARE, with Inspector Robb; is that your position under oath?

HARTNETT: That such an understanding was had with . . . Inspector Robb . . .

NIZER: Concerning Inspector Robb's authorization to talk to you and give you information or receive information; that that was an arrangement made with Mr. Milton, the witness who testified here?

HARTNETT: I believe so, yes.

NIZER: Don't you know that Mr. Milton under oath has denied that?

HARTNETT: I don't know that he did. . . .

NIZER: How many times do you say you talked to Lieutenant Crain about artists trying to get information from the Police Department of the City of New York?

HARTNETT: . . . about seventy.

NIZER: And you initiated all those seventy conversations; Lieutenant Crain didn't call you, you called him in every instance on your own?

HARTNETT: Or in virtually all instances, yes. . . .

NIZER: So you initiated calls about artists on television and radio, and you claim that Lieutenant Crain of the police department gave you, as a private citizen, information about those artists on thirty occasions; is that correct?

HARTNETT: Yes that is my testimony. . . .

NIZER: Don't you know, Mr. Hartnett, that Mr. Milton has contradicted your entire story that there was any understanding or arrangement with Inspector Robb in this matter?

BOLAN: Your Honor, I object to that statement.

THE COURT: Sustained.

Whereupon Lou took Milton's examination before trial and read from it on exactly this subject.

NIZER [reading from Milton's EBT]: "A: As to the . . . part of AWARE getting information from the police department, I doubt very much if we had asked for and certainly would have no right to expect it. Q: On what do you base that conclusion? A: Simply that the average citizen is not in a position to demand information from the police files, as I understand it. AWARE never did receive any information from that source."

Lou then looked steadily at Mr. Hartnett and continued.

NIZER: Now I ask you having read that testimony from Mr. Milton, do you still say that Mr. Milton made this arrangement with Inspector Robb for you to get this information? [Objection sustained]

Lou tried again. He wasn't about to give up this plum.

NIZER: Do you say in this court that it was Mr. Milton who sat with Inspector Robb and made an arrangement with the police department of New York to exchange information with you?

HARTNETT: It was my understanding that there was such a luncheon with Godfrey Schmidt and Paul Milton and with Inspector Robb, and that certain authorization was given. That was my understanding, sir.

NIZER: After this examination before trial at which this police department matter came up, you had a conversation with the police department, didn't you?

HARTNETT: I believe after that or some time around that particular examination, yes.

NIZER: And don't you know that Commissioner Stephen Kennedy called in Inspector Robb to ask whether there was any truth to your statements in this matter? Weren't you informed of that?

BOLAN: Your Honor, I submit this is highly—

THE COURT: Sustained and strike it out, the jury will draw no inferences from that question.

Lou was forced to drop this line of questioning and turn to the association between Johnson and Hartnett, a close, harmonious, and congenial relationship, during which they frequently exchanged information on artists and performers, as well as compliments on each other's fine character. The information they exchanged was rather detailed and they went to some lengths to obtain it; on one occasion Hartnett wrote to Johnson that he had called Jack Wren, an advertising executive in charge of artist clearance, about a woman in a crowd scene on a Robert Montgomery television show.

NIZER: And the woman in the crowd scene, just a person in a crowd scene, you protested against because you felt she had a Communist-front affiliation?

Whether Hartnett could remember his testimony on this matter or not wasn't important, but Lou took his examination before trial and read from Hartnett's EBT:

NIZER: "Q: You would go after them if they were in crowd scenes, even though they didn't take any speaking parts? A: If they were Communist Party members, someone with a significant party record, and if they were in a crowd scene, yes, I would consider that of importance."

Lou asked Hartnett about a magazine article he had written back in the early fifties for the *American Legion Magazine* which was critical of the Borden Company for hiring Communist-front entertainers on their program.

HARTNETT: I did write an article for the *American Legion Magazine* in which I was critical of the past employment practices of the Borden Company.

NIZER: And that article, before it was published, was brought to the attention of the Borden Company, wasn't it?

HARTNETT: No. I don't think it was.

NIZER: You had a conference with the Borden Company before that article was published, didn't you?

HARTNETT: I did. . . .

NIZER: And you were hired by the Borden Company before that article in which you criticized the Borden Company was published, weren't you?

HARTNETT: I was.

NIZER: Then the article came out thereafter and praised the Borden Company, didn't it?

HARTNETT: Both criticized and praised, I would say.

NIZER: By criticized, you mean they had once had not so good a record, but now they were very patriotic?

HARTNETT: It told the facts about the past infiltration and praised the Borden Company for taking measures.

NIZER: The measure which you praised that they had taken was that they had hired you: correct?

HARTNETT: No, that they had instituted their own policies. Part of this was retaining me. . . .

NIZER: In 1955 didn't you get $10,000 from the Borden Company? Didn't you receive that?

HARTNETT: I did.

NIZER: That was for your checking work, your so-called screening and security work?

HARTNETT: That is correct.

An aspect of Johnson and Hartnett's cooperation, which up to this point had not been explored, was now taken up.

NIZER: Mr. Laurence Johnson, you have told us, was close to Mr. Stuart Peabody of Borden, wasn't he? . . .

HARTNETT: Yes, I so testified in the EBT. . . .

NIZER: And didn't Mr. Laurence Johnson have something to do with your being engaged by the Borden Company?

HARTNETT: I have recently learned, he did.

NIZER: How recently did you learn that?

HARTNETT: I would say three, four weeks ago. . . .

NIZER: Didn't you know that approximately the time that this incident occurred, that Mr. Johnson had a meeting with Mr. Peabody just prior to your being retained by the Borden Company?

HARTNETT: He had had a meeting with Mr. Peabody shortly before, yes. . . .

NIZER: You say that you found out only three weeks ago that Mr. Johnson had helped get you that job at Borden's?

HARTNETT: Three or four weeks ago, yes, sir.

NIZER: By talking with Mr. Johnson?

HARTNETT: No sir.

NIZER: Who have you talked with? Just mention the name of the person.

HARTNETT: Mr. William B. Campbell of the Borden Company.

NIZER: And prior to three weeks ago, he had never told you that Mr. Johnson had visited him to hire you as a consultant?

HARTNETT: That is correct.

NIZER: Did you ask him about that fact three weeks ago?

HARTNETT: No sir.

NIZER: Are you still retained by Borden's?

HARTNETT: I am not.

NIZER: You went up to see Mr. Campbell of that company three weeks ago?

HARTNETT: No, I did not go to see him. He telephoned me.

NIZER: To tell you that Mr. Johnson had helped you in getting that job?

[Objection sustained]

NIZER: Mr. Laurence Johnson had also criticized the casting of Borden's "Treasury Men in Action" program before you were hired, hadn't he?

HARTNETT: Yes, I recall he did. . . .

NIZER: And after you were retained by the Borden Company, the protest of the Syracuse Post of the American Legion, the Veterans' Action Committee, and Mr. Johnson, in regard to the "Treasury Men in Action" stopped, didn't they?

HARTNETT: Yes, I think they surely must have.

NIZER: Did Mr. Johnson and the Syracuse groups, to your

knowledge, know that you had been retained by the Borden Company? . . .

HARTNETT: Some time not long after that, they did, yes.

On the final day of Hartnett's cross-examination—that is, Tuesday, June 19—the judge announced that the forelady of the jury, Miss Tindale, was ill and that her doctor said that she could not return to the trial. By the drawing of a slip from the jury drum, the alternate Ralph Rosenfeld was chosen to take her place, he became foreman.

I didn't think that Nizer could come up with anything on Hartnett that would prove any more embarrassing or contradictory than the matters that he had already gone over in the past week. But on that last day he found more.

NIZER: Did you hold yourself forth as an independent producer, a radio and television producer in 1950?

HARTNETT: That was the field I was in, sir, yes.

NIZER: What program did you ever produce as an independent radio producer? Can you mention one?

HARTNETT: No sir. The show actually did not sell. It was scheduled to go on the air on ABC Television. At the last minute it was canceled.

NIZER: Incidentally, you described your association with Phillips H. Lord as what? What did you testify you were at Phillips H. Lord?

HARTNETT: I was an assistant to the executive producer, John O. Ives, and supervisor of "Gang Busters" program.

NIZER: Supervisor? Weren't you just script man, hired for $100? Wasn't that your duty at that place?

HARTNETT: No sir, I was the supervisor. . . . I was the supervisor as I have evidence to prove, and I was not at $100.

NIZER: What was your salary at Phillips H. Lord?

HARTNETT: My salary when I left was $150 a week.

NIZER: Wasn't your salary at Phillips H. Lord no more than $110 a week, sir?

HARTNETT: No sir, my top salary was $150.

NIZER: Did you ever write an article under an assumed name of Foreman?

HARTNETT: I did.

NIZER: And did you in that article claim that *Red Channels* was a blacklist, that it was so charged by various people as a blacklist?

HARTNETT: Not in that language, sir. I wrote that some critics had assailed it as a blacklist.

NIZER: And then did you praise, under the name of Foreman, a man by the name of Vincent Hartnett?

HARTNETT: Whether I praised him or not, sir, I don't recall.

NIZER: Under the name of Foreman, you were referring to Vincent Hartnett as a fine man who was doing a good service on *Red Channels*, didn't you, in substance?

HARTNETT: Sir, I don't recall that is so.

NIZER: Do you recall that there was a group in AFTRA that met at the Blue Ribbon Restaurant to hold a meeting?

HARTNETT: Not a group in AFTRA as such, no. It included members of AFTRA. . . .

NIZER: You attended that meeting without telling them who you were, and carried this hidden microphone to record it, didn't you?

HARTNETT: I did.

Hartnett then testified that he gave excerpts from the secret recording he made to various people including members of AWARE and to some of his clients.

NIZER: Did you have a detective license that authorized you to carry hidden microphones in your holster?

[Objection sustained]

NIZER: Did you have any license at all as private detective?

HARTNETT: No. . . .

The weather grew warmer as June progressed, and the courtroom became uncomfortable. The huge fans which had been put in to cool off the jury were inadequate. Justice Geller made some pointed remarks about the lack of modern facilities in the courtroom. He also urged Nizer to cut short his cross-examination. Lou wanted to cooperate, but there was still a great deal of important material to be gone over with Hartnett. One night, however, he said that he felt we were taking advantage of the court's patience; perhaps we should bring the cross-examination to a halt. I looked at Paul and George and the voluminous material they had worked up, which was still unused. After a discussion of the matter, they agreed with Lou.

Nizer turned Hartnett back to Bolan. Bolan, anxious to repair some of the harm done on the cross-examination, went through a hopeless redirect examination. He made one telling mistake. Realizing that Nizer's question, several days before, about Hartnett's taking down the names of persons coming into the courtroom had left Hartnett in a bad light, Bolan sought to turn it to the defendant's advantage by asking Hartnett whose names he was writing down. Nizer objected strenuously to this, but he was overruled. After all, as Justice Geller pointed out, Nizer himself had opened the door to this line of questioning by asking Hartnett about the matter. He directed Hartnett to proceed with his answer. Hartnett promptly replied that he was noting the presence of actors who came into court—"like Eliot Sullivan, who was sitting next to Mrs. Faulk; John Randolph; Alan Manson; Jack Gilford." Bolan asked if some of them had refused to answer questions before HUAC? They had. He had made his point. They were associated with me; my wife sat next to them.

Nizer on his recross-examination of Hartnett, a little later, backed off across the room, and his voice took on a sarcastic tone as he addressed Mr. Hartnett.

NIZER: You have testified that Eliot Sullivan sat down next to Mrs. Faulk. Do you see Mrs. Faulk in the courtroom now?

Spectators, judge, jury, and reporters, all leaned forward expectantly as Hartnett frantically scanned the rows of spectators. At length he pointed out a woman.

HARTNETT: I believe she is the lady over here. I am not sure.

Nizer turned dramatically to the woman spectator and asked her name. The woman stood up and said, "My name is Helen Soffer. S-O-F-F-E-R."

Pandemonium broke out. Even Judge Geller could not escape the emotional impact of Hartnett's blunder. Lou waited for a lull and then in a searing voice addressed the defendant.

NIZER: Sir, is that an example of the accuracy with which you have identified your victims for the past ten years?"

Hartnett mumbled something to the effect that John Sibley, a reporter for the *New York Times*, who was present in court, had pointed out the lady to him as Mrs. Faulk. By this time, however, no explanation that Hartnett could give would in any way have gotten him off the hook.

Bolan announced a short time later that Mr. Hartnett was excused from the stand.

24

During the whole course of the trial, I had been worrying about CBS and what its role would be. Would its representatives testify in behalf of the defendants? Of course, if they were subpoenaed, they would have to take the stand. Lou had pointed out, however, that if CBS was firm enough with the defendants' attorneys, no one would be subpoenaed; it would be too risky. Lou had a strong conviction that it was never wise to subpoena a hostile witness.

I found out soon enough what their role was, however. One morning when I walked into the courthouse, I saw Carl Ward and another gentleman, who turned out to be a CBS attorney, standing in the corridor outside the courtroom. As I went in to take my place at the counsel table, Lou told me, "Ward is here and is going to testify all right—for the defendants." I felt a sudden resentment toward Ward, but I realized it was unjustified. He had not come willingly. He had been subpoenaed. I could tell from his expression that he did not particularly relish the role he was playing.

On the stand, Ward was the very model of a Madison Avenue executive. He was neatly dressed, and he had the air of complete detachment from the goings on in the court. In answer to Bolan's question, he said that he was now vice-president and director of affiliate relations for CBS television network. He had been general manager of station WCBS from 1951 until April 1957. Bolan had obviously brought him in to prove that my position at CBS had been shaky back in 1955, long before the defendants' attack on me. Ward testified that he had had discussions of my sagging ratings in February of 1955 and that he had discussed with my agent the possibility that I might be let out at WCBS. However, my ratings had gone up and I had been kept on. It was obvious that he was doing his best to be completely neutral in the case; he neither wanted to do me harm nor to be helpful to me.

Things picked up considerably when his cross-examination started. Although he was the defendants' witness, Lou made him sound as if were ours.

NIZER: Did you consider his [Faulk's] personality unique?
WARD: Yes, sir, I did.
NIZER: And very effective as a professional performer?
WARD: I do.
NIZER: You did at that time, too, did you not, Mr. Ward?
WARD: I felt that Mr. Faulk, by virtue of being an unusual personality, represented an opportunity for the station to develop some unusual audience attraction and radio following.

Lou then, to Bolan's obvious dismay and over his vigorous objection, introduced a whole batch of promotional material that CBS had sent out on me.

NIZER: Did WCBS, when you were general manager, attempt, in accordance with good management of a radio station, attempt to exploit Mr. Faulk's personality by issuing special folders featuring Mr. Faulk? I show you Exhibit 17 in evidence and ask you if you recognize that as one of the folders issued by WCBS with respect to Mr. Faulk's skills as a salesman of goods.

WARD: Yes sir.
NIZER: As a promotion for this artist, I show you also Exhibit 15 some twenty-one sheets which are in evidence. . . . I would like to hold this up for a second so that jury will see what it is I showed them.

I was keeping my fingers crossed, hoping against hope that Ward would give a clear and unequivocal account of our April 1956 conferences, at which he told me that Laurence Johnson was in town knocking my sponsors off. He had, at that time, asked me to give the affidavit which I had presented, and I wanted the jury to be very clear on exactly what had happened. His memory of those conferences was, alas, rather hazy.

It turned out that Ward could remember after a while that it was Libby's who had canceled their time on my program.

Then he couldn't remember whether he had sent my affidavit to any specific agencies or sponsors in an effort to offset Johnson's attack on me. However, when Lou presented him with a letter that he had written himself to Young & Rubicam agency in June 1956, his memory was refreshed again.

NIZER: Did you send, over your own signature, at any time in June 1956, this affidavit, defendant's Exhibit 20, to any leading agency?

WARD: On the basis of what I have just seen, yes.

It was Bolan, after Lou had completed Ward's cross-examination, who on redirect got from Ward the most definitive statement of CBS's—indeed the industry's—position on the matter of performers who were under attack:

BOLAN: If the sponsors had reacted negatively or had reacted against Mr. Faulk as a result of these statements you referred to, and canceled Mr. Faulk's spots with them, would CBS nevertheless have continued with Mr. Faulk?

WARD: If commercial sponsorship on the program had dropped below a certain level—I wouldn't know what they would be—but below a certain level his commercial value to us would have ended.

BOLAN: In other words the primary consideration with CBS was the commercial value of Mr. Faulk on CBS?

WARD: That would have been a factor, yes.

Ward left the stand looking as proper and unruffled as when he first got on it. He nodded curtly to me and departed from the courtroom along with several CBS lawyers.

During a recess I saw Sam Slate, flanked by two CBS attorneys, in the corridor outside the courtroom. He, like Ward, seemed to have little enthusiasm for the business at hand.

Sam was sworn in and took his seat on the witness stand. Bolan was not long in getting to the reason for having Sam as a witness. He wanted Sam to give the official CBS reasons for firing me. Sam testified that he had had a conversation with me in July of 1957.

BOLAN: Will you tell us what that discussion was, what you said to Mr. Faulk and what he said to you?

SLATE: To the best of my recollection, I had a conversation with Mr. Faulk that went something like this. I told Mr. Faulk that we were faced with a number of problems at the station which meant that we would unfortunately have to not renew his thirteen-week option on his contract. These—if you want me to explain what those problems were?
BOLAN: Yes.
NIZER: I object.
THE COURT: No, we want the conversation.
BOLAN: Did you discuss what those problems were with Mr. Faulk?
SLATE: To the best of my recollection, I did.
BOLAN: Will you tell us what you said?
SLATE: Yes. I told Mr. Faulk that we had a network commercial coming on at five o'clock, which automatically reduced the Faulk program, which was from five to six, to a half hour. We had also had some problems in the afternoon between the four and six period with a slight or gradual decline in the audience. . . . Well, as well as I remember, I simply told Mr. Faulk because of a number of changes that we were making in the program schedule, we would not be in a position to continue his services, and this is the gist of the conversation, to the best of my recollection.

Sam then testified that one of the factors that was responsible for my dismissal was my drop in ratings.

SLATE: The factors that we considered which led to a change in the afternoon programming, which included the Faulk show, showed a gradual decline in audience for the four-to-six period in 1957, roughly starting in January, and a slow decline the rest of the nine-month period, I believe.

BOLAN: Did you give Mr. Faulk all of the reasons why CBS decided to let him go?
SLATE: To the best of my recollection, yes.

Then Nizer rose to start his cross-examination.

Lou didn't start on the subject of my firing, however; he started on the meeting in April 1956, in Carl Ward's office, concerning Laurence Johnson's attack on me. Lou asked him to tell about the meeting.

SLATE: Mr. Nizer, to the best of my recollection, Mr. Ward talked to Mr. Faulk about this "AWARE" bulletin and asked him certain questions about it, and Mr. Faulk denied some of the allegations that were in the bulletins; and out of this conference came the affidavit that Mr. Faulk gave to WCBS.

NIZER: Was there a discussion with respect to the impact upon CBS in any way with respect to Exhibit 41? Was there any such discussion?

SLATE: Yes, there was a discussion at that time and we expressed concern about what might be the effect of this bulletin.

Lou then asked him if he could explain or remember what was said in general about the effect on CBS.

SLATE: Well, the substance of the conversation was that we had no way of knowing at this time what effect it might have on the commercial sponsorship of the Faulk show, and as I remember, I believe that Mr. Ward felt that if we lost a great number of sponsors, why then we'd have to take a good hard look at the show again to determine whether we would continue it or not.

Sam's memory seemed to be considerably clearer than Carl Ward's on the matter of Laurence Johnson's participation in my sponsors' affairs back in April 1956.

NIZER: At any of these conferences or talks, at any of these talks preceding or around this period on this subject matter, were the names of any outside persons mentioned who were making these accusations?

SLATE: The name that I remember is Mr. Johnson?

NIZER: Is that Laurence Johnson of Syracuse?

SLATE: I believe that's correct, Mr. Nizer.

NIZER: What was said about Mr. Laurence Johnson at any of these talks, the substance of it?

SLATE: The report that we had was that Mr. Johnson was making certain allegations against Mr. Faulk as in this bulletin, and also that he, I believe, was instrumental in having letters written to agencies and advertisers who were operating on the Faulk show.

NIZER: Did the jury hear that?

THE COURT: I am going to let this witness stand, but you must promise that you are going to speak louder. Stand up if it's going to make you speak louder.

SLATE: I will do my best.

And from that point on, Sam testified standing up, the first witness to have done so. At first Sam didn't seem to remember Tom Murray very well.

NIZER: Do you recall a gentleman by the name of Tom Murray bringing a letter to you from a sponsor who was on CBS?

SLATE: Yes, I have a vague recollection of that.

NIZER: Is Tom Murray—perhaps this is leading, but with your Honor's permission—associated with the Grey agency? Does that bring it back to you, sir?

SLATE: I don't know, Mr. Nizer.

NIZER: Did Mr. Murray represent the Hoffman division of the Pabst Blue Ribbon Beer? Does that come back to you?

SLATE: At the time, he did.

NIZER: At the time, I would like to show this to you, Mr. Slate, so that it can refresh your recollection.

Lou thereupon handed to Sam a copy of the letter that had been written to the president of the Pabst Brewing Company and passed on to Tom Murray for action. Sam said that he recalled seeing the letter.

NIZER: As to the letter that you do remember, which is Exhibit 35, that was a sponsor on the Faulk show wasn't it?

SLATE: I believe that's correct.

NIZER: Then Mr. Murray was the agency's representative of that show. Do you recall that now?

SLATE: That is correct.

NIZER: What did he [Murray] say to you on that occasion, in substance?

SLATE: Mr. Murray expressed concern about this type of letter and frankly was . . . He wanted to know what CBS's position would be on it.

NIZER: What did you tell him? If you recall?

SLATE: I told him, as I recall, I told him I'd let him know.

NIZER: Did you have any doubt personally about Mr. Faulk's loyalty and patriotism at this time?

SLATE: No, sir.

NIZER: Was there anything said about Mr. Johnson making the rounds of Madison Avenue, in substance? . . . By any of the salesmen giving information.

SLATE: Salesmen said or reported that Mr. Johnson was calling—to use their expression—the agencies all up and down Madison Avenue.

NIZER: Was that about Mr. Faulk?

SLATE: About Mr. Faulk.

NIZER: Were any steps taken in order to strengthen the position of CBS with respect to this problem you have described?

SLATE: The step taken was the affidavit in which Mr. Faulk denied the allegations in these two documents, Mr. Nizer. . . .

NIZER: What was done with this affidavit after it was prepared?

SLATE: Mr. Nizer, directly I don't know.

NIZER: I don't mean directly. Was it given to the salesmen?

SLATE: I believe it was, Mr. Nizer.

NIZER: And it was given to the salesmen with what instructions, sir, generally?

SLATE: To my recollection, the general instructions were to use this letter to vindicate or to—In case the question of these charges are brought up against Mr. Faulk, to use this letter in his sales talk.

THE COURT: Use this letter or affidavit?

SLATE: I mean the affidavit, I'm sorry, the affidavit.

Everybody in the courtroom connected with the lawsuit in any way knew that Sam Slate was the defendants' ace-in-the-hole. If his testimony could persuade the jury that my firing at CBS was in no way attributable to pressure from the defendants, it would cut sharply into my claim for damages. It struck me that calling Sam as a witness had been a bold move on Bolan's part. He must have known that Sam Slate was a close friend of mine, and he must have known further that Sam Slate had little appetite for the kind of goings on that the defendants indulged in. In many respects my sympathies were with Sam; he was in a difficult position. A feeling of gratitude and real affection would creep over me at various points in his testimony.

NIZER: Did you, at all times that Mr. Faulk was with you on WCBS, consider him an outstanding radio personality?

SLATE: I considered him one of our better people, Mr. Nizer.

NIZER: Did you consider him also a very effective salesman on the air in addition to being an entertainer?

SLATE: Yes, I did.

NIZER: In your opinion, was Faulk a unique and attractive personality in television as well, sir?

SLATE: On certain types of television shows, I thought Mr. Faulk was an excellent performer.

NIZER: Would a charge of his being affiliated with pro-Communist organizations make him [the performer] a controversial figure in the industry?

SLATE: That would be one thing that would make him one, yes.

NIZER: What is the effect of such controversiality on his getting employment?

SLATE: It certainly wouldn't help him any.

NIZER: No, I am sure of that, but would he become generally, in the practice of the industry, virtually unemployable for new jobs?

SLATE: I would say it would be very, very difficult for him to get new jobs, Mr. Nizer.

NIZER: Can you state with only reasonable certainty, sir, that if a man becomes controversial, whether it turns out ultimately that he is innocent or guilty, the very controversiality makes it very, very difficult, to use your words, for him to get a job? Is that correct?

SLATE: In a general way that's correct.

NIZER: After Mr. Faulk was let out at WCBS, it came to your attention that there was a station in Minneapolis that was trying to engage him? Do you recall that incident?

SLATE: Yes, through conversations with Mr. Faulk.

NIZER: Did you give Mr. Faulk advice with respect to accepting that offer if he could obtain it?

SLATE: I believe I did, Mr. Nizer. . . . As I remember the conversation, I advised Mr. Faulk to accept this job because, as long as this suit was pending and the—the combination of AWARE attack and the suit, and no one could predict how long this would last, and it might be a good idea for him to take the best job he could get.

However, at this point Sam's memory began to fail him badly. For instance, I remember very vividly the time in June 1958 when he called me down to his office and told me he had heard from Wendell Campbell who was offering me a job with KFRC in San Francisco. He was a good friend of Wendell's; but he didn't seem to have any recollection of the incident.

NIZER: You testified, Mr. Slate, that you became general manager of WCBS in April of 1956, is that right?

SLATE: If I did, I made an error, Mr. Nizer. It was in April of 1957.

NIZER: Did you not, in error, testify throughout your direct examination that you obtained the general managership in April 1956? Did you not on a number of occasions make that error yesterday?

SLATE: Mr. Nizer, if you say so, I accept it, but the facts are that I became in 1957—

NIZER: And in June of 1957, shortly after becoming the general manager, do you recall having a conference with Mr. Gerald Dickler, Mr. Faulk's manager, and Mr. Faulk, concerning the possibility of the Godfrey show taking over part of Mr. Faulk's hour?

SLATE: I am sure I did, Mr. Nizer.

NIZER: At that time, did you not tell both of these gentlemen that, so far as Mr. Faulk is concerned, he didn't have to be concerned at all, he would either continue on with the remaining half, or some other time that you would try to make available? Was that your position?

Sam answered the question in the negative.

NIZER: You say you talked to Mr. Faulk about the conversation you were telling us about yesterday when he came back from Jamaica in August? Is that your correction now?

SLATE: That is correct.

NIZER: By that time, he had already been discharged, had he not?

SLATE: We had sent a notification to Mr. Dickler.

NIZER: And you sent the notification of discharge to Mr. Gerald Dickler his general manager, didn't you?

SLATE: That is right.

NIZER: And you and Mr. Dickler met for a drink because he was astonished at this, wasn't he?

[Objection sustained]

NIZER: Did Mr. Dickler ask to see you when he got this notice that his client, Mr. Faulk, was discharged?

SLATE: We saw each other, Mr. Nizer.

NIZER: Yes, and did he tell you how astonished, in substance, he was at having received this notice when you had assured Mr. Faulk before he left on vacation that his position was secure?

SLATE: I don't remember Mr. Dickler making that statement.

NIZER: Not in those particular words, but didn't he in substance express that to you, Mr. Slate?

SLATE: Mr. Dickler was unhappy over the situation, Mr. Nizer.

NIZER: But in addition to being unhappy, didn't he say, in substance, that this comes as a great shock to him? Didn't Mr. Dickler tell you that at that meeting at the bar?

SLATE: I don't remember.

NIZER: You say you don't remember. You mean you don't remember one way or the other, he might have said that, but you don't recall?

SLATE: That is correct.

Lou continued to press Sam hard on this important meeting between him and Dickler at the Waldorf-Astoria Men's Bar. All Sam could remember was that Dickler was very unhappy. He agreed that Dickler was surprised. At this point Lou got down to a very crucial aspect of my firing.

NIZER: So that it is clear to you when you told him [Dickler] "I am sorry I have to do this," that Mr. Faulk being all the way down in Jamaica didn't know about his discharge at that time, did he?

SLATE: That is correct.

NIZER: So far as the legal reason for doing it on July the 30th, you could, at the end of August 30, the same cycle, have done this on August 30th after Mr. Faulk returned here, couldn't you?

SLATE: Mr. Nizer, I don't know, sir. I know that I was told by legal—I remember that Mr. Faulk's contract, there was something about a thirty-day notice in case of a network show, and we sent the letter out at that time.

NIZER: Your instructions about this came from the home office upstairs; is that right?

SLATE: No, sir.

Lou's voice had begun to betray irritation with Sam. He launched into the matter of my ratings and my share of audience, comparing them with those of WCBS generally as well as with those of several other performers during the 1956–57 period. Lou had mastered enough of the hocuspocus of ratings to prove one thing once and for all for me. I don't know about the jury, but as I listened to the testimony, I became more convinced than ever that ratings were whatever one chose to say they were.

Bolan obviously sensed that Sam Slate, a vital defense witness, was not doing the defense's cause much good. When he got up to conduct the redirect examination, he sought to shore up the places in Sam's testimony that were sagging sadly from the pounding of Lou's cross-examination. He had Sam recite in great detail once again, the official reasons for my being fired. Then, realizing that his own witness had stated quite clearly in previous testimony that my being controversial was a reason for my being unemployable, he sought to establish that I was controversial not because of the defendants' attack on me, but because I had brought the lawsuit. In this instance, however, it was not Lou who objected, but Judge Geller.

THE COURT: In your experience in the industry, Mr. Slate, does a performer become controversial by bringing a lawsuit of the type which is involved in this action?

SLATE: A lawsuit of this type would tend to make a performer controversial.

BOLAN: Would you read that back please?

[The last answer was read back.]

THE COURT: I think it is appropriate to advise the jury that it is the absolute right under our jury system of government for anyone who has a claim to bring a lawsuit so that the courts may determine the merits of the lawsuit.

BOLAN: The defendants readily concede that, your Honor.

THE COURT: All right. The jury said that they didn't hear me. Let me state it again. Under our system, it is absolutely the privilege of any citizen, if he has a claim, to sue, to bring a lawsuit, so that the courts may determine the validity or lack of validity of the lawsuit.

That is the privilege that we have under our system, and Mr. Bolan just conceded that that is correct.

Lou taking up the recross-examination, made his final thrust.

NIZER: You testified that a lawsuit of this type, repeating your exact words, would aid in making a man controversial. By this type, I take it one that involves the loyalty and patriotism of a performer, is that right?

SLATE: That is correct.

NIZER: And the controversiality, to use that word again, the controversiality which was the subject matter of the lawsuit, both of them being merged for this purpose, was in existence at the time he was let out, wasn't it?

SLATE: That's correct.

NIZER: And that factor was a factor in letting him out, wasn't it, that controversiality?

SLATE: No, sir.

NIZER: Was it not, sir?

SLATE: No, sir.

NIZER: You mean to say that of all the factors you considered, Mr. Slate, you are telling us that the one factor you didn't consider was the controversiality of this pending lawsuit and the subject matter of it? Is that your testimony?

SLATE: That is my testimony.

NIZER: That is all, sir.

BOLAN: Thank you very much, Mr. Slate.

Judge Geller announced that he had made arrangements, for the trial to continue in the Criminal Courts Building, in an air-conditioned room.

The next day, June 21, we gathered in the new courtroom, which was to be ours for the remainder of the trial. Judge Geller had assured the jury that the case would be in its hands by June 28, one week away. The jury had looked very pleased at this news; but no one was more pleased than I.

Throughout the trial there had been a running controversy between Bolan and Nizer over whether or not Laurence Johnson would testify. These arguments had taken place in the judge's chambers, outside the hearing of the jury. Bolan had maintained that Mr. Johnson was too ill to come and testify. Lou was not convinced. Lou pointed out that if Mr. Johnson indeed was too ill, he certainly did not want him to come, but he had had word that Johnson had been traveling about the country. Nizer wanted Johnson to submit to a medical examination by a specialist of Nizer's choosing. The judge explained to the jury the importance of the question. If a party to a suit fails to appear at a trial, without valid excuse, the jury is entitled to draw the strongest inference against him; they have the right to infer that he would not have been able to refute the evidence against him or substantiate charges made on his behalf.

This led to a duel of doctors. The defense announced that it would present a physician who would testify on Johnson's inability to come to the stand. Nizer chose as his specialist the foremost authority in New York on Johnson's particular disorder, Dr. Jerome Marks; Johnson agreed to come to New York for the examination.

The defendants called to the witness chair Dr. Wardner D. Ayer from Syracuse, a distinguished and learned physician with many degrees and an unimpeachable professional record.

Nizer had sat with Dr. Marks for hours going over in detail the nature of Johnson's disorder and familiarizing himself with all the medical terminology in the case. His cross-examination of Dr. Ayer reflected the thoroughness of his preparation; although Dr. Ayer was the very model of a thoroughly competent physician on the stand, Nizer was able to throw serious doubt on Ayer's evaluation of Johnson's physical condition.

Dr. Jerome Marks, in his turn on the stand, testified that in his opinion Johnson was fully able to come to court. I watched the jury's reaction to the conflicting testimony of these two distinguished doctors, and it seemed that they regarded Dr. Ayer as a fine gentleman, but that they considered Dr. Marks the better qualified authority on Johnson's particular disorder; it seemed clear that they accepted his judgment that Johnson was well enough to appear as a witness if he wanted to.

However, either Bolan did not want to put Johnson on the stand, or Johnson refused to go through the ordeal of testifying. He did not make an appearance.

After Dr. Marks was dismissed from the stand, the defense stated that it had no more witnesses to call. Justice Geller announced that he expected both sides to finish off all presentation of evidence by the next day.

Lou had several rebuttal witnesses ready to go and he ran them off in fairly rapid order. First there was John Sibley, a reporter from the *New York Times*, who had been covering the case from the first; it was he who Vincent Hartnett had claimed pointed out my wife to him. His testimony was brief and to the point.

NIZER: Did you ever point out Mrs. Faulk to Mr. Hartnett?
SIBLEY: I did not.

Lou then called Ted Poston, a long-time friend of mine, and a reporter on the *New York Post*. Ted and I had known each other since I first arrived in New York in 1946. We were both interested in interracial affairs and had seen each other socially as well as at public affairs gatherings. One of the allegations against me in the AWARE bulletin was that I had appeared—presumably to entertain—at Club 65 on a certain date in 1946. The affair had been given under the auspices of the *Amsterdam News* unit of the Newspaper Guild of New York. I had denied having entertained at the gathering or even being present, although it would have made little difference one way or the other, for it was a perfectly respectable social affair, as Ted Poston, who had been there, testified. However, he made it perfectly clear that I had not been there and stood firmly by that answer during Bolan's cross-examination of him.

The following day, Friday, June 23, Nizer presented his final rebuttal witnesses. Hartnett, in an effort to prove that he had at least relied on ordinarily belief-worthy sources for the statements he had published about me, had claimed that he had based one of those statements—namely, that I had appeared at a function at the Jefferson School—on information he had received from a Mr. Jack Wren, an advertising executive with the firm of Batten, Barton, Durstine, and Osborn. Hartnett had further testified that he had been a friend of Jack Wren's, who had been something of a clearance officer for B.B.D.&O. in the early fifties, and that they had frequently exchanged derogatory information on various television personalities. When Wren came into the courtroom, Bolan and Hartnett evidenced considerable surprise. By the time he had been sworn in and had taken the stand their surprise had turned to chagrin.

NIZER: Prior to February 1956, did you have any conversation with Mr. Vincent Hartnett in which you gave him any information about Mr. John Henry Faulk, supposedly appearing or scheduled to appear at the Jefferson School on or about February 16, 1948? . . . Did you have any such conversation with Mr. Hartnett?

WREN: Absolutely not, sir.

NIZER: Your witness.

Bolan and Hartnett huddled for a few moments, then Bolan launched his cross-examination. His attitude and that of Hartnett, sitting directly across the table from me, suggested that they were furious with Mr. Wren.

BOLAN: Mr. Wren, what were your duties at B.B.D.&O. in late 1955?

WREN: Well, my duties, among other things, was to protect our clients against false charges made that we loaded our shows with Communists, by Vincent Hartnett, who made these charges against us, who wrote poison-pen letters behind our backs to our clients, wrote to our officers accusing us of loading our shows with Communists.

BOLAN: Anything else in your duties, Mr. Wren?

WREN: Yes, my duties were to read television scripts to make sure that they were accurate, especially dealing with realism.

BOLAN: Did you ever exchange information with Mr. Hartnett during the year 1955?

WREN: No, sir.

BOLAN: Was your relationship with Mr. Hartnett in the year 1955 and early 1956 a friendly one?

WREN: Unfriendly.

Bolan then produced a letter dated February 16, 1956, from Hartnett to Wren.

BOLAN: Did you have any communication at all with Mr. Hartnett toward the latter part of 1955 and early 1956?

WREN: Absolutely not. None to my recollection.

BOLAN: Did you ever call his office on the telephone?

WREN: Not in that year.

BOLAN: 1955?

WREN: Not in that year, sir.

BOLAN: How about in 1956?

WREN: Not in that year, sir.

BOLAN: Are you positive of that?

WREN: Quite.

BOLAN: Did you ever send any communications to Mr. Hartnett at any time?

WREN: It is entirely possible I sent communications in the early fifties, especially when Mr. Hartnett was engineering picket lines around our clients' shows, and I had to treat with him as a merchant treats with a racketeer who sells protection.

Lou, through Fred Mitchell, an advertising executive had secured the expert of experts on the subject of Pulse ratings, a genial, soft-spoken but very persuasive gentleman, Marvin Antonowsky. Antonowsky had taken his B.A. and M.A. degrees in statistics and was working on his Ph.D. in statistics. Lou had worked with him for several nights mastering all the details of the mysterious items called ratings. Then Lou had had them construct huge charts so that the jury could easily see what was being discussed from the illustrations on the charts. It was Lou's thought that we should once and for all clear from the jury's mind any question about my falling ratings having been responsible for my being dismissed from CBS.

The large charts were placed in a strategic spot before the jury, and Mr. Antonowsky held forth under Lou's questioning like a professor explaining a diagram to a class. He was a thorough scholar in the matter. With his charts and his testimony, Lou proved precisely the opposite of what the defendants had sought to maintain. As a matter of fact, he rather startled me; I had no idea that my ratings had been so high until Antonowsky started testifying. I got mad at WCBS all over again. Bolan, of course, knew that Antonowsky's testimony was doing a great deal of harm to the cause of the defendants, but he hadn't spent the time mastering the matter that Nizer had and was unable to shake any of Antonowsky's testimony on cross-examination.

After Antonowsky was dismissed, Bolan called Hartnett back to the stand to rebut some of the strong testimony that Jack Wren had given.

BOLAN: Mr. Hartnett, was your relationship with Mr. Wren in January and February, 1956, a friendly relationship?
HARTNETT: It was.

The jury was left to decide whether Mr. Hartnett or Mr. Wren was to be believed. We were getting toward the end of the day and Judge Geller was urging the lawyers to cut short any further discussion; he wanted to let the jury go home.

But Bolan was anxious to get more direct rebuttal testimony from Hartnett concerning his finances. He also wanted to get a stipulation from Nizer that the defense counsel's accountant could go over my recent financial records, to ascertain my income since I had been fired. At one point it looked as though things were going to blow up in the courtroom. Mr. Bolan appeared to be verging on tears as he exploded at the judge.

BOLAN: . . . I wish you wouldn't be shouting at me throughout the trial as you have done from the very beginning. It gets to the point where the pressure is too great for me, your Honor. You have done it from the beginning.
THE COURT: Nonsense, you put the court under pressure.
BOLAN: It's not nonsense.
THE COURT: Just a moment. We're going to stop this right now.

After a brief recess, Mr. Bolan returned to the courtroom, his composure regained.

BOLAN: . . . Your Honor, may I say that I apologize for getting excited a few moments ago.
THE COURT: Your apology is accepted.

Within a matter of moments thereafter, I heard the welcome words from Nizer: "That is all. The plaintiff rests." The defense rested, too. Darkness was gathering over Manhattan as the jury was excused until Tuesday, June 26, at which time Bolan would give his summation.

25

I woke up at dawn Tuesday morning and lay in bed thinking. As far as I was concerned, school was out. All that remained now was the graduation exercises. Each side had had its say. All the evidence was in. Nothing could be added, nothing taken away. No surprise turn now. Bolan's summation of the defendants' case today and Lou's summation of ours tomorrow; the judge's charge to the jury, the jury's deliberation, and its verdict on Thursday. I had no thought past that moment.

When we arrived in court, first thing I noticed was that Vincent Hartnett was there with his wife and six lovely, bright-faced children. I felt a strong impulse to go up and congratulate them. They looked as though they had come to see their father receive a diploma of some kind. They were arrayed up near the front of the courtroom in front of the jury. Lou took exception to what he regarded as a crass bit of staging for the benefit of the jury. He spoke to the judge in chambers, and the Hartnett family was moved back several rows to a less conspicuous place.

When court convened, Judge Geller stated from the bench that it was the responsibility of the court to dismiss from consideration by the jury all issues that had not been supported by evidence in the trial; and then, to my considerable amazement, he proceeded to state that the defendants' two affirmative defenses—namely, truth and fair comment—were stricken: the defendants had presented no evidence that would establish the truth of their charges against the plaintiff; and the defendants had not proved that their libel had been provoked. He then proceeded to strike their first partial defense of partial truth and partial fair comment, and instructed the jury that they could not consider these issues. He stated: "This leaves as the affirmative defense of the defendants, AWARE, Inc., and Hartnett, the partial defense of reliance on sources, which goes to mitigation of punitive damages. These defendants, you will recall, offered no direct proof of truth, but did present evidence of alleged reliance on sources, mostly in the form of documents which were not admitted for the truth of their content but merely for the limited purpose of claimed reliance on sources."

Judge Geller then turned his attention to the matter of the summations, pointing out that the function of the summation by the lawyers was to sum up or draw together the various lines of evidence and to argue and try to convince the jury to arrive at conclusions that each lawyer advanced. He wanted them not to be swayed by the oratory of the two lawyers. "So listen carefully to both counsel. Reject what you consider to be unfounded or unsupported arguments and accept what you deem to be fair and reasonable inferences based on the believable evidence as you find it in this case."

He then told Mr. Bolan to proceed with his summation. Bolan moved up to the table that had been placed in front of the jury, set his papers out in front of him on the table and started in a low, easy voice. He explained to them that he was going to give the highlights of the case.

BOLAN: Why has this case lasted so long? It is probably a record for a libel case in New York County. And the answer is simple: because the plaintiff at the outset knew he was not going to be able to prove his case. . . . Had we confined this case to Mr. Faulk and the defendants, we would have been out of here many weeks ago.

Why was somebody like Tony Randall the movie actor brought in here before you to testify? What did he testify to? Did he know Mr. Faulk? Did he have anything to do with Exhibit 41 or any of the issues in the case? All Mr. Randall testified to was that he was afraid to go to AFTRA meetings because he didn't want to be seen publicly taking a position against AWARE. That's all he testified to.
. . .
The plaintiff's plan here was obvious. That he sought to saturate you with a mass of irrelevancies; week after week of testimony having nothing to do with Exhibit 41; weeks

and weeks of testimony to the effect that blacklisting is a
bad thing, that this is a general practice in the industry,
and it is a bad thing. . . .

Now, did the plaintiff, however, produce the key witnesses, the important witnesses in this case? Namely, his
employers at CBS. No, he did not. He did not produce one
witness from CBS. The defendants did. The plaintiff had
the burden to show his damages, but he did not produce
anybody from CBS. . . . We subpoenaed for you all of the
records at CBS relating to Mr. Faulk, and you may consider
that very seriously, ladies and gentlemen, in your deliberation, why didn't the plaintiff produce anybody from CBS?"

I was beginning to feel drowsy again as Bolan droned on.
The jury was listening with interest, however, and I tried to
do the same. Suddenly his summation took another turn.

BOLAN: . . . Mr. Faulk, has deliberately lied to you on numerous occasions in this case on matters of great importance.
There are so many lies that it is hard to list them all. I will
give you about nine or ten for a start and mention many
more throughout my summation.

I was suddenly wide-awake and furious. I was not prepared
for this turn of events. To sit and listen to a man calling me a
liar and be unable to do anything about it was a grim experience. I glanced at Martinson and Nizer and Berger; they
seemed to be taking it all very calmly. I became angry at
them. Bolan was riding along citing instance after instance
where, he claimed, I had lied. He said that I had lied about
how well I had been doing at WCBS in 1955, had lied about
my loss of sponsors, had lied about my popularity as a TV
performer, had lied about the reasons for my being fired
from CBS.

BOLAN: . . . I submit that on this series of lies, they are so
deliberate, so flagrant, that you could question anything
Mr. Faulk told you at this trial, but I am going to give you
quite a few others that are almost as bad, if not worse in
some cases. . . .

And as is evident throughout much of his testimony

Mr. Faulk lied when he knew—when he believed that there wasn't any occasion to contradict him. . . . He wanted to show you that he was quite a performer before the alleged libel, before the publication of Exhibit 41. The fact is that it wasn't until after the publication of Exhibit 41 that Mr. Faulk really got sponsors. . . .

I submit that Mr. Faulk got more publicity out of this lawsuit, as a result of this lawsuit, than he had ever had before in his life. He had never been mentioned to any extent at all in the New York papers.

As I sat there in my chair, immobilized by court rules, listening as he heaped opprobrium upon me, a feeling of despair and loneliness crept over me. I realized that it would be impossible ever to communicate to anyone, even my dearest friends, how utterly crushing this experience was to me. Although intellectually I understood that to Bolan I was only a symbol and not a person, it was still impossible for me to shake off the terrifying pain of his brutal attack on my character.

BOLAN: . . . Mr. Faulk's lies spread over a tremendous area. Every area in which he testified, he lied or exaggerated. . . .

When at long last Judge Geller announced a lunch recess I rose numbly from my chair. Friends were smiling sympathetically, but I regarded their sympathy as a smirk. Out of the entire group of spectators only one person seemed to understand my state of mind. That was Mildred Nizer. She came forward and caught my hands and kissed me warmly and looked at me steadily, squeezing my hands affectionately.

When I got back to the courtroom, Vincent Hartnett's children and family were gone. I realized why he had brought them: He had wanted them to hear about the evil man who had caused their father so much trouble. Bolan slashed into me again in the afternoon session, at first citing Sam Slate's testimony as evidence of what a hard-hearted liar I was. He then began to ridicule my ability as an entertainer, pointing out that I was never more than fourth-rate at best. After reviewing my various shows he went on with more.

BOLAN: This is another hoax which the plaintiff is seeking to perpetrate at this trial. The plaintiff, from the start of his career, has been primarily a radio disc jockey and nothing else. . . . His ability or lack of ability was very well known in the industry . . . The fact is that Mr. Faulk was not a star performer. He was ranked third or fourth amongst the radio disc jockeys in New York.

He delivered a splendid eulogy of Vincent Hartnett and AWARE, Inc., and their fine work, and he pointed out that there was a need for their services. At one point he said, "Is there anything wrong about Mr. Hartnett's getting paid for this work?" I wondered if his words sounded as ironic to the jury as they did to me. I was emotionally exhausted, without even the strength to be angry. When court finally adjourned that afternoon a grim taciturnity had settled over me. I nodded curtly to my friends and departed for the hotel. I had no appetite for conversation. I desired only solitude and the release that only sleep can bring.

The effects of Bolan's unbridled attack on me still hung over me the next morning. My mood wasn't improved any when I saw the *New York Times*, which carried the full story of the diatribe against me.

However, by the time I got down to the courthouse that morning my spirits had been raised. I was astonished to discover there were hundreds and hundreds of people gathered at the courthouse long before the court was to convene. I saw dozens of friends I had not seen for a long time. They had all come to hear Nizer's summation of the case. The courtroom would not hold even half of them, and there was some confusion about setting up chairs and what not. I slipped into the courtroom as soon as possible and took my seat at the counsel table. I was in no mood to stand around being the premature victor. Vincent Hartnett sat down opposite me stiffly. He began to read the *New York Times*, smiling to himself as he read of Bolan's attack on me.

Nizer was all business, arranging huge piles of exhibits on the table in front of the jury, checking his notes, and making sure that everything was in order. He seemed to be in perfect form, fresh and alert. George leaned over to me and commented, "You'd never know that he has not been to bed at all last night, would you? He worked on this summation the entire night. Only finished it a couple of hours ago."

There was an air of climax in the room, one that suggested "This is it." I studied the faces of the jurors as they took their seats, to see if there was a trace of any sympathy for me after the drubbing I had received yesterday. Not one of them looked at me. They were chatting amiably and then quieted down as the court came to order.

Lou began quietly addressing the jury, thanking them for their extraordinary dedication to duty and for the patience that they had shown in serving on this case. He pointed out that this was not an ordinary service that these jurors had rendered. He said perhaps the jurors would derive some compensation from the extraordinary nature of their service, from the fact that this was a historic case with historic implications.

NIZER: It is a case by John Henry Faulk against these defendants, but certain cases involve extraordinary principles. There are in the history of litigation just a few of these, sometimes only one in a generation, and I stand here with a very deep sense of responsibility because I have upon me the burden of presenting this case to you. . . . For six years we have waited for this day, six years. We have worked during those six years day and night. You see the exhibits, the documents, the unraveling of that which was very difficult to prove in a courtroom under oath; and so we too have been under strain. It has been a great responsibility, which we take very earnestly and you ought to have, I hope, the satisfaction that your work, whatever it be when this case is over, will have significance in the history of litigation nationally and, I think, internationally.

The last day was a very bitter day, because we would have thought that, after everything that happened in this courtroom, there could have been a different position taken by the defendants. I would expect them to defend themselves, but they didn't have to spill their malice and hate in this courtroom until I felt that I was neck-deep in mud. When a man has no generosity in his heart, he has real heart disease; and I think the defendants yesterday demonstrated the malice with which this case from the first moment has been steeped.

Here we were with the learned court, whose research and learning on the complicated question of libel law have awed us all, instructing you that the defenses of truth were stricken out of this case; they couldn't plead the truth because there wasn't a shred of evidence to show that there was any truth. . . .

There wasn't even partial truth. There was a defense of partial truth; that was stricken out. There wasn't even a defense left of fair comment; as his Honor instructed you learnedly, in certain libel cases you can say, "Well, I was wrong but it was a comment, a fair comment." That was stricken out because it must meet certain standards which are missing here. . . .

So they stood bare in this courtroom as libelers who had destroyed this man and his family. Don't you think it would have been the decent thing under those circumstances for the defendants to take the usual, proper position for a defendant, "I was wrong; I am sorry?" . . . But no! Even under those circumstances they came into this court and called my client a liar for coming into court and testing his rights. . . . I admire Mr. Faulk for keeping silent under that attack, because I had to grip my seat. At the last moment we were libeled again.

And who is it that is held forth as a truthful man? Mr. Bolan says, "I gambled my case on the integrity, on the truth of Mr. Hartnett." I accept that unhesitatingly. Why, Exhibit 41, the bulletin that he wrote, has already been held to be a complete lie, and he is the author of it. So how can he be a truthful man? At least he ought to say, "I lied about this whole exhibit, but forgive me, I was mistaken. I didn't mean to." . . . I repeat that when the defense of truth is stricken out of a case and the defense of partial truth is stricken out of a case, the document is not only libelous but a complete lie. I stand by that, and I wouldn't be as strong about it if they hadn't called Mr. Faulk a liar. And I repeat it. . . . The whole summation was symbolic of this case.

In the first place, there is no issue of Communism in

this case. John Henry Faulk, from the first moment he could understand and breathe, has been anti-Communist, and no one has proved otherwise. . . . So Communism is not an issue. . . .

The question is whether we will permit our government to protect us under proper judicial and other procedures, or whether we're going to permit private vigilantes like this gentleman seated here with the thin mouth and the blue suit [pointing at Hartnett], who sneaks into a restaurant, the Blue Ribbon Restaurant, when there is a meeting of some union people, with a hidden microphone in his lapel. That is the question, or are you going to permit private vigilantism for profit? If he was a real patriot and he dug up any evidence, he would have sent it to the F.B.I. like all of us should, against a Communist. . . .

If any citizen has any evidence of any kind and he is really a good-natured and proper and loyal citizen, he sends it to the governmental authorities, not to this gentleman; he charged $20 a throw.

The issue is not Communism at all. It is private vigilantism, and the only time that Mr. Bolan came near to touching the issue in this case is when he told you yesterday all about the Fifth Amendment fellows. He said, "If a fellow takes a Fifth Amendment, haven't we a right, when I want to employ the man, to take it into consideration?" Why, you don't need the Fifth Amendment. I as an individual employer can refuse to hire anybody because I don't like the color of his tie. I can refuse to hire anybody because I don't like his speech, I don't like the way he dresses. That is my privilege as an American, but that isn't blacklisting. That doesn't mean that I send around a list to all the employers that this man will go to, and they all agree that they can't hire this man. That is what is evil about it. As an individual, cannot the electric company say, "I want to charge twice as much as my competitor?" They're fixing a price. That is legal. But what they can't do is get together with all their people and fix prices among them. That is a crime under our law, not only an anti-trust violation, it's a crime under the criminal law.

And the question is not whether somebody should have a right to reject a man who took the Fifth Amendment.

The question is whether Mr. Hartnett can send around a list to all the agencies and sponsors and put them into their grips and say, "If you use this man we're going to see to it that you get pressure from the American Legion Post 41 and the Veteran's Action Committee, and thus, by concerted conspiracy, hit a man behind his back when he doesn't know what has hit him, and deprive him of his livelihood, and send him, like Mr. Faulk, away from New York and back to his home town. . . . And why? He never faced any accuser. The only time we have had a chance is by waiting six years to come into this courtroom and struggle through every witness, objection after objection, and then we are maligned for coming into an American court. We are told we're liars. We have no right to be here, I suppose.

And incidentally, the issue is not the American Legion. . . . That is not the issue. No one is attacking the American Legion. We are attacking Post 41 in Syracuse, Mr. Dungey, who is the tool of Mr. Johnson. You can get a local of any kind to be corrupt, and this is a conspiracy between Mr. Johnson, who controlled Mr. Dungey, and the reason they didn't bring Mr. Dungey into court is that we would have found out what his financial arrangements are with Mr. Johnson. We would have had a chance. Why didn't they bring Mr. Dungey down to say, "Oh, I didn't know Mr. Johnson was doing this. I did it on my own." Why isn't he here?

And why isn't the Veteran's Action Committee of Syracuse Supermarkets here, Mr. Neuser? After all, he is an employee of Johnson; that is conceded. He is his fruit and vegetable buyer. But notice these letterheads. You saw them, red, white and blue. After all, if you were a sponsor of a television company and you get a letter of that kind, American Legion Post 41, Syracuse, Onondaga County, red, white and blue, well, you get scared. This is how this conspiracy worked. But this was just a tool of Mr. Johnson. He ordered these letters sent, as I will prove to you. There is no question about it. We have it in writing. . . .

And the Veteran's Action Committee is another tool of Mr. Johnson. That also has a beautiful red, white, and blue letterhead, and it's signed with this auspicious signature,

"Chairman of the Internal Subversion Committee, Francis W. Neuser." And who is Neuser? The fruit and vegetable buyer of Mr. Johnson.

But when the sponsor gets this letter, he doesn't know that. He says, "My God, I'm paying $100,000 for two weeks of this program and I have got the Veterans and the American Legion after me." . . .

The real issue in this case, ladies and gentlemen, is that there are people who try to take the law into their hands. They try to, because they believe fanatically and in this case there was no fanaticism; it was malice. They didn't think Faulk, even fanatically, was a Communist. They struck at Faulk for another reason which I am going to give you. That is what makes it malicious. But when they struck at other people, they did it fanatically, and if people can take the law into their own hands that way, then the Ku Klux Klan is a good organization. They too, think the government isn't doing enough. Then the Silver Shirt organization, that is Pelly's group, that is a very good group if that's right, because they say, "We are impatient."

You heard Mr. Hartnett testify that is the philosophy of these people. Mr. Hartnett said it's unrealistic to depend on the government. I couldn't believe my ears. He actually said it from the witness stand. . . . And there you had an insight into the evil that we're striking at, private vigilantes taking the law into their own hands. . . .

When you and your neighbor are not safe from somebody who does not like you, and he tips off Mr. Milton or Mr. Johnson and Mr. Hartnett and he can, through these organizations, ruin you and your enterprise and your business by writing a letter behind your back to your employer, and you suddenly find yourself economically strangled, which is what happened to Mr. Faulk (he didn't earn one cent in his profession from 1958, 1959, 1960)—Mr. Bolan forgot all about that—When you are strangled because your neighbor or someone who is fanatical can take these measures against you without recourse, without your facing an accuser, without your showing you are innocent, then you have Communism under the guise of fighting Communism. . . .

This man was shipped off to Siberia. I don't mean to ma-

lign Austin, Texas, but that is not where he belongs now after he had been in New York living in a beautiful apartment and becoming one of the great stars of our culture.
. . .

We allege a conspiracy to control the radio and television industry, and it was our duty to show you that this happens to all sorts of artists.

Why, one man, Mr. Dickler, testified that he knew of two people who committed suicide. I think he mentioned Philip Loeb, and this woman, Mady Christians, a wonderful actress, because they didn't know what hit them. They were great stars. Then suddenly they got into an agency—"No, we are sorry, we can't use you."

Although the room had more than its capacity of spectators, there was not a whisper as Nizer delivered his summation. It was a wonder to watch the skill with which he could reach for an exhibit, display it to the jury, and talk about it, all at the same time. At those times when he referred to Hartnett's conduct, Hartnett sat tight-lipped, writing away as though he had no connection whatever with what was going on in the courtroom. Lou spoke of the terrible difficulties that Kim Hunter experienced as the result of Hartnett's activities. He recalled her testimony and the hardships she had suffered.

NIZER: . . . And what was the price for her continuing working? She had to meet Mr. Hartnett's demand to send a telegram to the union not to condemn AWARE. And this man who, if you hadn't met him in the courtroom and seen him cross-examined, you would think this was some great powerful figure—All these dictators, they shrink when you see them.

Lou then recited dramatically how the courageous Tom Murray of the Grey advertising agency had stood up to Johnson when Johnson had come to New York threatening reprisals if the agency continued to buy commercial time on my program. Lou went through the whole thing, repeating the conversations between Johnson and Murray. He told of

Johnson's threat to have the American Legion write a letter to my sponsor and how he fulfilled that threat. Then he grew solemn.

NIZER: That is the kind of action and conspiracy which operates here, and there are bones on these roads, of wonderful artists, men and women in their profession, crushed by this.

And we have had the courage—I say "we"; I mean Mr. John Henry Faulk—You rarely find them. The reason I'm spilling out my heart and feeling in this case is—well, when do you find that kind of American? Everybody rushes to shelter. Why put up the fight? Why should I starve with my children for the industry? I know Americanism is being violated, but why is it my duty to be a martyr?

But this man, from the first moment, said, "I am going to see this thing through if I have to drive a taxi." And, incidentally, he couldn't even do that. He tried to sell the *Encyclopedia Britannica*; he failed. He went into mutual welfare funds; he failed.

And the thing that touched me most, I must admit to you I had to stop, I am sure you didn't notice, but I cried when he was on the stand and said, "I finally got to the point where I went over, . . . and said, 'Have you got any kind of a job for me in television?' and the fellow said, 'You know, let's be blunt about it. You are controversial. I can't take the chance.'" . . . And the result of that situation is that Faulk asked for a $10 sit-in job and the fellow said, "We haven't got a sit-in," and he can't earn $10 to sit in a chair because these people have crushed him. And yet he wouldn't surrender this lawsuit, nor would we.

And we examined these people. Mr. Bolan told it to you as if this were a crime on our part, twenty-seven sessions of Mr. Hartnett. Tens of thousands of dollars for these huge mountains of minutes, yes, and we did it and we are proud of it, and we finally have reached the day of vindication, and your word is going out to all the world that Americanism will not stand for this kind of corruption, of private vigilantism.

Lou then described how Wren had called Hartnett a liar from the stand and accused him of being a blackmailer and a racketeer. He then reminded the jury that this was an issue in the case, whether Hartnett, Johnson working in conspiracy with Post 41 of the American Legion, and Mr. Neuser, his own fruit and vegetable buyer, could control the entire radio and television industry.

NIZER: This is dangerous, ladies and gentlemen. It is far more dangerous, dangerous as Communists are. This is far more dangerous to permit the culture, the entertainment medium to be controlled by a few people for profit. That is the real issue; that is the framework.

At recess, I slipped outside to smoke my pipe. In the corridor were hundreds of people who hadn't been able to get in—every seat in the courtroom had been taken, and a number of people had been lined up along the walls. Kim Hunter was there in the corridor; she had been unable to get into the courtroom. She came forward and kissed me and asked me how it was going. She squeezed my hand tightly and whispered, "This is your day, you waited so long." Many other performers who had suffered at the hands of AWARE were on hand. They had come to witness the day of reckoning. I made it a point to see to it that Kim Hunter was able to get into the courtroom so that she could hear the remainder of Nizer's summation. As he resumed, he had cause to turn on Hartnett again, and I listened.

NIZER: If he [Hartnett] is a good investigator and he is so precise, he knew about it, and he deliberately omitted it, that man with the thin mouth and the blue suit, as somebody said, who goes to the police department. There was something here that shocked us out of our wits, and I think it should shock any American. He sets up, he claims, an alliance with the police department of New York. He says he had sixty or seventy conferences, secretly, with a certain gentleman whose name I will mercifully omit. You remember it, Lieutenant—I will mention it; there is no reason to shield him—Lieutenant Crain. Mr. Milton who has more sense, says that's untrue, Mr. Hartnett couldn't have done that because it's illegal to do it. So Mr. Milton calls Mr. Hartnett a liar, not we. Mr. Milton calls him a liar.

And isn't that a terrible thing? A private vigilante works his way—you see how this works—works his way into the police department. He gives them information which is misleading. They may arrest you or your neighbor or your husband or your sister because he thinks she is pro-Communistic, and he has given them some data on her, and on the other hand they are supposed to feed him, he says.

So here is a brilliant student, a teacher at Texas, a liberal democrat—yes, liberal, very liberal in the greatest tradition of the South. You have heard his testimony. . . . He is a liberal democrat, always was. . . . When that Middle-of-the-Road slate won, Mr. Hartnett was in trouble with that collection agency of his for patriotism, because they were going to stop blacklisting if they had to go to the courts or to the government to stop him.

That's why Mr. Hartnett and all the directors of AWARE and Mr. Johnson met. I am going to show you the meeting. I am going to piece together the writings in this case that we were able to dig out of their hide. They met and decided to destroy this man before he destroyed their income, their illegitimate income. That is the reason for the malice in this case.

And you have a chance; that is why I say this case is historic. You have a chance in this case to give a clarion call to the world on this, to make an award of punitive damages in several million dollars, of compensatory damages of over a million dollars.

It doesn't matter whether it can be collected or not. Let the word get out that this kind of thing must stop. Give, by your verdict, a clear answer to the kind of un-Americanism which this case represents. Aren't we free people? Do we have to knuckle under? Would you, before you get a job, want Mr. Jones or Mr. Smith to pass upon you so that you can't earn your livelihood if he thinks you're not a good American?

Behind his [the artist's] back he suddenly becomes unemployable, unemployable, unemployable. That word never passed Mr. Bolan's lips. They did not use that word "unemployable" in their entire summation of the whole day. The word "unemployable" wasn't mentioned, and it is the most important word in this case. When a man becomes controversial, he becomes unemployable. Let's not forget that word. They forgot it. Don't you forget it.

Lou knew how to wring every bit of the value out of the testimony of such witnesses as Kim Hunter, Ken Roberts, and Everett Sloan. After recapitulating the testimony of Sloan as to how he had gotten clearance from the United States Government and still been turned down by the defendants, Lou continued.

NIZER: The United States Government says he is loyal, but he still can't get a job because Mr. Hartnett didn't say he was loyal. . . . Milton . . . says, "This isn't good enough." And Sloan is amazed. Remember him on the witness stand? He says, "Isn't good enough, what do you mean?" He [Milton] says, "Well, our standards are different." You see, this is unrealistic. This is the same as Hartnett. "This government stuff is unrealistic. We have different standards, but I'll tell what I will do for you. I will make an appointment for you to see Mr. Hartnett." You see, that is the acme. Lord knows who Mr. Hartnett is until you get him into a courtroom and see his size. . . . An incident which ought to make an American hang his head in shame.

Lou was building up a real head of steam now. The courtroom was entirely silent as he highlighted the conspiracy against me. He went back to 1955 when John Crosby in the New York *Herald Tribune* had written, "Not long ago the American Federation of Television and Radio Artists, the terror-stricken union of radio and television performers took a courageous and long overdue stand by condemning the viciously un-American practice of blacklisting actors." Lou referred to AWARE and Hartnett as a wolf pack of vigilantes. Then he quoted from another article. "Unholy alliance, AFTRA and the blacklist. Something like a state of terror spreads through the union. Actors who might have sought after office were afraid to do so. Many members have told me that they were afraid to speak at AFTRA meetings for fear that their names would be noted and their opportunities for work would diminish. Several have told me they were afraid even to attend meetings."

He quoted a line from Robert Frost: "The people I am most scared of are the people who are scared." He told how Hartnett, when I was running for office in AFTRA in November of 1955, had written to the House Un-American Activities Committee. "He [Hartnett] is trying to get Faulk in trouble with the House Un-American Activities Committee because Faulk is a candidate, and if the Middle-of-the-Road slate is elected, the House Un-American Activities Committee should call Mr. Faulk and they would issue statements to that effect, they would crush the Middle-of-the-Road ticket." He pointed out to the jury that the reason I hung on a year after I had been attacked at CBS was because Collingwood and Ed Murrow had stepped in in my behalf and spoken to executives at CBS.

Lou was sailing along through the testimony, pointing out first Hartnett's then Johnson's malice, when suddenly Judge Geller declared a short recess. This was about four o'clock in the afternoon. A reporter, Miss Stephanie Gervis, touched my elbow and drew me aside. "Laurence Johnson just died," she said. I stared at her. She was deadly serious and nodded her head as a kind of reaffirmation. "It's true," she said. "That's the reason for this recess. The lawyers and the judge are trying to decide whether to go on or not."

"But how could he? Now?" I mumbled. Somehow, I knew that it was a fact. I moved over to the counsel table and sat down heavily in my chair. Paul and George entered from the judge's chamber, somber-faced. My eyes met theirs as they took their places beside me. They nodded sympathetically and looked straight ahead. Lou came in and walked behind my chair. He leaned over and put his hand on my shoulder. "They have just found a body in a Bronx motel," he whispered. "They think it is that of Larry Johnson."

I sat pondering—trying to come to some conclusion, trying to grasp the meaning of this strange turn. I could only think, over and over, "What a frail thing life is!" What would Johnson's death mean to our case? I was suddenly embarrassed with myself to think that I only considered the effect of this man's death on my interest. What a cold-blooded lot lawsuits make of all of us! I glanced at Lou. He was busily going over his remaining notes. The jury came back in, completely unaware of the news, and took their places. Judge Geller came in, took his place, and nodded for Lou to resume his summation.

George Berger told me later what had happened in the judge's chamber. Mr. Bolan's secretary had called him shortly before four o'clock and informed him that a body identified as that of Mr. Laurence Johnson had been found in a motel in the Bronx and was at that moment at the morgue in the Bronx. The judge asked that this information be withheld from the press until a positive identification of the body could be made, but Mr. Bolan had already informed two reporters. The judge called these two in and asked them if they could withhold the story until it was positively established that it was Mr. Johnson who had died. The reporters refused, saying that they had already called in the story. Bolan moved for a severance of Johnson as a defendant. To keep the jury from being influenced by the news of Johnson's death, Judge Geller arranged to have them sent to a hotel that night. The judge then instructed both attorneys to prepare memoranda on how they thought the matter should be handled.

Lou continued his summation without giving the slightest hint that anything had gone awry. He dwelt at length on the matter of damages, both compensatory and punitive. He then called upon the jury to award $1 million in compensatory damages and $1 million separately against each of the defendants for punitive damages.

When Nizer had completed his summation, the judge informed the jury that they would all go together to a hotel for the night, and they were not to read any newspaper or to listen to any radio or television. The jury was understandably mystified and obviously distressed at this news. The judge assured them that the case would be through by tomorrow, and accompanied by several court attendants they left for their hotel.

I could scarcely wait to hear from Nizer just exactly what this development would do to our suit. He explained it to me in detail. He also said that he was going to put every available man in his office to work on research relating to the legal problems that Johnson's death had raised.

Later I went up to Nizer's office. He had all hands available working on the case. The consensus seemed to be that there was no precedent for such a situation.

The next morning's papers carried the news of Johnson's death under such headlines as "Faulk Case Figure Dead." They reported little that I hadn't already learned. Mr. Johnson's body, clad in pajamas, had been discovered in a Bronx motel. He had died, apparently, of natural causes.

Since a dead man cannot be party to a lawsuit, but his estate may, a legal mechanism had to be found whereby the position of the late Laurence Johnson as defendant could be immediately transferred to his estate, without any discontinuation of the proceedings. After an all-night session, Paul Martinson and George Berger submitted next morning to Judge Geller a Creditor's Petition; they argued that as the New York Supreme Court is a court of general jurisdiction, Justice Geller was entitled to accept this as a Surrogate, and to grant letters of Temporary Administration to an executor of his choice. He agreed with this course, and named an independent lawyer as administrator, who then sat in that afternoon when the court reconvened, as a defendant in the place of the late Laurence Johnson.

I went to court that afternoon with Lou, Paul, and George. We were astonished to see Bolan and Lang sitting at their ease on a table that had been placed before the judge's bench. They were sitting there cross-legged, laughing gaily and chatting, facing the spectators' section and apparently counting the number of persons entering the courtroom. Nizer was indignant. He observed that their posture and attitude "is of such arrogance as I've never seen in court before." The courtroom quickly filled up and as the spectators composed themselves we sat at the counsel table waiting for Justice Geller to enter. Paul and George chatted amiably with me as Louis Nizer sat and sketched the faces of court attendants and others. Bolan and Lang, still laughing, continued to swing their legs from the table and look out over the spectators. Finally Mr. Bolan tore a crossword puzzle from the *New York Times* and took his place at the counsel table, where he proceeded to work out the puzzle.

After what seemed to me an eternity, Justice Geller took his place on the bench. The jury was brought in and Justice Geller informed them of Johnson's death. One woman juror gasped and placed her hands over her mouth, but there was no noticeable reaction by the other jurors. Justice Geller then proceeded to deliver his charge to the jury.

"Now we have reached the hour of decision," he said, and he carefully explained that the verdict must be based solely on the evidence the jury had heard in the case. It was up to the jury to decide what were the true facts of the case and what inferences should reasonably be drawn from them. They were the sole and exclusive judges of the facts. The judge's function was to see to it that only legal evidence relevant to the issues of the case should be submitted to them, and to instruct them as to the principles of law to be applied to the case; on these they must accept the judge's direction.

Moving on to the subject of libel, he explained the laws involved.

THE COURT: The good reputation of a person has always been rightly regarded as a cherished possession among the peoples of the civilized communities.

Where action has been brought for alleged libel, it is for the defendants to bear the burden of proof; in this case, the only defense remaining was that of the quality of proof on which the defendants had relied.

With three defendants, it would be for the jury to determine the degree of conspiracy.

THE COURT: A conspiracy is an agreement or understanding between two or more persons, which may include a membership corporation, to do an illegal act. A libel is an illegal act.

If all three were found to be parties to a conspiracy, damages must be awarded against all of the conspirators.

The judge then discussed the two kinds of damages the jury must consider.

THE COURT: Compensatory damages are intended to compensate a plaintiff for all the damage he has suffered, that is, to make him whole. The damages awarded must be based upon the injury to his reputation and in his profession. He is also entitled to be compensated for the mental anguish, mortification, and humiliation which you find and believe he experienced in his public and private life.

The amount of these damages was up to the jury to determine. They should use their common sense and good judgment. In respect to damages for loss of income, the judge referred to the testimony given by experts during the trial, and warned the jury to evaluate it as they did the testimony of other witnesses. Substantial damages could only be based on substantial injury. If the jury should consider there had been no substantial injury, then damages awarded should be only nominal.

Punitive damages, on the other hand, are to punish a defendant, to deter him from the repetition of an offense, and as a warning to others not to commit a like offense.

THE COURT: Punitive damages are intended to protect the community and to vindicate public decency.

The award of punitive damages, in addition to compensatory damages, would depend on the extent to which the defendants had been actuated by malice.

THE COURT: Malice would include the notion of hostility or intent to injure. You may consider, if you deem it indicative of malice, any testimony given by either of the two defendants in this case.

Of course, now that Johnson was dead, he was no longer concerned in this consideration of punitive damages.

The judge carefully pointed out that the defendants' partial defense of reliance had no effect on their liability for compensatory damages. But there could be a mitigation of punitive damages if the defendants had shown great care, accuracy, and truth in use of the information on which they had relied; again, it was for the jury to decide on this. The judge was careful to remind the jury of his ruling that, as a matter of law, none of the organizations described by the defendants as "officially designated a Communist front" was, in fact, so designated.

Finally, the judge explained that a unanimous verdict was not necessary in this case, and that as soon as ten of the jurors were in agreement, they should bring their deliberations to an end. If they found for the plaintiff, they must include in their verdict the amount of compensatory damages against all the defendants, and if they decided to award punitive damages, these must be named against each Hartnett and AWARE. "If your verdict is for the defendants, you must so state."

As the full meaning of Judge Geller's charge sank in, I was almost shocked. In this charge, he had literally ruled out Bolan's entire case, leaving the jury to decide but one thing—how much compensatory and punitive damages to award. In other words, the years of effort that the defendants had put into building their defenses, had been thrown out the window by Justice Geller in the last hour.

Bolan arose and made his exceptions to the charge and the judge then excused the alternate juror, Mr. King, who came over and shook my hand as he left the court. At exactly 5:35 P.M. Justice Geller said, "Members of the jury you may now retire and deliberate." And the jury rose and filed out. As they walked past the counsel table, I tried desperately to get some clue from their faces as to their feelings. There was none. Each juror looked straight ahead.

Nizer suggested that I stay near him. Most of our friends went over to Gasner's to have cocktails and dinner. Lou suggested that we go to a quiet place away from the court crowd. It was pointless for me to try to linger over the meal and feign indifference. I wanted to get back to the courtroom. Nizer speculated that if the jury were out a short time, it would mean a good verdict for us. If the jury got locked up in wrangling, there would have to be compromises and it would probably go badly for us. He offered no speculation whatever on whether the jury's verdict would be for us or against us.

At nine-thirty I could stand it no longer. I went back to the courtroom. There were several court attendants and a couple of reporters and good George Berger lolling around the tables and taking it easy. I sat down and jotted thoughts down on a piece of paper. Spectators wandered in and out. Suddenly an attendant called, "Will everybody be seated!" and word went out through the corridors and to the surrounding restaurants that something was about to happen in court. Bolan was summoned from his office several blocks away. When we were all seated and Bolan had arrived, Justice Geller asked an attendant to bring the jury in. My heart was pounding as they filed in and took their seats.

Justice Geller then said that the jury wanted to ask a question and he wanted it done in open court. The foreman rose and asked, "Can the jury award more damages than the plaintiff's attorney asked?" There was complete consternation on the face of everyone in the courtroom. George Berger and Paul Martinson stared at one another in disbelief. Louis Nizer fell back in his chair in amazement. In his entire legal career a jury had never come in and asked to give more than he, Nizer, had asked them for. The judge was obviously astonished by this question too. However, he carefully explained to the jury the law on this point.

The newsmen at their table and the spectators quickly got word out through the public that a historic event was about to take place. Nizer remarked to me that the record libel verdict in history was half a million dollars. He warned me, however, not to become too sanguine now. "Let's wait until the verdict's in," he said.

I sat at the table alone, thinking of the long, long road I had come along from South Austin, Texas, to this moment, in the courtroom in New York where a decision was being made that could possibly make history. The soft June night outside was filled with the sounds of Manhattan after dark. Some of my friends wandered down to the night court, several floors below, to watch the never-ending drama there. Anything to while away the time. Scenes from my childhood kept floating before me. What would Daddy and Mama think about this? and Dobie? I realized how important the approval of those I loved was to me.

At last, word came out that the jury had reached a decision. It was necessary to send to Bolan's office for him again. The courtroom filled up quickly. Some minutes later Bolan came in. Hartnett sat opposite me, in his accustomed place. The jury filed back into their box. It was twenty minutes before midnight when the clerk of the court addressed the foreman of the jury, "Have you agreed upon a verdict?" "We have," he replied. "How do you find?" "We, the jury, have arrived at our decision in favor of Mr. Faulk. We have awarded the plaintiff, Mr. Faulk, compensatory damages in the sum of $1 million against AWARE, Inc., Mr. Vincent Hartnett, and the estate of the late Mr. Laurence Johnson. We have also awarded the plaintiff, Mr. Faulk, punitive damages in the sum of $1,250,000 against AWARE, Inc., and $1,250,000 against Mr. Hartnett." Bolan immediately jumped to his feet and demanded that the jury be polled. One juror had voted against the decision. Since only ten jurors were necessary for a verdict, this made no difference. The judge thanked them and excused them. The full impact of the verdict had not fully hit me as I went up to shake hands with each one as they left the jury box. For the first time in three months, their faces betrayed their genuine feelings. As I clasped the hand of each, we could only smile and bob our heads. Several were weeping. I was near tears myself.

Suddenly, photographers and reporters were all over the place. The courtroom wheeled about me in a great blur. I tried to be honest, answering reporters that the decision numbed me. Lou suggested that we should have a quiet celebration. We left the courthouse for the last time and adjourned to the Algonquin Hotel. I still couldn't comprehend the meaning of such a settlement—$3.5 million dollars! Myrna Loy phoned, too ecstatic to do other than repeat, "Wonderful, wonderful." I called my friend Cactus Pryor, program director for Lyndon Johnson's radio stations, my sister Mary, and my sister Texana, and J. Frank Dobie, in Austin, to relate the news to them.

I slept more soundly than I had in many, many, many days.

26

The news of the record-breaking award and verdict set off a chain reaction of front page news stories around the country. Indeed, by the evening of the next day, I was getting calls from London and Paris newspapers. The *New York Times* and the New York *Herald Tribune* carried the story on their front pages. I was beseiged by radio and television newsmen, bringing along their cameras and recording equipment for national newscasts. They all came clamoring. All, that is, but CBS.

Newspapers across the land carried editorials, praising the verdict and declaring that blacklisting had been exposed for all to see. The *New York Times* editorial on the suit commented, ". . . the libel verdict should have a healthy effect in curbing the excesses of the superpatriots. . . . The case should assist in establishing the limitations on the lengths to which private groups, arrogating to themselves the mantle of public protection against subversion, can go in blacklisting and defaming their fellow citizens. . . ."

Nizer was convinced that the networks would come bustling with offers. They did not. In fact, I fell to trying desperately to find work, but soon found that the broadcasting industry had not taken kindly to my lawsuit. It had exposed their collaboration with AWARE and the ugly business of blacklisting. I was *persona non grata* with them.

The defendants naturally appealed the decision. Several months later, Nizer called me into his office. He told me that he had discovered that the Laurence Johnson estate was worth, in toto, only about $250,000, a fraction of the millions Johnson reputedly had. We laughed at the grim humor of it. Every network and advertising agency in New York had trembled before Johnson. Any one of them could have bought him out with one week's advertising budget. However, Nizer had good news, too. He said the administrators of

Johnson's estate had offered to settle the estate's damages for
$175,000, on condition that the estate would be released
from further responsibility in the suit. Although the costs of
the suit, to the Nizer firm, were well over $500,000 I agreed
with Lou that we might as well accept what we could get
and release the Johnson estate. Lou allocated me a generous
share of the settlement, although I felt I should not take anything. He pointed out that I could pay off my indebtedness
and start out fresh, with enough left over for me to coast
awhile.

The Appellate Division of the New York Supreme Court
affirmed the verdict in every respect, except for the $3.5 mil-
lion damages. They cut it to $500,000 with interest. They
held, in affirming the verdict unanimously, to a decision too
long to reprint in full.

> So we have, as found by the jury and amply supported by
> the evidence, a vicious libel, deliberately and maliciously
> planned and executed with devastating effect upon the
> plaintiff, all without a semblance of justification. . . .

The New York Court of Appeals and the United States Supreme Court upheld the verdict also.

AWARE, Inc. went out of business shortly after my case
was completed. I had to content myself with going about the
country on lecture tours, and doing after-dinner speeches. I
am frequently asked if the destruction of my career in broadcasting did not embitter me. My answer, of course, is that it
did not. If anything, I consider that it was a rare, and indeed,
a great privilege to have had the opportunity to stake my
convictions against those who shared AWARE's attitudes
about our constitutional freedoms. My fight against AWARE
was neither heroic nor courageous. It was nothing more than
any American citizen should do, when forces of repression
and fear threaten to undermine our character of government,
constitution, and the heritage of freedom that has served us
so well the past two centuries. If there is a hero in my case, it
is the American judicial system—and by implication—the
American people who maintain it and make it the most via-
ble system of justice on earth today.

EPILOGUE

When *Fear on Trial* was first published back in 1964, I felt pretty sure that I had included everything of importance that there was to say about my lawsuit against AWARE. I also believed that I had pretty much said all there was to say about putting citizens' names on a secret list for the purpose of harassing them.

It was not until fourteen years later that I found out, almost by accident, that there had been another dimension to my trial that neither Louis Nizer nor I had suspected, and from a quarter that we never suspected: the FBI.

One day at lunch in Houston in early 1978, a friend and I were chatting. We were talking about the public revelations of FBI misconduct in connection with the harassment of Martin Luther King. It had been pretty shocking.

My friend asked if I had sent to the FBI a request for any information that their files might contain regarding me.

"Why, no," I replied. "I've never even thought of it."

"Well, you know that the Freedom of Information Act makes it possible for any citizen to make a government agency cough up any information the agency might have on the citizen. A lot of people are making the FBI come across."

"But why would the FBI collect information on me? I've never applied for government employment. I've never been charged with breaking the law or even been suspected of criminal acts. Why would the FBI be investigating me?" I asked.

My friend gazed at me in wonder at my naïvety.

"Don't you know that J. Edgar Hoover managed to accumulate records on millions of American citizens who spoke out on social and political issues? Any and everybody who ever expressed a dissenting opinion is in the FBI files. It became such a scandal that Congress had to pass the Freedom of Information Act to protect the citizen's right to know what derogatory information Hoover was storing on him."

I had known for years that Hoover had exercised formidable power in Washington and was an ardent admirer of Senator Joe McCarthy, HUAC, and other repressive forces, but for some reason or another it had never occurred to me that his activities extended to a relatively unimportant person such as I was.

"Tell you what I'll do," my friend continued. "I'll bet you a brand new Stetson hat that, if you'll write to the FBI and ask if they have a file on you, they will tell you that they do. And a big one."

I wrote to the FBI, and a month or so later, I bought my friend the Stetson. The FBI had not only a file on me, but a very fat one, it seemed. They said that I could have it at 10¢ a page, in compliance with the provisions of the Freedom of Information Act.

I was shocked and angered as I went through the dossier. I knew that J. Edgar Hoover had been guilty of some pretty shady activities, but I had never dreamed that our tax money was going to finance such a shameful abuse of a citizen's basic constitutional freedoms.

The material assembled in the dossier consisted of the same political claptrap, gossip, and distorted and false information that had characterized the AWARE, Inc., bulletin that had triggered my lawsuit. However, some of the material in the file dated back to 1942, before AWARE even existed. It dealt with alleged associations and attitudes of mine forty years ago.

There was not one scintilla of evidence in it that the bureau had ever suspected me of criminal activity. There was, however, an abundance of evidence that J. Edgar Hoover had been obsessed with my lawsuit against AWARE. There were dozens and dozens of pages with a single entry—a clipping from the Washington or the New York papers reporting the daily developments in my lawsuit while it was in progress.

The most shameful and revealing thing about the whole shabby business was the memos to and from Hoover regarding me. One can only guess that they were probably left in the dossier by oversight, and certainly before the Freedom of Information Act made it possible that I might see them some day. They exposed activities of the bureau that were inexcusable.

One of them related to material in my dossier that had been turned over to a political opponent of mine by Hoover personally when it could do my career great harm. Another revealed a collaboration between the FBI and HUAC in an effort to get "dirt" (their actual word) on me so that I could be called before the HUAC for a public pilloring. And to make it even more reprehensible, this latter bit of duplicity was hatched up in 1964—*two years after I had won my law-suit against AWARE!* Other entries suggested strongly that the FBI had collaborated closely with AWARE, Inc., during my lawsuit.

The revelation of how grossly the FBI, an agency of my own government, had knowingly and consistently violated the spirit and the word of our basic law, the Constitution, had a profound effect on me. With a much greater clarity than even my experience with blacklisting had afforded me, I came to understand what wisdom and genius our Founding Fathers possessed when they framed our constitution.

As men who had lived under the tyranny and arbitrary power of the British Crown, they understood the stratagems of repression. They sought to erect absolute barriers against the exercise of that arbitrary power and political repression by the government. As James Madison observed when he wrote and presented the First Amendment to the Congress, the absolute freedom of conscience, speech, the press, and the right of the people to peaceably assemble and to petition the government for the redress of grievances were the Great Rights of the people and essential to a self-governing republic.

Since the people were the masters and the government was the servant, in the new United States, the right of censorship resided in the people over the government, *never* in the government over the people. An agency of government, even one headed by such a self-infatuated patriot as J. Edgar Hoover, that engages in the secret collection and storage of political information on American citizens has more in common with totalitarian police states than it does with the United States Government.